Materializing the Bible

Bloomsbury Studies in Material Religion

Bloomsbury Studies in Material Religion is the first book series dedicated exclusively to studies in material religion. Within the field of lived religion, the series is concerned with the material things with which people do religion, and how these things—objects, buildings, landscapes—relate to people, their bodies, clothes, food, actions, thoughts and emotions. The series engages and advances theories in 'sensuous' and 'experiential' religion, as well as informing museum practices and influencing wider cultural understandings with relation to religious objects and performances. Books in the series are at the cutting edge of debates as well as developments in fields including religious studies, anthropology, museum studies, art history, and material culture studies.

Christianity and Belonging in Shimla, North India, Jonathan Miles-Watson
Christianity and the Limits of Materiality, edited by Minna Opas and Anna Haapalainen
Figurations and Sensations of the Unseen in Judaism, Christianity and Islam, edited by Birgit Meyer and Terje Stordalen
Food, Festival and Religion, Francesca Ciancimino Howell
Islam through Objects, Anna Bigelow
Material Devotion in a South Indian Poetic World, Leah Elizabeth Comeau
Qur'anic Matters, Natalia K. Suit
The Religious Heritage Complex, edited by Cyril Isnart and Nathalie Cerezales
Museums of World Religions, Charles D. Orzech

Materializing the Bible

Scripture, Sensation, Place

James S. Bielo

BLOOMSBURY ACADEMIC
LONDON • NEW YORK • OXFORD • NEW DELHI • SYDNEY

BLOOMSBURY ACADEMIC
Bloomsbury Publishing Plc
50 Bedford Square, London, WC1B 3DP, UK
1385 Broadway, New York, NY 10018, USA
29 Earlsfort Terrace, Dublin 2, Ireland

BLOOMSBURY, BLOOMSBURY ACADEMIC and the Diana logo are trademarks of
Bloomsbury Publishing Plc

First published in Great Britain 2022
This paperback edition published 2023

Copyright © James S. Bielo, 2022

James S. Bielo has asserted his right under the Copyright, Designs and Patents Act, 1988, to be identified as Author of this work.

For legal purposes the Acknowledgments on p. x constitute an extension of this copyright page.

Cover design: Toby Way
Cover image © Rory M. Johnson, PhD

All rights reserved. No part of this publication may be reproduced or transmitted in any form or by any means, electronic or mechanical, including photocopying, recording, or any information storage or retrieval system, without prior permission in writing from the publishers.

Bloomsbury Publishing Plc does not have any control over, or responsibility for, any third-party websites referred to or in this book. All internet addresses given in this book were correct at the time of going to press. The author and publisher regret any inconvenience caused if addresses have changed or sites have ceased to exist, but can accept no responsibility for any such changes.

A catalogue record for this book is available from the British Library.

Library of Congress Control Number: 2021938959

ISBN: HB: 978-1-3500-6504-8
PB: 978-1-3502-6025-2
ePDF: 978-1-3500-6506-2
eBook: 978-1-3500-6505-5

Typeset by Deanta Global Publishing Services, Chennai, India

To find out more about our authors and books visit www.bloomsbury.com and sign up for our newsletters

For Sara, Simon, and Charlie

Contents

List of Figures	ix
Acknowledgments	x
Introduction	1

Section I: Variations on Replication

1	1:1	21
2	Miniaturizing	31
3	Reenacting	39
4	Imagineering	49
5	Plastic Jesus	59
6	Ways of Remaining	67

Section II: The Power of Nature

7	Flora	81
8	Fauna	91
9	Ingesting the Word	99
10	How Stones Do Things	107

Section III: Choreographing Experience

Circulation — 119

11	Miracles and Lavatories	123
12	Greetings From . . .	131
13	Like-able Me, Like-able There	141

Design — 149

14	In Place, In Motion	153
15	Interactivity	165
16	Engulfed I	175
17	Engulfed II	187

Classification — 195

18 In the Garden — 199
19 Rev. Ruth's Yard Poetics — 209
20 Four Crosses Over Waterbury — 219

Conclusion — 229

Notes — 239
Bibliography — 254
Index — 270

Figures

1	Tabernacle replica	20
2	Model of Jerusalem at Clear Creek Bible College	30
3	The book of Job	38
4	Ark Encounter, exterior view	48
5	Biblical Sand Sculpture by Randy Hofman	58
6	Inside the World of Jesus of Nazareth at the Museum of the Bible	66
7	Entry to Biblical Garden at Paradise Valley United Methodist Church	80
8	Sign at Creation Museum Petting Zoo	90
9	Print for sale at Biblical History Center gift shop	98
10	Holy Land stone on display at the Garden of Hope	106
11	Brochure for Saint-Anne-de-Beaupré shrine	122
12	Postcard for Tabernacle replica	130
13	Instagram "selfie-spot" at Museum of the Bible	140
14	Jesus praying in the Garden of Gethsemane at the Shrine of Christ's Passion	152
15	Inside the Hebrew Bible Experience at the Museum of the Bible	164
16	Postcard of the Cyclorama of Jerusalem	174
17	Virtual Reality at the National Geographic Tomb of Christ Experience	186
18	Tour group at Garden of Hope	198
19	Rev. Ruth in his Bible Park	208
20	Holy Land, USA	218

Acknowledgments

This book was nearly six years in the making, and I received a wealth of support and collaboration throughout the process. The ethnographic portions were made possible by the people who generously spent time with me and helped me to understand their worlds. In particular, I thank Jon from the Ark creative team; Steve, Ed, and Samuel from the Garden of Hope; and, Matt, Alin, Nate, and Bill for sharing their work on the Museum of the Bible. Staff at the following institutions graciously contributed to the archival portions: Miami University Libraries; Cincinnati Public Library; Kenton County Public Library; Northern Kentucky University's Steely Library Special Collections; Western Kentucky University Libraries; San Francisco Botanical Garden Society Library; Field Museum; Zoar Historical Society; Amherst College Archives and Special Collections; Marian Library at the University of Dayton; Georgetown College Library; University of Florida Special Collections; American Folk Art Museum; Leelanau Historical Society; Central Michigan University Library; Buffalo and Erie County Public Library; the Provincial Archives of Alberta; and, the Newberry Library. Special thanks are also due to the undergraduate research assistants who helped with data collection and analysis at various stages (Amanda White, Claire Vaughn, Kaila Sansom, and Lou Lou Wingert), and to the Miami University Humanities Center for assistantship funding.

I am grateful to be in relationship with a network of colleagues who inspire as much with their kindness as their intellect. So many generously engaged with aspects of this project in wonderfully different, yet always generative, ways. In particular, I want to thank Andreas Bandak, Tim Beal, Jon Bialecki, Anderson Blanton, Tom Boylston, Jason Bruner, Judith Brunton, Kyle Byron, Larissa Carneiro, Saliha Chattoo, Simon Coleman, Amy DeRogatis, Philip Deslippe, Kate Dugan, Omri Elisha, Aron Engberg, Jackie Feldman, Peter Gottschalk, Mathew Guest, Grey Gundaker, Naomi Haynes, Eric Hoenes del Pinal, Ingie Hovland, Brian Howell, David Howes, Hillary Kaell, Rebekka King, Fred Klaits, Rachel McBride Lindsey, Jim Linville, Marc Loustau, Alyssa Maldonado-Estrada, Devin Manzullo-Thomas, Caroline Matas, Jana Mathews, Monica Mercado, Moxy Moczygemba, Urmila Mohan, Yasmin Moll, David Morgan, Christina Pasqua, Crispin Paine, Seth Perry, S. Brent Plate, Sarah Porter,

Sally Promey, Katja Rakow, Amos Ron, Lena Rose, Steve Selka, Daniel Silliman, Matt Tomlinson, Suzanne Van Geuns, Travis Webb, Isaac Weiner, Amy Whitehead, Lieke Wijnia, and Laurel Zwissler.

One difference between this and previous projects I have completed is that the time and space to write was largely afforded by friends and family who provided childcare. This book would absolutely still be in progress were it not for the trusted help provided by Maddie Shultz, Claire Leitzen, Esther Claros-Berlioz, Hannah Teetor, Bailey Miller, the Vath family, Judith Bielo, and Dave and Mary Ann Williams. To my mother, Judith, and my mother-in-law, Mary Ann, I owe a special debt of gratitude for the time, energy, and care you gave so lovingly.

Songs, prose, and prayers kept this project (and its author) from unraveling. Any spirit that animates the writing owes a great deal to Tony Rice, David Grisman, Miles Davis, John Coltrane, Caitlin Canty, Tyler Childers, Lucinda Williams, Jason Isbell, Brandi Carlisle, Greg Brown, Todd Snider, Guy Clark, and, always, John Prine.

This book is dedicated to three people who I wake up every day aching to continue loving. Sara, whatever awaits, we will flourish together. Simon and Charlie, our beautiful children, your joy is an evergreen inspiration. May our days be prayers of thanksgiving.

Introduction

How do people, especially Christians across cultures, materialize the Bible? That is: How are the written words of scripture transformed into experiential, choreographed environments? This book examines this question and, in doing so, moves among different times, places, theological traditions, performative contexts, and sensory arrangements. To name a few: we consider "full-scale" and miniature replications of Jerusalem and other sites used to imagine biblical pasts; imagineered versions of biblically themed environments, from Noah's ark to first-century Nazareth; a traveling drama troupe who reenacted the book of Job; attractions filled with dioramas, sculpted or cast in wax, sand, stone, plaster, concrete, bronze, and other materials; attractions of cultivated nature that care for plants and animals mentioned in biblical texts; the cooking of biblically themed meals; brochures, picture postcards, and Instagram posts as technologies of circulation; cycloramas and virtual reality headsets as technologies of absorption; and a diverse mix of immersive environments, some choreographed by an ensemble of digital technologies and others by hand-painted wooden signs.

Most of the examples analyzed closely are set in the United States, though the phenomenon is global and reference is made to sites in Brazil, Israel, Italy, and elsewhere. Some sites are still extant, and some are not. Some are popular (even, infamous), while others are largely forgotten (or were never widely known). They emerge from multiple traditions: Protestant, Catholic, fundamentalist, charismatic; interdenominational; and some claim stances of being interreligious or nonsectarian. Their genres of self-identification range as well, including museum, theme park, garden, zoo, shrine, theatre, fair, and memorial. Given this diversity, how can we bring together these performances of material Christianity?

The answer developed here is what I term *Materializing the Bible*. Christians engage this process in many ways, grounded in different traditions and driven by divergent ambitions. Whenever written scripture is transformed into experiential environment, it happens amid a series of interlaced contexts: biographical, local social, political, economic, and intersectional conditions (racialized, gendered, and theological). Expressions of power—status, legitimacy, authority, economic and symbolic capital, claims to territory, erasures of history, assertions of authenticity—are a defining dimension of this phenomenon.

The organizing argument is that materializing the Bible works as an *authorizing* practice that intensifies *intimacies* with scripture and *circulates* potent ideologies. By *authorizing*, I mean the ways in which material performance illuminates the assertion of and struggle over legitimacy and value. *Intimacies* is also a load-bearing term; it marks the affective attachments that are forged, embodied, shared, and negotiated through material performances and their social contexts. *Circulation* references the public life of materiality: the ways in which our worlds are "infused with the communicative norms and materials forms" of religious traditions (Handman 2018: 158). Being attuned to circulation means attending to the pathways and traces of religion's movement, the actors involved in making materialities move, and the institutions and conditions that orient movement.

This argument builds on a robust framework established by scholars of material religion, beginning with the insight that "belief" is not merely a cognitive-linguistic phenomenon. Rather, belief and believing are constituted and lived through religion's materialities: the sensory experience of bodies in place, the relations of those bodies with technologies, and the infrastructures that contextualize those experiences and relations (e.g., Morgan 1999; Engelke 2010; Plate, ed. 2015; Meyer 2014; Promey, ed. 2014; Mohan and Warnier 2017). In an early articulation of this framework for the study of Christianity, Colleen McDannell (1995) captured the core of it well: "the sensual elements of Christianity are not merely decorations that mask serious belief; it is through the visible world that the invisible world becomes known and felt" (272).

A Material Religion Project

Throughout the process of research, analysis, and writing for this project, I have understood it to be inspired by, and a contribution to, the interdisciplinary study of material religion. Practices of materializing the Bible draw our attention to things like visitors ritualizing at sites of tourism and pilgrimage; artists creating choreographed environments; the circulation of natural, artisanal, and mass-produced objects; and lively encounters between people and landscapes. One way to conceptualize the interests of material religion is through three analytical moorings: body, technology, and infrastructure. Of course, in the midst of moments, lives, cultures, and histories, these three are always entangled. I separate them here for introductory clarity, but their ties should not be severed in the empirical analysis.

Body. The sensory experience of bodies is a cornerstone for understanding how religion works among individuals, communities, and societies. How people learn to see, touch, hear, smell, and taste their way through the world is vital for understanding ritual practice, social attachments, and the ways in which theologies are internalized. Plate (2012) offers the beautiful metaphor of our senses being the "skin" of religion, "a semi-permeable membrane that mediates input and output, the flows of religious behavior and belief, and the creation of sacred environments" (12). If we closely attend to bodily techniques becoming favored, naturalized, contested, and rejected, then we begin to understand how sensory attunement plays a vital role in the making of religious worlds (Blanton 2015). With materializing the Bible, tracing these embodied forms helps reveal how people learn to pray, congregate, worship, witness, remember, and the ideological work that is done through claims of "experiencing the Bible" or "bringing the Bible to life."

Technology. Considering bodily experience swiftly leads to the simple and complex stuff that bodies engage with. I understand "technology" in the broadest way possible, encompassing any materiality mobilized in social practice. In the chapters to come, everything from landscape objects (rocks, soil, flowers) to engineered apparatuses (stereographs, virtual reality headsets) are featured. "Mobilize" is a useful term, signaling the creative and routinized ways that people use technologies to live their Christianity, to make it active in the world: to practice devotion, to evangelize others, to memorialize the biblical past, to celebrate claims of authentic tradition. However, it is also a limited term, and we should resist any tendency that reduces technology to being merely instrumental (Stolow 2012: 7). Analyzing technology is also about exploring the ways in which technological affordances create and constrain; that is, "the deep conditions of possibility for religious adherents to proclaim their faith, mark their affiliation, receive spiritual gifts, or participate in any of the countless local idioms for making the sacred present to mind and body" (5; cf. Morgan 2013).

Infrastructure. The sensory experience of bodies happens in relation to technologies and, always, in place. The third mooring addresses the layers of spatial context that function as both stage and prop for material performance. Like "technology," "infrastructure" encompasses a range of phenomena: from natural and cultivated landscapes to diverse architectural additions that foster place-making. As with "technology," we are best served when we engage with infrastructures as materialities that people make use of and that structure the conditions of possibility. As Pena (2017) observes in her analysis of Catholic devotional practices in relation to the apparatus of the US-Mexico border, "physical infrastructure not only animates religious practice and dictates devotional rhythms . . . but also informs movement to and from [sites] of worship" (467).

The chapters to come move among this holy trinity of body-technology-infrastructure. There are occasions when a particular technology is highlighted for its rich history of practice (e.g., Chapter 12 and the picture postcard), but the overarching goal is to maintain the interrelatedness of these three moorings. "Engulfed I," for example, examines representations of Jesus's crucifixion in the cyclorama, an attraction that showcases large panoramic paintings. To understand this expression of materializing the Bible, we must attend equally to architecture, the integration of visual and sonic technologies, and the sensory dynamics of immersion in a choreographed environment.

Body-technology-infrastructure helps us understand material religion's remit but does not differentiate among theoretical approaches. That is, this triad names what we care about, but not how we make sense of it. Religious studies scholar Sonia Hazard (2013) distinguishes among four theoretical orientations that are realized in material religion scholarship. (1) Interpretive approaches decode the meanings embedded in and trafficked by objects and embodied practices; focused on the symbolic potency of materialities. (2) Disciplinary approaches reorient toward the role of materialities in shaping religious identities and communities; focused on the training of bodies to authorize and participate in particular theological traditions. (3) Phenomenological approaches highlight relationships among materiality, physical experience, and social context; focused on the constitutive role of materiality for human being and becoming. (4) New Materialist approaches seek to understand the "materiality of things themselves" (59); focused on the agentive capacities of human and nonhuman entities and their functioning as networked assemblages that animate religious life.

This book pledges no theoretical loyalty, aiming instead for promiscuity. I draw on all four approaches, ideally marshaling the generative insights of each. In various moments, I grapple with how theological and ideological meanings are circulated in and through biblically themed environments. For example, several chapters return to the historical accumulation of Protestant imaginings of the Holy Land and how those imaginings guide projects of material replication. Interpreting such meanings happens alongside attention to processes of legitimation and authorization, to the position of meaning-making within enduring power dynamics. Phenomenological interests appear as well, as many chapters examine the sensory effects of how materialities are engineered and choreographed. The chapters are also inspired by New Materialism's interest in the distribution of agency among humans and nonhumans; the power of artists and visitors to act and influence is recognized, but so are guiding materials, physical landscapes, and technologies in print and digital form.

The Material Life of Scriptures

Proposing a material religion approach to the social life of scriptures exposes a useful tension. The field of material religion cohered as a critical response to a logocentric bias toward written texts, language, and meaning (Meyer 2014: 220). Privileging bodies, technologies, and infrastructures arose as a counter to the historic over-privileging of linguistic practices for understanding religious world-making. The category of "scripture" is closely implicated in this because of emphases on literacy and hermeneutics. But, people do much more than read and speak about scriptures, and there is nothing inherently oppositional about scriptures and materiality. Indeed, their intersection is a rich vein for scholarship.

One way to resolve any apparent dissonance between scriptures and materiality is to examine the sensory qualities of scriptural texts and the mobilization of those texts as a material technology (e.g., Watts 2019). This approach has been incredibly productive, opening up the comparative study of how sacred texts are used in ritual, cultural ideologies surrounding the decommissioning or destruction of sacred texts, and the use and circulation of sacred texts as cultural symbols. With respect to "the Bible" and Bibles, we are flush with insightful analyses, such as illustrated Bibles (Gutjahr 2001), mantic uses of biblical books (Malley 2006), and Bibles in digital formats (Rakow 2017). Front and center in this approach is the fact that scriptures are textual products with artifactual properties that we physically interact.

Another resolution comes by examining the ways in which scriptures circulate in transmedial form; that is, they exist across multiple kinds of media (Beal 2010). People transform written scriptures into songs, stained glass, paintings, sculpture, film, and games (e.g., Plate, ed. 2004; West III 2019; Gonzalez 2014). Scriptural expressions in other media are distinct from, but always tethered to, their written textual analogs. The cultural potency of a scripture travels across media genres, and non-textual expressions continue to bear attributions of authority and the capacity to mediate divine presence.

This book engages with the second resolution, focusing primarily on spaces people create that are transmedial representations of biblical texts. While they self-identify in various ways (theme parks and museums, gardens and shrines), places that materialize the Bible consistently make a promise to visitors. They promise that by transforming written text into choreographed environment, the sacred scriptures will be experienced anew. As a phenomenon, materializing the Bible is about experiencing scripture through multiple material forms, in multiple sensory configurations. Just as the Bible is an interpretively inexhaustible text, it is also an experientially inexhaustible transmedial form. Ultimately, this promise of experience is oriented toward reflecting and recreating ideologies and identities that are forged in relation to "the Bible" and Bibles. Amid this reflection and recreation, bodies, technologies, and infrastructures work in concert to engage people in affectively charged forms of authorization.

Processes of heritagization are a prime example of how the material life of scriptures ensnares Christians and other social actors into debates of authority. Heritage-making is always a sociopolitical process, defined by acts of classifying, claiming authenticity, and circulating the status of being worthy of recognition (Meyer 2019; Isnart and Cerezales 2020). Often a resource-rich process with financial and symbolic capital at stake, heritagizing is an industry equally enmeshed in market dynamics and the (re)narration and (re)display of history (Coleman 2018). To heritagize is to experience transformation. This might mean a broadening of value, from strictly devotional to claims of universal, nationalistic, or ethnic significance. In other contexts, it might mean transforming a past that was unknown or of little interest to one that people want to claim for religious, aesthetic, or political reasons (Bowman 2020). In some cases, this transformation is a secularizing force, reorienting value away from religious purposes, while in others religious actors lead the search for heritage classifications (Isnart and Cerezales 2020). Heritagizing is a potent cultural force and is often a source of tension: as when a community's active devotional life is put on display for tourist consumption (Nielsen 2021), or when the felt authenticity of a place is thrown into question (Coleman 2018). Dynamics of heritagization animate the chapters to come, as sites that materialize the Bible negotiate their place in public life, if and how they will be remembered, what value they have and for who.

Experiential Frames

The expressions of materializing the Bible examined in this book are largely place-based. For some amount of time—days, decades, centuries—they exist in particular places, entering into local landscapes and histories. Some operate fully in the registers of tourism and pilgrimage, while others are more ambiguous. In any case, they are marked as different from the places that surround them. When we encounter them, we know we are encountering something set apart from the routines of everyday life. In turn, it is useful to understand these places in terms of the experiential frames they seek to immerse visitors into.

I use "frame" as Erving Goffman (1974) does, as a way to trace how people differentiate one kind of social context from another. Experiential frames provide us with structures of expectation and interactional norms that can be accepted or challenged. By knowing the frame we are in, we gain a general sense for what actions and feelings are likely to be prompted, and for what is normative. In short, frames guide us in how to interact with these places: what to do, how to be.

Four experiential frames are prevalent in this book. Some sites are devotional, designed to foster prayer and worship, often abiding by formalized ritual tradition. Some are pedagogical, mobilizing materiality toward instructional ends, teaching theology, scriptural hermeneutics, and social ideologies. Some are evangelistic, addressing visitors as spiritually wanting people in need of conversion or recommitment. And, some are sites of leisure, fusing recreation and reverence. Many places are polymorphic, strategically integrating multiple frames. Similar to what Ketchell (2007) observed with the religious tourism industry of Branson, Missouri, many materializing the Bible sites offer visitors devotional leisure, moralized education, and other hybridized expressions.

Site producers choreograph these frames, from religiously committed artists who invest decades of devotional labor to build an attraction to professional design firms hired to create memorable, affectively charged experiences. And, visitors of all stripes interact with these frames: devout pilgrims, skeptics, curious passersby, and dedicated researchers. Sensory engagements and technologies are integral for keying these frames, drawing visitors into embodied negotiations: to embrace or distance the devotional invitation, imbibe or disrupt the educational stance, accept or reject the call to have fun. Sound is a prime illustration. "Engulfed II," for example, juxtaposes two virtual reality exhibits housed in museums and promising immersive tours of the Christian Holy Land. Among their differences is the respective choice of instrumental musical scores piped into visitors' ears: one indexes excitement and adventure, the other contemplative meditation.

Experiential frames are also activated through forms of language use: printed signage; live tour guide performances; and the pre-scripted performances of guide books, brochures, and recorded narrations. I pay close attention to these linguistic performances and, in doing so, address another tension in the study of material religion. In her study of lived Christianity and material culture, McDannell (1995) observed: "As 'multimedia events,' religious practices are areas where speech, vision, gesture, touch, and sound combine" (14). However, given the critique of logocentrism baked into the study of materiality, the "speech" dimension of McDannell's observation is sometimes downplayed. Birgit Meyer (2008) reminds us that sensory experience is never un-mediated: "instead of celebrating the appraisal of the body as a return to what really matters—life!—and dismissing language and other semiotic forms as secondary to that, it needs to be stressed that the body itself is formed through mediation" (10; cf. Engelke 2010). While material religion scholarship has excelled in foregrounding bodies, technologies, and infrastructures, it has not always attended as closely to the interplay of material experience and linguistic performance. This is unfortunate. We are not playing a zero-sum game in which analysis in one area (e.g., embodiment) requires neglecting others (e.g., discourse) (cf. Opas and Haapaleinen 2017: 5).

Material religion is not the only scholarly field to be troubled by this kind of zero-sum logic. Ochs (2012) explains that interdisciplinary collaboration, for example, among psychological and linguistic anthropologists, has been limited because the symbolic properties of language are often emphasized over indexical and performative dimensions. That is, when language is understood solely as a referential vehicle for meaning, it becomes complicit in the kind of logocentric bias that devalues materialities. However, when we understand language more fully—that is, more accurately—as a marker and creator of social realities, we can analyze language as it exists in relationship with bodies, technologies, and infrastructures. Shankar and Cavanaugh (2012) expand Ochs's explanation, observing a robust "convergence" between language and materiality: from semiotic codes that are intrinsically physical (e.g., sign languages; Morse code; gestural systems) to the semiotically entangled nature of discursive and nondiscursive signifiers in lived reality and the material dimensions of all discursive forms (e.g., writing and print technologies; bodily materialities, such as vocal chords and eardrum vibrations). If a goal of this book is to examine the experiential frames constructed and negotiated among expressions of materializing the Bible, then it is imperative to address multiple, intersecting mediations: bodily, technological, infrastructural, and linguistic.

Materializing across Theologies

In the following chapters, we move among performances of materializing the Bible that use various media and operate with diverse ambitions. Most are place-based sites located in the United States, created between 1870 and the present. But, materializing the Bible is a global and historic phenomenon. This project has catalogued more than 500 extant sites in 44 nations. Roughly half are located in the United States, with others in Argentina, Australia, Austria, Bahamas, Bosnia, Brazil, Canada, China, Croatia, Czech Republic, Denmark, Egypt, England, Ethiopia, France, Germany, Hungary, India, Ireland, Israel, Italy, Japan, Kenya, Latvia, Lithuania, Malta, Mexico, New Zealand, the Netherlands, Northern Ireland, Pakistan, Philippines, Poland, Portugal, Russia, Scotland, Slovakia, South Africa, South Korea, Switzerland, Taiwan, Ukraine, and Wales. We have also catalogued more than fifty nonextant sites, again mostly in the United States.

There is no single moment that marks the genesis of materializing the Bible. Some of the earliest examples observed in this project date to the twelfth century and anticipate later forms: such as the Church of Santo Stefano in Bologna, Italy (a replication of the Sepulchre of Jesus), and the Ethiopian Orthodox architectural complex of Lalibela (a spatial mimesis of Jerusalem). However, a series of northern Italian shrines, started in the late fifteenth century, do mark a turning point for a self-conscious tradition of Christian place-making. The first, the Sacred Mount of Varallo, inspired several nearby complexes: San Vivaldo (1500), Ossuccio (1635), Varese (1656), Domodossola (1656), and Belmonte (1712). They are now classified collectively as the *sacri monti*, protected and legitimized as UNESCO World Heritage sites.

Authorized by a papal commission in 1486, Franciscan friars began building the Sacred Mount of Varallo in 1493. Inspired by their pilgrimage to Jerusalem in the 1470s, the friars wished to recreate some of the holy city and its biblical past for those who could not (or would not) make the long and difficult trip east. Built on a hilltop above the town, the finished attraction features more than forty chapels, connected by walking paths, each filled with elaborate murals and life-sized clay figures that replicate the Stations of the Cross and other scenes from the life of Jesus (e.g., Lasansky 2017).

In his analysis of Varallo, David Leatherbarrow (1987) argues that location is integral to the site's design and efficacy—built at a time when pilgrimage to the Holy Land was becoming increasingly difficult yet pilgrimage as a form of popular piety was becoming increasingly popular. The town's off-the-beaten-path location satisfied pilgrim desires for experiencing a journey, a separation from the everyday and entry to the liminality of pilgrimage (Turner and Turner 1978). The mountain setting resonated in two further ways: with the scriptural tradition of mountaintop experiences (think: Moses on Mt. Sinai, Jesus tempted in the wilderness), and with the embodied rituality of ascending slopes to reach a pinnacle experience. "Up steep slopes and across the terraces," Leatherbarrow writes, "the pilgrim was directed through dense woods, openings in tree screens and architecturally built-up areas. . . . The rule of uniqueness of place is beautifully celebrated at Varallo" (114). The site capitalizes on tree lines and topographic changes to heighten the immersive experience, keeping visitors on the intended route while obscuring subsequent chapels on the ritual path. Early site designs reveal that this spatial choreography was purposeful: "it is clear that the route up the hillside was designed very carefully to structure the sequence of spaces that would aid the memory of the pilgrim" (115).

Varallo elaborated a number of themes that became integral for later sites: a mimetic relationship with the Christian Holy Land, and Jerusalem in particular; the functionality of providing a surrogate pilgrimage experience; design choreographies oriented by the replication of places and paths associated with biblical stories; dynamic integration with and mobilization of the immediate landscape. All of these came to figure heavily in performances of materializing the Bible across time, space, culture, and Christian tradition. For several centuries, materializing the Bible was primarily a Catholic practice. Like Varallo, many sites sought to replicate Holy Land pilgrimage. Others replicated biblically oriented sites celebrated in Catholic tradition, such as the Holy Stairs (*scala santa*) and the Holy House of Loreto (*santa casa*). Protestant performances of materializing the Bible developed in tandem with two interrelated historical changes.

First, Protestants began proclaiming a special connection to the "land of the Bible" through the register of scientific modernity, often as a direct challenge to more long-standing Catholic and Orthodox presences in the Holy Land. For example, a US scholar named Edward Robinson led early efforts to survey, map, measure, and excavate archaeological sites associated with scriptural events. Published simultaneously in English and German, *Biblical Researches in Palestine, Mount Sinai and Arabia Petraea* (1841) inaugurated the fields of biblical archaeology and geography. Robinson traveled with a distinctly evangelical agenda. Infuriated by the increasing prominence of biblical textual criticism, he dedicated himself to the archaeological and topographic verification of "the absolute authority of the Bible" (Davis 1996: 35). As Protestants redefined the Holy Land in their own terms and sought to cloak those claims with scientific authority, Protestant expressions of biblical replication began to flourish.

An early and influential example is Palestine Park at the Chautauqua Assembly in western New York state. Chautauqua was founded in 1873 by two leading Methodist figures to be an institution dedicated to training Sunday school teachers. One of the founders, John Heyl Vincent, was celebrated in the Sunday school movement for his "Palestine class," a youth curriculum designed to immerse children in the land and culture of biblical history (Kimball 1913). At Chautauqua, he expanded this immersive pedagogy by designing a landscape model of "biblical Palestine." Constructed in collaboration with another influential Methodist, W. W. Wythe, the original Palestine Park stretched 170 feet in length (extended in 1879 to nearly 400 feet), and presented a scale topographic model of scriptural lands that marked the locations of cities and bodies of water. Vincent, much like Robinson, trumpeted the need to develop a land-centered understanding of biblical history. In an 1884 Introduction to a popular Bible Atlas, he explained the need this way:

> Every Bible reader should be acquainted with the outlines of Biblical and geographical antiquities. Without such knowledge it is impossible properly to understand the divine word. How often, through ignorance of sacred archaeology, we overlook the force and beauty of the allusions which abound in the narrative, poetic and prophetic parts of Scripture. And there is, moreover, an air of reality imparted to all history by familiarity with the geography involved in it. (v)

Palestine Park relied on bodily attunement to meet this geographical imperative, cultivated by the emplaced experience of walking between spots on a miniaturized replica. With Chautauqua Lake serving as the Mediterranean sea, classes were brought to the model by boat and encouraged to imagine themselves stepping onto the land of the Bible. The park was "an immediate success," teachers and visitors attended lectures dressed in Middle Eastern garb, adding elements of theatrical role-playing to the virtual reality fostered by the model (Davis 1996: 89). As Long (2003) observed about the park, "Realism was the driving aim, fantasy the enabling impulse" (30).

Second, the late nineteenth-century expansion of Protestant forms of materializing the Bible was informed by the emergence of modern tourism. While Catholic and Orthodox pilgrims had visited the lands of the Bible for more than a millennium, mass travel to the Holy Land was popularized in the 1860s. Expanding communication and transportation technologies combined with increasingly elaborate international travel infrastructures to make the trip more plausible and more attractive for unprecedented numbers of people (Kaell 2014). Increased travel to the Holy Land meant that more people were following the lead of Varallo's Franciscan creators: drawing from their own Holy Land travel to design a surrogate pilgrimage experience composed of replications.

At the same time, other pilgrimage sites took the form of mass tourism and modeled the integration of sacred travel, leisure, and capitalist consumption. The Lourdes shrine in France is a prime example (Kaufman 2005). Pilgrims began traveling to this site of Marian miracles soon after the first apparition in 1858, and by the turn of the century it was a fully realized national shrine attracting half a million visitors annually. Lourdes "recast devotional practices long associated with the act of pilgrimage within the structures and experiences of a newly commercialized society" (2) and pioneered practices that influenced secular tourism (e.g., strategic use of public infrastructures, such as railways and newspapers, and developing densely packed souvenir shops) (26, 28).

The Protestant and Catholic histories of materializing the Bible set up a key insight developed in this book. While different performances do conform to particular theological contexts, as a phenomenon materializing the Bible is not more at home in one tradition or another. Especially in vernacular forms, the material practices of Protestants and Catholics have more in common than not. The following chapters will present examples that emerge from and cater to a range of theological traditions, from Roman Catholic to Reformed Calvinist, charismatic to Southern Baptist. In turn, this project joins an interdisciplinary groundswell that critiques "unqualified notions of aniconism as the normative and conceptual default" (Meyer and Stordalen 2019: 2). Despite theological, historical, and social scientific assumptions to the contrary, materiality is always constitutive in Christian lives (Protestant, Catholic, Orthodox, and otherwise). Bodies, technologies, and infrastructures mediate divine presence, social belonging, claims to authenticity, imaginings of the past, and scriptural ideologies. The question is not if Christian traditions are material, but how and the ways in which material performances are integral to assertions of legitimacy, value, and authority (Meyer and Stordalen 2019: 4; cf. Opas and Haapalainen 2017).

Project Methodology

The research for this book was rewarding and challenging, equal portions puzzle and surprise. I collected data that speaks to the production of biblical tourism sites by designers, founding artists, and caretakers; the circulation of people, technologies, and discourses related to those sites; and, the consumption of different sites by visitors. To address these three interests, I engaged with ethnographic, archival, and mass media research methods. I outline some general methodological reflections here, and details about the data informing each chapter's analysis are included in the notes of each chapter.

Ethnographically, the book draws on data from three fieldwork projects and a series of supplemental qualitative interviews and observations. The chapters are informed by three years of fieldwork with the design team for Ark Encounter and visitors to this creationist theme park; two summers of fieldwork with tour guides and visitors at the Garden of Hope in northern Kentucky; and eighteen months of noncontiguous fieldwork with exhibit designers and visitors to Washington, DC's Museum of the Bible. These sites make multiple appearances, but they are only three of many that are analyzed closely. For most of the other sites, I interviewed individual founders, artists, or visitors. From 2014 to 2020 I traveled to forty-four sites that materialize the Bible: recording extensive field notes and photographs, taking guided tours when possible, and collecting materialities designed to help choreograph the visitor experience (e.g., guidebooks). For select site visits, I conducted informal interviews with guides, caretakers, and visitors.

To complement the ethnographic data, this book is informed by roughly 1,500 items in print or digital format sourced from multiple contexts. Some items were available through public domain, discovered in online repositories (from digitized special collections at university libraries to the Internet Archive website). I also interacted in person or online with seventeen formal archives housed at universities, museums, and historical societies. In some cases, this was an inquiry about a single item (e.g., a guidebook for a nonextant biblical garden at the San Francisco Botanical Gardens). In others, I enjoyed the experience of sifting through boxes, binders, and folders and talking with dedicated archivists (e.g., the Georgetown College Archives and Special Collections enabled access to a score of materials related to the book of Job play featured in "Reenacting").

I also assembled a personal collection of material culture items related to biblical tourism. Like other material religion scholars, I have found that the process of building one's own archive yields substantial analytical insight as well as a trove of objects to engage with as sensorial technologies (e.g., Morgan 2016; Primiano 2016; Bowman 2016). Altogether, the project collection consists of over 900 items organized into several categories: brochures, cards, DVD-CDs, flyers, guidebooks, manuscripts, newspaper-periodical articles and editions, objects, pamphlets, photographs, and postcards.

Nearly 200 items were collected or purchased at biblical tourism sites and about sixty items were donated to the collection by family, friends, and colleagues. Most of the collection, over 60 percent, was purchased through online and in person second-hand venues. Anderson Blanton was the first colleague to recommend eBay as a source for acquiring items, a method he practiced when assembling a collection of mid-twentieth-century prayer cards from Oral Roberts ministries (2015; cf. Hillis, Petit, and Epley, eds. 2006). My first eBay acquisition was in February 2017: a 1936 guidebook to Chautauqua's Palestine Park for US$9.99. Since then, I have purchased over 300 items through this online marketplace. In step with the modern tourism industry, biblical tourism sites are often prolific producers of souvenir goods, many of which find their way onto eBay through estate sales and other forms of exchange. For some sites—such as Fields of the Wood in North Carolina, Ave Maria Grotto in Alabama, and the Cyclorama of Jerusalem in Saint-Anne-de-Beaupre—new items appeared regularly over time, which meant periodic searches always yielded opportunities to consider new acquisitions. Along with providing access to actual material culture items, the eBay search process was useful in other ways. For example, I discovered the existence of several nonextant materializing the Bible sites for the first time through experimenting with search terms.

The success of finding items on eBay prompted me to begin exploring a brick-and-mortar predecessor: antique stores. In May 2017, I stepped into a small, delightfully cluttered shop in the college town where I work (Oxford, Ohio) and walked out with a series of 1904 Holy Land stereoscope cards, US$0.99/each. Over the next two years, I would visit seventeen more in-person antique venues: mostly in the tristate area of southwestern Ohio, southeastern Indiana, and northern Kentucky, but also in Phoenix, Arizona, and southwestern Florida. In only a few cases did I leave empty-handed, and altogether these stores yielded over 230 items. Exploring these contexts is, of course, quite different than the targeted searching enabled by eBay. Here, you wander the aisles, picking through well-ordered and chaotically jumbled stacks, crates, and folders. Invariably, I left immediately looking for a sink and soap: caked onto my fingertips was the accumulated dust and grime from piles of worn paper. Every store visit felt like a treasure hunt, never knowing if I would find materials of interest, how many, or of what kind. Typically, stores did have relevant items, and I was struck by how I came to expect to find at least a few things (and was both surprised and disappointed when I didn't).

This collection informs many of the chapters to come, and the process of assembling has been enjoyable and analytically useful. Given this book's focus on materiality and sensation, it is unsurprising that being able to engage with the physicality of these items is instructive. It is one thing to read the text of digitized brochures and quite another to experience the tactile qualities of brochures from different eras: varying paper textures, differing mechanics of unfolding and viewing. It is one thing to see the images on a digitized stereoscope card, and quite another to place that card into a wooden viewer and experience the optical illusion.

Building this collection has also prompted reflection on common categories in the market and scholarship of material culture. "Ephemera," for example, is a term that I have experienced a significant reorientation to. This term is usually assigned to mass-produced items, made for easy distribution and temporary use that are prone to being easily lost, forgotten, or discarded. Yet, for nonextant biblical tourism sites my knowledge of them owes a great deal to the continually circulating ephemera they once produced. In many cases, the material culture of postcards, brochures, and guidebooks long outlives the physical place they first served to promote.

Finally, I have discovered what others have about collecting; it can become obsessive, prompting a want to continually expand the contents, to work toward an ever-receding horizon of completeness (Morgan 2016). Building this collection has yielded an unexpected pleasure and a nagging desire to keep searching and acquiring. It has a hold on me beyond the scope of any single site, analysis, or book. I am tempted to continue, and suspect I will. Yet, I wonder: Will the experience change when the collection is no longer servicing a book project but has become an end in itself?

The third method that informs the chapters to come is the collection and analysis of mass media texts drawn from online sources. For every biblical tourism site that appears in this book, I searched for related news and journalistic reports, official websites, personal blogs written by visitors and designers, podcasts, and video footage documented on YouTube and Vimeo. For many of the extant sites, I subscribed to email and newsletter listservs and followed sites on social media platforms (namely, Instagram, Twitter, and LinkedIn). In a few cases, social media also served as visitor data. Focusing on Instagram, I analyzed hundreds of self-posed images that people posted when visiting biblical tourism sites (e.g., Chapter 13).

The mixed-methods design of integrating ethnographic, archival, and mass media data emerged in response to the way I approached the phenomenon of materializing the Bible. The comparative dimension of moving across time, place, and tradition demands a methodology that can address extant and nonextant sites and the global circulation of people and things. The interest in both producers and consumers likewise demands a methodology that can speak to differently positioned actors. This book, again, is not about any single expression or genealogy of Christian material culture; it is more ambitious (perhaps, foolish) than that and required a method to match.

Conclusion

On several occasions, while working on this book, I remembered something the musician John Prine used to say about a song he recorded in 1978, "Sabu Visits the Twin Cities Alone." A decade later, when recording a live album, he told an audience the story. He joked semi-seriously: "When I wrote this I stayed in my room for three days. I was afraid somebody was gonna ask me what this song was about."[1] In moments of self-doubt, or maybe just brutal honesty, I've felt a bit the same about *Materializing the Bible*. In its conception and writing, it is an unconventional book. Truthfully, it's a bit weird, and that is one reason I kept going with it. More hopefully, we might call it an experiment in scholarly storytelling. If it is a failed experiment, that is ok. At the least, it can be a reminder that we, as scholars and storytellers, have more options available to us than the standard conventions of the academic monograph.

What follows are twenty short chapters divided into three sections: Variations on Replication, the Power of Nature, and Choreographing Experience. The sections are prefaced with their own brief introductions, providing less a chapter play-by-play and more a proposal for what makes each set cohere. Each chapter takes up a different expression of the materializing the Bible phenomenon. Some chapters focus on a single site as a case study, while others move among several sites. The chapters are mostly noncontiguous, which means you, the reader, can decide where you want to begin and which order you want to follow.

Ultimately, I hope this book will be a generative provocation in the study of material religion, one that encourages creative imaginings and renderings of research. Building on the inspiring work of colleagues, I also hope this book makes a valuable contribution to understanding the material life of Christianity—that is, the ways in which bodies, technologies, and infrastructures help constitute lived experiences and relations of power (e.g., McDannell 1995; Morgan 1997; Engelke 2007; Meyer 2015; Kaell 2014, 2020). Much of this project has been about trying to find the beauty where others see it—rather than, say, "kitsch" or "spectacle." I hope this search comes across in the reading and that readers are willing to do the same. As much as any other ambition, though, I hope the book is an enjoyable journey through the social life of materializing the Bible. I encountered a lot of fascinating stories in the course of doing this research, and I hope to be a good steward of them: to share them well, keep them in circulation, and make clear their value for the interdisciplinary study of material religion.

Section I

Variations on Replication

In six chapters, Section I explores practices of material replication—that is, of isolating an aspect, event, or era of the past (actual or imagined) and physically recontextualizing it in the present. The chapters examine (1) so-called "full-size" replicas, such as biblical story spots located in contemporary Israel-Palestine and the Wilderness Tabernacle detailed in the book of Exodus; (2) miniature models of the city of Jerusalem; (3) a theatrical re-enactment of the Book of Job that toured in the United States and internationally for over twenty years; (4) a literalist recreation of Noah's ark that fuses Disney entertainment and Protestant fundamentalism; (5) the linking of materiality with theology, such as stone's durability and sand's ephemerality; and (6) an aesthetic reimagining of first-century Nazareth.

As materializing the Bible performances engage with replication, they enact a consequential religious practice. Contrary to secular ideologies that devalue replication (Baudrillard 1994), Christians have a long history of using replication efficaciously. Ethiopian Orthodox churches mark sacred space by adding a consecrated replica of the Ark of the Covenant (Bolylston 2018: 25); Mormons remember the nineteenth-century pioneer experience of journeying west to Salt Lake City by performing Trek reenactments (Patterson 2020); Protestants create a range of biblical replications, from landscape models to panoramic views of biblical places (Long 2003); and, Catholics are serial replicators, channeling divine presence through prayers cards (Orsi 2005), portable Marian statues (Morgan 2009), and shrine complexes (McDannell 1995).

Replication accomplishes the powerful cultural work of promising experiential access to a sacralized past. Replication's efficacy is grounded in a claim that material re-presentation enables a new or renewed relationship with the past element being recontextualized. Replication seeks to free moments of sacred history from a singular space-time location and collapses the temporal divide, creating an affective bridge between past and present. Irrespective of the scale (life-size or miniature) or relational claim (exacting or inspired by), this promise is anchored by the body's experience of technology and infrastructure. The power of the replica rests on sensorial encounters; we feel our physical presence in relation to their materiality. And, as Chapters 5 and 6 explore, the materiality at stake is not merely instrumentalized by human actors but is itself an agentive force. The chapters in this section explore the sensory dynamics and ideological dimensions of materializing the Bible's experiential promise, asking what replications of the biblical past have to say about their makers, visitors, and the social conditions of their making.

The examples profiled in this section also make clear that replication is always interdiscursive, integrating multiple discourse genres, frames, and histories (Bartesaghi and Noy 2015). For example, we see the non-scriptural discourse of science used to render scriptural expression. Chapters 1 and 2 engage with the dramatic increase in Christian Holy Land replicas in the wake of a scientific (re)discovery of Palestine in the early to mid-nineteenth century. As Protestants and Catholics mapped, measured, excavated, studied, and extracted from the "lands of the Bible," a new confidence cohered for rendering the Holy Land authentically, gauged by the register of scientific accuracy.

Section I reveals important ways in which authority is claimed, negotiated, and performed through replication. The experiential promise of accessing the sacred past is about fostering spiritual intimacy, but in ways that classify experiences as legitimate, valuable, compelling, trustworthy, and, ultimately, authoritative. Biblical replication is certainly about reflecting and recreating textual ideologies of scriptural authority, but it is also about mobilizing the cultural power of other discourses (e.g., science, entertainment) to bolster the authoritative claims of actors who embody theologies, traditions, and identities.

Figure 1 Tabernacle replica (Timna Park, Israel). Photo credit: Wikimedia Commons.

1

1:1

Life-size. Full-size. Full-scale. Exact scale. Exact copy. There are different ways to make the same claim about a replication: that its spatial dimensions are on a 1:1 scale with an original. This claim of direct proportionality can also extend to other physical elements, such as material contents, composition, and relations to forms of practice, such as movement. Ultimately, this is not strictly about physicality and is not merely a claim of accuracy. It is a promise of affective experience and is thoroughly sensorial.

The promise of being 1:1 is about the presence of the body in space and the body's engagement with materiality. It's about a body sensing the height of a ceiling, the width of a room or walkway, the proximity between objects, the density of matter, environmental scale and shape from a human vantage. Corporeal experience is vital for 1:1, but it is actually grounded in the limitations of the body. Without additional technological mediation, we can only know the world through our senses and 1:1 trades on this restricted capacity. Any promise of 1:1 is an illusion, a seduction to accept one sensory experience as standing in for another. What is the promise that masks this sleight of body? The promise is that the replication will deliver a direct and immediate sense of presence, of being elsewhere, of being connected to an original via the copy.

Claims of being 1:1 figure centrally in the history of materializing the Bible. From Noah's ark to Moses's Tabernacle in the Wilderness to Solomon's Temple and Jesus's tomb, producers have claimed to have made "life-size" replicas of biblical stories, scenes, and settings. The illusion of exactness is inevitably partial, full of gaps, distortions, omissions, and erasures. Consider, for example, the surrogate pilgrimage experience of an early twentieth-century Holy Land replication.

From April to December 1904, St. Louis, Missouri, hosted an extravagant World's Fair, the Louisiana Purchase Exposition.[1] Located at the fairgrounds' center was one of the Exposition's most elaborate displays, a roughly 10-acre exhibit of the Old City of Jerusalem. Designed as a 1:1 replication, Jerusalem in St. Louis included 300 structures and 22 streets. Several months before its opening, a San Francisco journalist assured readers and potential visitors of the model's accuracy: "The architect visited Jerusalem personally and studied with minute care the construction of the walls, towers and interior dwellings and other edifices which they were to reproduce at St. Louis, so that in all essential respects the 'New Jerusalem' will be identical in appearance with the original."

Centered on this recreated architecture, the exhibit's promise of 1:1 faithfulness extended to other features. The land was graded to mimic Jerusalem's hills and valleys. The feel of the ground in the Church of the Holy Sepulchre's courtyard was to be copied: "pavement worn by the feet of innumerable pilgrims, is to be reproduced accurately."[2] And, a series of living imports would be an animate element of the experience: between several hundred and a thousand people—including Muslims, Jews, and Greek Orthodox Christians—were purported to be brought from Palestine; several hundred animals also from Palestine, including camels, donkeys, mules, and horses, and food items, "the luscious oranges, lemons, dates, and grapes which so attracted the spies of Israel."[3]

Exhibitors celebrated the sensory promise of this new Jerusalem's exactness, from the scale of buildings to the feel of "worn" pavement and those "luscious" fruits. Of course, they did not advertise the many ways in which Jerusalem in St. Louis distorted Jerusalem in Palestine. For example, only select sacred sites were included, most of which were geared toward Christian visitors (e.g., the Via Dolorosa). Walls were built of wood and buildings of plaster, not stone. Most of the houses were either empty or used as vending stations. The cardinal orientation was askew—for example, the Church of the Holy Sepulchre was in the replica's southwest corner instead of the northwest. Many of the purported Jerusalemites were, in fact, from Syria, Lebanon, other areas of Palestine, or US cities. The replica only included four of eight city gates and added two additional gates that had no analogue in the actual Jerusalem. Several sites that exist outside the Old City were brought inside the replica, primarily to kindle Christian interest (e.g., a miniature Garden of Gethsemane and imagined Bethlehem manger). There were also anachronistic biblical additions, such as a miniaturized Solomon's Temple and a painted canvas depiction of the Israelites at Mt. Sinai. The visual experience from outside the gates also differed dramatically from Palestine's Jerusalem: namely, a large Ferris wheel was unavoidably visible behind the Dome of the Rock when looking southeast.

The point of cataloguing these distortions in the 1:1 promise is not to dismiss the skill of the designers or the immensity of the project; it was at the time, and still remains, the largest documented effort to replicate Jerusalem. The point is that all 1:1 projects are partial and that any suspension of disbelief entails an erasure of distortions and omissions. Indulging that suspension is common. The exhibitors for Jerusalem in St. Louis boastfully marketed the illusion and, based on reviews at the time, visitors seemed to embrace it.

The sensory promise of 1:1 replication exemplifies a cultural shift that took root among US Protestants in the second half of the nineteenth century. This shift was defined by a move from "a conceptual realism initiated by narrative and sermon heuristics to an external, materially based, simulated reality epitomized by various interactive and performative pedagogies" (Jackson 2009: 4) and was performed via diverse media, from traveling panoramas (Morgan 2007) to magic lantern (Schaefer 2017) and stereoscope (Lindsey 2017) shows. By training bodies to trust their experience of these material performances, this participatory pedagogy mobilized the senses in service of ideological ends. In the case of Jerusalem in St. Louis, the bodily experience of being immersed in a 1:1 replica drew together surrogate pilgrimage, a sense of scriptural intimacy, and an Orientalist gaze that recreated white Protestant claims of dominance.

The replica worked as virtual pilgrimage in multiple ways. Visitors could perform rituals that originated in the actual Jerusalem, such as walking and praying the Stations of the Cross. They could buy artisanal souvenirs from would-be Palestinians dwelling within the exhibit. They could eat "luscious" foods and rent a camel to ride (the latter being one of the distorted participatory elements, as renting a camel to ride inside the actual Old City walls was not common practice). Pilgrimage is defined by movement to places set apart (Coleman and Elsner 1995), which resonated with the replication's setting: being centrally located inside the already set apart experiential frame of being inside the Exposition.

In the exhibit's prospectus, a fundraising document used to entice investors, the creators emphasized the capacity of the replication to intensify visitors' attachment to scripture. "A day spent here . . . will give Sunday-school scholars and teachers a more vivid and lasting impression of hundreds of Bible texts than months of study in the class room."[4] Much the same was declared in the exhibit's opening address, July 11, 1904. The president of the Jerusalem Exhibition Company, a sitting US senator from Missouri, said to the gathered crowd: "There are many Scriptural passages, the full significance of which has never dawned upon even the close Bible students until they have become conversant with the architecture, topography, products and other features of the Holy Land, and the manners and habits of the people residing there."[5]

The efficacy of the virtual pilgrimage and the renewed intimacy with scripture were both thoroughly grounded in an Orientalist vision of the Holy Land. Just after boasting about the "full significance" of scriptural meaning, the senator invoked a particularly audacious version of an ideology of biblical timelessness: "It is a remarkable fact that Palestine has changed but little since the days of Christ, and in some respects but little, if any, since the days of Abraham." This replication's sensory promise of 1:1 was full of such Protestant claims about the Holy Land, a yearning for the "land of the Bible" to be as biblical as imagined. The troubled ideology of timelessness was extended to the people who exhibition designers enthusiastically objectified. As Lindsey (2017) observes in her analysis of Jerusalem in St. Louis, "inhabitants of the Holy Land were simultaneously configured as ethnographic icon and biblical relic" (162).

The Wilderness Tabernacle

If Jerusalem in St. Louis represents an especially elaborate example of 1:1 biblical replication, then the most common example is the Tabernacle described in the book of Exodus. As of June 2020, there were at least twelve extant Tabernacle replicas.[6] The appeal of the Tabernacle ensues partly from the level of detail provided in Exodus 25–30. As the story goes, the Israelites wandered in the desert for forty years. During this time, Moses encountered God on Mt. Sinai for forty days and forty nights; it was then that God gave Moses precise instructions for creating a mobile sanctuary. This sanctuary, the Tabernacle, would be God's earthly dwelling place.

The account of God's instruction to Moses for the Tabernacle begins with a catalogue of materials: "gold, silver, and bronze, blue, purple, and crimson yarns and fine linen, goats' hair, tanned rams' skins, fine leather, acacia wood, oil for the lamps, spices for the anointing oil and for the fragrant incense, onyx stones and gems to be set in the ephod and for the breastpiece" (25:3-7, NRSV). The text that follows details the size dimensions of various elements, construction specifications, color compositions for different cloth components, arrangements of items (e.g., where to place the Ark of the Covenant), dress for the high priest, and ritual guidelines (e.g., incense recipe). Compared to other biblical accounts that have been replicated in which the details are relatively sparse—Noah's ark, for example—the Tabernacle is quite closely outlined.

An early and influential site in the US history of materializing the Bible was Palestine Park, a scaled topographic model of the Holy Land developed on the grounds of western New York's Chautauqua Assembly. In 1875, for its second summer season, one of Palestine Park's designers added a new attraction: a replica of the Tabernacle (Long 2003). The next documented account is of a Seventh-Day Adventist preacher, O. O. Bernstein, who crafted a traveling exhibition that premiered at the 1933 Century of Progress Exposition in Chicago.[7] In 1948, a Baptist pastor in St. Petersburg, Florida, opened his version of the Israelite sanctuary to the public as an object lesson for his church and as an attraction for tourists. This replica was purchased by the Eastern Mennonite Board of Missions and relocated in 1975 to the Mennonite Information Center in Lancaster, Pennsylvania, where it still welcomes visitors.[8] Most 1:1 Tabernacle replicas have been located in the United States, but not all. A widely reported example was created in 1986 by German missionaries in southern Israel, within the state-owned Timna Park, which was purchased by the US Southern Baptist Convention in 1999. Like Bernstein, others have conjured the portable nature of the Israelite Tabernacle by making their replica a mobile version—for example, the Tabernacle Experience was founded in 2000 and is based in southern California, and Messiah's Mansion was founded in 2003 and is based in central Oklahoma.

Like Jerusalem in St. Louis, Tabernacle replicas reflect and recreate a participatory pedagogy.[9] On group tours, guides move visitors from outside the perimeter walls to inside the "holiest of holies." Tours are largely staged as a ritual explanation, with guides retracing the high priest's movement through the different areas and interactions with ritual items (e.g., sacrificial altar). Guide performances are marked both by constant movement and by constant meta-corporeal observation about that movement—for example, noting where they are moving and its relationship to preceding spaces. Goh (2017) analyzes a Tabernacle tour at the Great Passion Play and observes how the performance emphasizes an "up close experiential aspect" (318), which trades on visitors following the guide's gestural and bodily cues. To open a two-hour tour of Messiah's Mansion, the guide and project founder speaks, standing behind a miniature model. He invokes the foundational sensorial promise of 1:1 replication to frame the tour:

> As we travel today through this sanctuary, you're gonna see in just a little bit, you're gonna see that we're gonna go through a sanctuary like this. This is, of course, a model of the Mosaic sanctuary. The one that we're actually gonna go through today, later, as we continue from here is going to be a full-scale model

of the Mosaic sanctuary. It's gonna be the size it would have been if you were one of the children of Israel in days of Moses. So, you're gonna be able to see the furniture. You're gonna see how it looks, the shapes and the sizes of everything as we travel through the sanctuary.

Being "up close" and "traveling through" a "full-scale model" is the corporeal engine for any Tabernacle teaching performance. Engaging 1:1 Tabernacles in this way exemplifies what Morgan (2012) calls the "embodied eye," in which visuality is produced in tandem with other sensations. For the Tabernacle, this is primarily about the experience of the body in space, capitalizing on scale and proximity to create a sense of accessing the biblical past.

Other ways of sensing are also used, such as olfactory visuality. Included in the Exodus account's many details is a recipe for incense: sweet spices, stacte, onycha, galbanum, frankincense, and salt (30: 34-35, NRSV). For the tours analyzed here, each attraction's version of this incense mixture is lit as tours begin, which means the enclosed tent is heavily perfumed by the time visitors enter. Consider the following example from the Great Passion Play:

> Guide: Now, if I could get you to turn and look at me please. Just look at me. Many people don't realize that incense is an important thing, because a lot of our churches don't use it. Do you use it in your church usually? Alright, learn the lesson of the incense quickly, then. Two things, very simple. The first one is, {sniffing air}, hey, it smells good. Isn't that a simple lesson? And yet, God's Word says, "I want your life to have a sweet-smelling savor before Him." He wants to enjoy being with you. In other words, don't be a stinker. Okay. The second lesson is very simple. I want you to learn this one so you can say it in your sleep. As the smoke goes up it says, "let your prayer and your praise reach up to God." {shifts to chant and increases rate of speech} Your prayer and your praise reach up to God. Your prayer and your praise reach up to God. Your prayer and your praise reach up to God. Your prayer and your praise reach up to God. {ends chant} What did I say?
>
> Crowd: Your prayer and your praise reach up to God.
>
> Guide: Oh, you've got it.

Here, the guide attunes visitors to the olfactory experience and puts the pungent moment to work in several ways. He begins by invoking a dominant evangelical self-critique that contemporary "churches" have forgotten key biblical teachings, suggesting the participatory pedagogy of the Tabernacle as an antidote. He then presents two Christianized interpretations of this ritual element, both grounded in the logic of iconicity: ethical character to resemble sweet smell, prayers to resemble rising smoke. As with orienting the body in space, this moment of olfactory visuality is designed to create sensorial access to the biblical past.

Participatory pedagogy mobilizes the affective power of sensation to intensify experience and circulate ideologies. Given the theological diversity of Tabernacle replications, what is the common ideology being recreated? This project's catalogue of Tabernacle replications includes Methodists (Palestine Park); 7th Day Adventists (Bernstein); a Baptist creation bought by Mennonites (the St. Petersburg replica moved to Lancaster); a replica in Israel jointly operated by Southern Baptists and Messianic Jews; a mobile replica operated by Latter-Day Saints from 2016 to 2019;[10] and, the Tabernacle Experience emerged from the neo-charismatic milieu of southern California.

One ideology that recurs across this theologically diverse set is supersessionism. When Christian replications of the Tabernacle use the Exodus story as a prefiguration of Jesus, they recreate an enduring and destructive theology that understands Judaism as a stepping stone toward Christianity. Any Jewish understandings of Hebrew Bible texts, including the Tabernacle, are displaced in favor of a Christianized "Old Testament." Goh (2017) observes this ideology in his 2016 tours of Tabernacles at the Great Passion Play and Florida's Holy Land Experience, and Long (2001: 36) observes the same for Palestine Park's 1875 replica. Writing about the traveling Tabernacle Experience for *The Interfaith Observer* in 2016, biblical studies scholar Jonathan Haumrighesen describes his reaction to the replica's participatory pedagogy as "ambivalent." He found the sensory engagements deeply compelling, "the re-enactment made the words of Exodus 25-27 become flesh." But, he found the thorough supersessionism deeply disturbing, "these profound rituals were [presented as] only deficient foreshadowings of the Jesus to come."[11]

Coda

The promise of 1:1 replication is definitively sensorial. It's a compelling proposition for designers and visitors alike. While claims about dimension, scale, shape, color, activity, and smell might be figured as matters of historical authenticity, they are not reducible to this. Ultimately, they are about the presence of the body in space, in relation to materiality, and the seduction that the replication is not only physical but experiential. Through this sensory choreography, the biblical past is presented as accessible.

In this project's record of 1:1 biblical replications, the promise of being in a "full-scale" environment is never an end in itself. These materializations are used to teach, and in doing so, they recreate enduring ideologies (e.g., Orientalism and supersessionism). Since the mid-nineteenth century, Protestants have invested in technologies, techniques, programs, and institutions that rest on a participatory pedagogy (Jackson 2009; cf. Morgan 2007; Schaefer 2017). Replications pitched as 1:1 exemplify this approach. Productions like Jerusalem in St. Louis and the Wilderness Tabernacle are materializations designed to engage audiences by activating the senses, in which efficacy is bound to bodily experience.

Figure 2 Model of Jerusalem at Clear Creek Bible College (Pineville, Kentucky). Photo credit: James S. Bielo.

2

Miniaturizing

Come and See Jerusalem in Miniature! Variations on this invitation have circulated since the late 1500s and continue still more than four centuries later. The media form is a scale model replication of the city, typically the Old City and surrounding landscape, and the promise is that this representation creates access to the biblical past. Makers, guides, and guiding materials say to visitors, "come and see, see and imagine, imagine and understand better the stories of scripture, understand them better and experience renewed intimacy with the truths of scripture."[1]

The earliest documented Jerusalem miniature was produced in the 1570s by a German wood-carver, Jacob Sandtner. He had created similarly styled models of numerous Bavarian cities, and the Jerusalem model attributed to him now resides in Munich's Bayerisches Nationalmuseum. Sandtner's model represented contemporary Jerusalem in the late sixteenth century, though it was more idealized than real, not based on firsthand measurements (Rubin 2000).

The practice of producing Jerusalem miniatures escalated in tandem with the expansion of militarism, imperialism, and scientific engagement with the lands of the Bible (Foliard 2017). Figures like Edward Robinson led early efforts to survey, map, and excavate archaeological sites linked with scriptural stories. Robinson was infuriated by the increasing influence of biblical textual criticism and dedicated himself to verifying "the absolute authority of the Bible" through archaeological and topographic analysis (Davis 1996: 35). Robinson and others treated landscapes as biblical object lessons and imbued those lessons with the cultural capital of science, embodying modern impulses to wed faith and reason and assess truth through discourses of measurement, in which authenticity is anchored by scientific legitimacy (Cintron 1997). As the Holy Land became newly legible through the register of empirical science, a "rash of [Jerusalem] models" proliferated throughout western Europe (Altick 1978: 394; cf. Kark 1987).[2]

A prominent example from this "rash of models" was produced by Brunetti, a Dubliner of Italian origin. Brunetti's 1846 model represented Jerusalem in the first century (i.e., Jerusalem in the time of Jesus), premiering in Dublin before touring extensively in England and Scotland. In 1849, Brunetti's model was the first Jerusalem miniature to exhibit in the United States, touring New York, Boston, and other cities (Rubin 2000). No remains of the model itself are known to have survived, but guidebooks from its exhibitions are extant, including an 1847 copy of "Description of the Model of Ancient Jerusalem, Illustrative of the Sacred Scriptures, and the Writings of Josephus."

This thirty-page booklet moves visitors from spot to spot on the model, narrating each location's appearance in scripture and link to the life of Jesus. It begins with Jerusalem as the "city of David" and concludes with the destruction of the Jewish Temple in 70 CE as a prophetic fulfillment. The guidebook uses various techniques to entice a sense of intimacy with the biblical past, encouraging visitors to imagine themselves transported as they move around the model. Eighty locations were labeled and most use spatial indexicals to place the visitor onsite: "And *here* [David] erected the palace (1) in which he passed his eventful life" (emphasis added). An opening "advertisement" offers instructions for viewing that orient the body and transition from distance to proximity: "In order fully to see the beauty of the Model, it is recommended to take a distant view of it from each of the corners, and to bring the eye to the level of the Model by sitting down, so as to have the same view as one has from the natural level of the ground." Throughout, the book fosters a visual imagination, such as this description of the Mount of Olives: "The view from the summit is most beautiful. Jerusalem, spread out beneath the feet like a map, on the one side; and on the other a varied and extensive view of the mountains of Moab and the vale of Jordan to the Dead Sea."

To compliment these imaginative techniques, the guidebook makes various appeals to authenticity. Figures invested with scientific legitimacy, including Robinson, are repeatedly referenced directly or indirectly, often in support of continuities between the biblical past and the present: "In the outer enclosure, on the same side, is the golden gate (32), through which the Redeemer entered, amid the hosannahs of the multitude. The gate still existing is by some supposed to be the same, but there is no doubt that it at least stands upon the same site." The guidebook also appeals to sensory ideologies of nature that promise direct, metonymic access to the past through biblical botanicals (see Section II). For example, in describing olive trees in the Garden of Gethsemane, visitors are instructed: "that group of aged olives were the witnesses of a superhuman agony inflicted upon him by the collective crimes of a guilty world." Finally, the book's mobilization of the authentic looks to the future, fostering a promissory ideology of biblical archaeology: "A Turkish mosque now covers [David's burial site], but it is supposed that the sepulcher below still exists, and will one day be discovered." Here and elsewhere, an authentic Christian Holy Land is envisioned in ways that erase non-Christian presences, anticipating an Orientalist gaze that clears away anything that obscures or interrupts access to a biblical past defined by Jesus (Feldman 2007; cf. Kersel and Rowan 2012).

The success of Brunetti's model anticipated other nineteenth-century miniatures of contemporary Jerusalem. For example, a model was created by Stephen Illees, a Hungarian Catholic, for the 1873 Vienna World's Fair, and subsequently toured Europe for five years (exhibiting in London, Munich, Cologne, Zurich, and Geneva, among other cities). Since 1985, Illees's model has been on display at Jerusalem's Tower of David museum (Rubin 2007). In 1879, a model was created for visitors to the Methodist camp meeting site at Ocean Grove, New Jersey (Messenger 1999), which was extant until 1959. Visitors to the Ocean Grove model were led on virtual tours, mimicking group tours of Palestine that had just begun in the 1860s. A 1919 description by an Ocean Grove Camp Meeting Association trustee performs again an aura of authenticity grounded in a discourse of measurement, boasting that the model featured 1,200 trees and was "so accurate in the reproduction that scores of travelers who have visited Jerusalem have found keen delight in identifying its different sections and even individual buildings" (106).

Jerusalem miniatures continue to resonate with contemporary sites of religious tourism. One model of biblical Jerusalem, *c*. 66 CE, is a permanent display at the Holy Land Experience (HLE) in Orlando, Florida.[3] Located 11 miles northeast of Walt Disney World, HLE opened in 2001 as "a living, biblical museum." Founded by a Christian Zionist ministry, it was purchased in 2007 by Trinity Broadcasting Network, a charismatic televangelism ministry (e.g., Mathews 2015). A 2019 schedule of events presents the model with this invitation: "Visit our model, the largest indoor replica in the world, and see where Jesus walked, ministered, healed, and performed other miracles." Twice daily, thirty-minute guided presentations of the model are performed.

The model is situated by cardinal direction, with a landscape painting of springtime hills and valleys beneath a blue sky to the north and a replica of the Western Wall to the east (complete with artificial weeds sprouting from the crevices). The floor on the east-west sides inclines slightly, enhancing the panoramic gaze when moving around the model. In March 2014, the first tour began promptly at 10:30 a.m. "Dr. Bill," a man in his early seventies who introduced himself as a longtime guide for pilgrimages to Israel, stepped onto a small speaking platform atop the model. He joked in the register of biblical literalism when first stepping up, "The Bible says there were giants in the land, and here I am."

Speaking with a headset mic, Dr. Bill used a flashlight to pinpoint locations on the model throughout the presentation. The small audience listened attentively, seated in chairs or leaning against the model's sides, periodically snapping photos with iPhones, point-n-shoots, and more professional cameras. His performance was a mix of historical claims, identifying the locations of biblical scenes and Protestant-inflected anecdotes about scripture. For example, we were taught: this was Jerusalem at its population peak of ~90,000 people, four years before the Roman siege; Herod was as architecturally gifted as he was morally corrupt; Satan tempted Jesus to jump from the temple's highest point, where the Last Supper was located and where Peter and Jon healed a man on the temple steps in the book of Acts. Dr. Bill closed his sweeping historical narrative with a modest ambition that recalls the promise of Brunetti, Ocean Grove, and all Jerusalem miniatures: "I hope the scriptures come a bit more alive with the model in your mind." He then invited us to purchase a souvenir laminated map of the model, which would aid individual and group Bible study back home.

HLE's miniature is a featured exhibit at a much-visited attraction, but other models are more tucked away on the US religious landscape. Since 1979, a miniature model of Jerusalem at the time of Jesus has resided at Clear Creek Baptist Bible College in central Appalachia.[4] Clear Creek's small campus in Pineville, Kentucky, is located 40 miles east of I-75, near the Tennessee and Virginia borders. Like so many Holy Land replications, Clear Creek's miniature Jerusalem emerged from a visit to Israel-Palestine. Robert Fitts, a former Bible professor at Clear Creek, participated in an archaeological dig in 1977 with faculty from New Orleans Baptist Theological Seminary. Fitts completed the model in two years with assistance from students and colleagues. It garnered a news feature by a local TV station, which briefly made the model an attraction for area residents to visit. After Fitts's retirement in 1986, the model sat mostly dormant until 2016 when it was refurbished and relocated to a newly constructed building.

Since 2016, the model has sat front and center in the central administration office, the main welcome center for all campus visitors. Campus tours visit the model, which includes two nine-minute audio narrations, "The Last Week of Jesus Christ" and "Jerusalem—Walk Through." Both recordings are accompanied by an overhead laser that is timed to identify the spots as they are being discussed. The former is replete with Gospel references and provides a scriptural play-by-play of the days preceding and following Jesus's crucifixion. The latter highlights geographical spots integral to Christian scripture, with references to both the Hebrew Bible and the New Testament. Throughout, these guiding narrations reflect and recreate enduring elements of the miniature's promised access to the biblical past. The opening minute of the Last Week narration combines two of these elements, authenticity grounded in a discourse of measurement and a call to be imaginatively transported: "What you're looking at has been the result of years and years of archaeological and literary research related to the first century AD Jerusalem, or the Jerusalem as Jesus would have known it. . . . We pray you find it helpful to imagine what Jesus experienced his last week. Imagine being alive about two thousand years ago."

Subtly, and perhaps unintentionally, past and present performances of the promise of miniaturizing intermingle at the Clear Creek model. In a small hallway, adjacent to the main room where the model sits, a framed picture of the model sat on a table. The picture is an artifact of the model's initial display, and the caption text references its previous technological choreography: a taped narration and timed lighting installed underneath the model. The text concludes by, again, appealing to authority and intimacy: "Scholarly research and careful construction allows the viewer to receive both educational enlightenment as well as inspirational uplift. Christians will be delighted with this close encounter." Michael, the college staff member who led me on a tour of the model in March 2019, echoed this with his own rendition of the promise of miniaturizing: "a picture speaks a thousand words, so a model must speak a few more!"

Imagine

The social life of miniatures has ranged widely across time and cultural context, from children's toy to military stratagem, museum display, decorative and commemorative object, didactic and instructional device, surrogate and mimetic travel, and a memorializing media (e.g., Rubin 2000; Mikula 2017). Perhaps it is the "hybrid character" of the miniature—its resonance with art and science, the imagined and the actual, distance and proximity, play and analysis—that affords this diverse potential (Mikula 2017: 152). For the last 450 years, Catholics and Protestants have mobilized the miniature as part of an unquenchable desire to draw closer to a biblical past defined by the life of Jesus.

In the US context, the Jerusalem miniature reflects and recreates an embrace of the object lesson as a pedagogical tool (Boylan 1988; cf. Carter 2018). Along with maps, chalk talks, diagrams, Bible lesson picture cards, and other miniature replications (e.g., Moses's Tabernacle, Noah's ark), Jerusalem miniatures were part of a media complex that taught through materiality (Morgan 1999: 242). "Any winning and reverent device which may serve to attract young minds and hearts to the priceless truth hidden away in the Holy Book, deserves a welcome," writes one champion of using material media in the Sunday school classroom and at home (Beard 1908: 3). The Jerusalem miniature, unlike many of its media counterparts, gained traction beyond congregational and familial contexts, attracting audiences as a tourist display.

As an object lesson used in religious tourism, Jerusalem miniatures integrate imagination, affect, and embodiment. Guidebooks and tour guides that narrate miniatures do not merely relay on facts and figures and scriptural stories; they ask visitors to "imagine" the city at a particular moment in time. The goal is to envision scriptural stories as lived history more so than chapter and verse. "This" is the path Jesus took; "here" is where he prayed. The imaginative capacities of the miniature are bolstered by emotional attachments developed through embodied engagement. "Affect is precipitated by the activity of corporeal movement around the object. We walk around the model, we gaze at it, we look deeply into its hidden spaces" (Whitcomb 2010: 48). Encircling, inspecting nooks and crannies, leaning in and over, pointing to a spot, taking a picture: through these bodily techniques, visitors play in the biblical past and foster the intimacy they seek with scripture.

Miniatures have been a source of tourist fascination, but they have also been a source of scholarly concern. Like all forms of material replication, miniatures are susceptible to processes of erasure (Kersel and Rowan 2012). Histories and presences on the landscape are erased that do not fit the past being conjured. For miniatures of Jerusalem, envisioning Jesus in place is the primary interest. The centuries of dwelling, flourishing, and contestation that followed are often treated as "oriental clutter," impediments to this desired past (Feldman 2007: 365).

Critics of the miniature have also argued that this form of object representation freezes a place in a particular moment of time, creating static and overly nostalgic representations (Stewart 1984). In the case of miniature Jerusalems, this seems less a hidden or nagging dilemma and more something that is quite self-consciously the point of it all. Miniaturizing the city where Jesus's life on earth culminated suspends this event in time, isolating it for study and imagination.

For examples like the HLE model, miniature Jerusalem has a Janus-faced quality, looking back and ahead in time. It is dedicated to both the past when Jesus lived and a messianic future when Jesus returns.

In the mid-nineteenth century, the Holy Land was extensively mapped and measured, borne of science and imperialism. Miniatures of Jerusalem began proliferating at this time, performing scientific modernity's discourse of measurement (Cintron 1997). The authenticity of models was figured first in mathematical terms: celebrations of dimensional, topographic, and architectural accuracy. Precision was, and continues to be, important. Precision highlights the miniature's capacity to work effectively as an object lesson for scriptural study. Ultimately, much like the "full-scale" models featured in Chapter 1, obsessions with precision are a means to a different end. In the desire to create an experiential bond with the biblical past, understanding comes through envisioning and precision is oriented toward imagination. In this way, miniaturizing Jerusalem embodies the capacity of the miniature to "condense" and "enrich" values: "The cleverer I am at miniaturizing the world, the better I possess it. . . . One must go beyond logic to experience what is large in what is small" (Bachelard 1964 [1958]: 150).

Figure 3 The book of Job (Pineville, Kentucky) postcard (author's collection).

3

Reenacting

For many materializing the Bible performances, the experiential frame coproduced by designers, caretakers, visitors, and materialities is clear. Some work devotionally, designed to foster prayer and worship, often abiding by authorized ritual scripts and routines. Some work pedagogically, mobilizing technology to teach theology, scriptural hermeneutics, and sociopolitical ideologies. Some work evangelistically, addressing visitors as spiritually wanting people in need of conversion or recommitment. And, others work as entertainment, fusing fun and faith. Some strategically integrate multiple frames. Following Goffman (1974), the frame shared by participants is mutually understood, providing structures of expectation, norms of appropriateness to be followed or challenged, and a general sense of "what is going on here."

However, things are not always so clear. In some materializing the Bible performances, the experiential frame is more ambiguous. Intents and effects are unclear, polysemous, or contested. The confidence of "what is going on here" becomes an uncertainty: "what is going on here?" This chapter presents one such case: a dramatic interpretation of the Hebrew Bible's book of Job that was produced from 1957 to 1980.[1] This example operates in the genre of theatrical reenactment. The scriptural story is recreated not through architectural and landscape replicas but through bodily gesture, voices, textuality, and dress. For a variety of reasons outlined here, this example of performing Job illustrates how an ambiguous experiential frame is conjured and engaged with by director, designer, actors, critics, and audiences. While obviously biblically based, was the book of Job a "religious" play? For example, was it working devotionally or evangelistically? Or, was it art, designed to inspire and provoke without theological baggage?

The Drama of Job

Orlin and Irene Corey created *the* book of Job, a married couple who devoted their careers to theatrical arts. Born in the mid-1920s, they met as undergraduate students at Baylor University and married in 1949. In 1952 they accepted academic appointments at Georgetown College, a liberal arts school near Lexington affiliated with the Kentucky Baptist Convention. After several years of experimenting, they debuted *Job* on Georgetown's campus with students as players on October 11, 1957. Orlin arranged the script and stagecraft, and Irene designed the costumes.

They selected Job because they claimed it held universal appeal. In texts ranging from the original script preface to his 1988 autobiography, Orlin describes Job as a book that articulates life's ultimate existential questions. He characterized it as a "timeless debate about human suffering and Divine purpose"[2] and an "enduring and universal vision of God and human existence [that] touches all."[3] Orlin and Irene attended Baptist churches, but they were convinced that Job possessed fundamental value for everyone, irrespective of theology or tradition. For them, it was not only a Christian book but very much a human book.

Orlin considered Job's engagement with the problem of theodicy to be a gravely necessary message for the mid-twentieth century. "Secular idealism" had wrought "a global hell, the slaughter and near extermination of more people than all history records before 1900."[4] Elsewhere, he characterized the prevailing social conditions in the United States as plagued by a warped certainty:

> We do not live in a period of great questions. Ours is an age of answers. Confident of our ability to release the energy of the atom, or to cruise beneath the polar ice cap, we are impatient to escape this world and explore the darkest distance of the universe. We require conclusions. Impossibilities are out of date. We demand and daily receive miracles.[5]

In response to this nuclear and space age discontent, he pitched Job as "a reminder that the eternal search for meaning in life remains man's greatest adventure"[6] and as "a revelation because [Job's] is a wisdom larger than the finite limits of our inch-worm logic and our inherent limitations of mind."[7] Clearly, Orlin was pitching the theatrical production as a kind of prophetic cultural critique and an argument for the enduring relevance of an ancient scriptural text.

The Coreys were not the first to reimagine Job in dramatic terms or materialize Job on stage. In a history of Broadways' biblical plays, Bial (2015) suggests that Job is "perhaps the single narrative in the Bible that most lends itself to dramatic interpretation" (32). Alfred Walls, a Methodist Episcopal theologian, published a version of Job in 1891 formatted as a theatrical script, though not intended for staging. On Broadway, a one-act play based on Job premiered in 1918, and other adaptations followed in the 1950s and 1970s. Theirs was not the first, though it would prove to be the most popular.

Corey's arrangement of *Job* was an eighty-minute production with ten players. Apart from Irene's intricate costume work, it was a materially sparse production: no stage props or scenery. The script was drawn, verbatim, from the King James Bible. Job's forty-two chapters were abridged, focused on the dialogic portions. Accompanying Job as the main character were four male friends (Eliphaz, Bildad, Zophar, and Elihu) who spoke alternately as themselves and in the roles of "God" and "Satan." And, there was a "chorus of five women" who served a polyvocal role. A *New York Times* critic noted in 1962 that the female chorus were the "voices of Job's other self or selves; of his conscience; of his sense of wrong and injustice; of his questioning search for the meaning of life; of his intimations of immortality and of his sense of himself as a child of God."[8]

Following its Georgetown College debut, *Job* toured England, Wales, and was staged at the 1958 Brussels World's Fair. This success prompted the Coreys to organize an acting troupe, which they named the Everyman Players, echoing again their ambition to prize themes of universal human experience. The Everyman Players toured from 1959 until 1980, completing forty-three US and fifteen international runs. In addition to England, Wales, and Belgium, the Players took their art to the 1964 New York World's Fair and multiple cities in South Africa, the Netherlands, Canada, and Italy. Their repertoire eventually included twelve stage productions—others that were Christian-themed (e.g., a play based on Bunyan's *Pilgrim's Progress*), theatre classics (e.g., *The Tempest*), and children's fables (e.g., *Reynard the Fox*). But, *Job* was always their cornerstone. It was their only production for the first five years and ultimately accounted for a third of the troupe's roughly 6,000 performances.

Job's signature status for the Players was solidified by a twenty-year gig at a public park in southeastern Kentucky. Every summer from 1959 to 1978, *Job* was performed nightly, Monday through Saturday, starting in late June and ending in late August or early September (depending on the season). The venue was Laurel Cove, an outdoor amphitheater at Pine Mountain State Park, just outside the rural town of Pineville. A park director initially invited *Job* to perform, hoping to revive tourist interest in Pine Mountain. Orlin recounts in his autobiography that the park was on the brink of closure when the Players began, and the production's success renewed attention, drew visitors, and helped keep the park open.[9]

While some local residents attended, *Job*'s Pine Mountain audiences were largely comprised of incoming travelers; religious tourists drawn to a biblical drama and theatre tourists who had read favorable reviews of the Players.[10] Locals were supportive, at least insofar as the production was good for attracting tourist bodies and dollars. In a 1960 review published by the Nashville *Tennessean* newspaper, one critic observed the pervasive presence of a community-based marketing campaign: "Every place of business displays 'Job' posters, and business men wear placards which ask 'Have you seen Job?'"[11] Other residents, however, had concerns and were not shy about making them public. "A standard diatribe developed by several, belittled Job vis-à-vis Jesus," Orlin noted in his autobiography, recalling a consistent objection from local street preachers. He continued, parroting the oral poetics of Appalachian sermonizing, "And in that last hour—ah!—when your coffin nails is hammered home—ah!—will it be Job—ah!—or will it be Jesus—ah!—to whom ye will turn—ah? Ah!—it will be Je-sus—ah!—it will be Je-sus—ah!"[12]

Pine Mountain is set amid lush State and National Forest lands, near the borders with Tennessee and Virginia. The deep rural setting meant that for most tourists it was not a stopover location, but a place sought out. This set apart quality limited audience numbers, but it also added to the sense of a pilgrimage experience (Coleman and Elsner 1995). Orlin invokes the language of a sacred destination in a description of the location from his autobiography:

> To reach that loveliest of places, people had to persevere, traveling twisting secondary highways, dodging roaring coal trucks, turning down a wide trail that was notoriously celebrated in the twenties as "Thunder Road"—an artery of the bootleg era—and drive to a starlit silence. They believed that they had personally discovered us. Their very presence attested to a desire to see what we performed.[13]

Whether playing Pine Mountain or touring, *Job* was celebrated for a series of sensory designs in the production's choreography. Bial (2015) refers to this dimension of performance as "spectacle": "lights, bodies, scenic elements—[what] exceeds the written text, with a particular emphasis on those elements that convey magnitude or exoticism" (27). Job's most celebrated feature was the costuming designed by Irene Corey.

Irene and Orlin decided to style the costuming as Byzantine mosaics, creating a visual effect in which the actors resembled stained glass figures. In her design treatise, *The Mask of Reality*, Irene explains that the mosaic style was chosen for *Job* to echo the play's organizing claim of universality: "As a timeless art form, it gave us a universal garment in which to clothe Job, that ancient symbol of man's endurance and faith."[14]

Irene used two techniques to transform actors into "living images."[15] First, she dressed the players in black body-length robes, gloves, and wigs shaped from organdy. She covered these surfaces with small squares of differently colored rayon satin. She selected this material because it imitated the capacity of glass to "catch and refract the light."[16] Second, each face was hand-painted with tile shapes shaded by different colors. For Irene, creating a seamless transition between makeup and dress was a signature aesthetic and was designed to generate awe: "The actor, cloaked in non-human identity, freed of individual inhibitions, can move into a new realm of relationship with the audience: that of a super-human, mystical power."[17] For the rayon swatches and the makeup, coloration was treated symbolically. Blues and purples were used for the four male players to signify their "antipathy toward Job"; reds and oranges for the female players to signify "empathy"; and greens for Job's "ever-verdant faith."[18]

Along with Irene's costuming, *Job*'s auditory dimensions were also widely celebrated. The production had two distinguishing vocal elements. First was the decision to use the King James translation, which Orlin described as vital for keying the kind of ritual performance he wanted. In his autobiography of the Players, he variously described the language of the translation as "sacred," "lofty," and "magnificent." Many reviewers agreed, such as a critic for the *Dayton Daily News* in 1969, who referred to the "pure beauty" of King James English.[19]

Second was the vocal choreography, arranged as a chorus that alternated between individual and collective voicing. Starting with Pine Mountain in 1959, Orlin began each performance with a spoken prelude, which included this reflection on the vocal arrangement: "[Players] also work together as a choir, speaking, crying, mourning, chanting, humming, intoning, and singing."[20] Many reviewers honed in on this design, citing it as an effective sonic device. A *New York Times* critic wrote that the sound "is bound to linger for a long time in memory."[21] And, the same *Dayton Daily News* reviewer cheered the vocal dimension following praise of Irene's costuming:

> Were they not ever to speak, the sight of the Everyman players would be worth the visit. But, they do speak . . . and chant . . . and talk-sing . . . and hum . . . and bewail . . . and lament and so much more that bespeaks of the trials and tribulations of that man of consummate patience . . . Job.[22]

For the Pine Mountain run, the natural setting also shaped *Job*'s sensory choreography. As others note about outdoor theatre, landscape can be instrumental for establishing an affective atmosphere (e.g., Stevenson 2015).

Vocally, the Laurel Cove amphitheater afforded amplification for the players and encouraged silent attentiveness for the audience. Orlin described the venue as one of "incredible natural acoustics [where] a single whisper could be distinctly heard 100 yards away."[23]

In addition to sound, Laurel Cove presented multiple visual affordances. A small pool was situated between the stage and the audience's seating, which mirrored the players' images. In tandem with Irene's already reflective costumes and the stage lighting, the visual effect complemented the artistic vision of stained glass. For the 1969 *Dayton Daily News* reviewer, this "echoe[d] the colorful—yet somber—figures and turn[ed] them back into flat-planed, almost mono-dimensional portraits of the stained window art."[24] Similarly, the elongated projection of the players' shadows onto the vertical cliff behind the stage was consistently praised by critics. In a 1970 interview with the *Cincinnati Enquirer*, Orlin explained the effect: "The shadows (of the actors) are 80 to 100 feet high—right up the side of the cliff to the tree-tops above. The result is an enormous kind of pageantry of light and color and shadow against the stars and the trees and the cliff."[25]

Job's sensory dimensions were certainly part of its critical and popular appeal. From dress to sound to interaction with landscape, the production's intricate choreography helped create affective bonds between audiences and scripture, irrespective of their theologies. Given this orchestrated effort to work ritualistically, we can now return to the question of the play's experiential frame and the ambiguity it generated.

In 1970, the Coreys were commissioned to adapt *Job* as a sixty-minute broadcast for Chilean television. Sponsored by governmental, Catholic, and Baptist organizations, they traveled south for filming. In recounting this piece of *Job*'s history, Orlin recalls: "Wherever we stopped—Panama, Ecuador, Chile—customs officials were baffled, then impressed by the 'ecclesiastical vestments' as [the costumes] were certified."[26] This recollected moment of confusion is more than a humorous anecdote; it marks a defining dynamic in the design and reception of *Job*.

An enduring tension marks theatrical performance in the US context. On the one hand, "drama is ordinarily understood as a secular genre" and "the theatre as a secular space" (Bial 2015: 12). And yet, theatre is renowned for its capacity to produce sacred sentiments of transcendence and awe, and there is a long history of churches staging religious dramas in a devotional frame.[27] Opposition to theatrical drama staged outside church walls circulated widely among US Christians in the mid- to late nineteenth century. Famously, the first attempt to stage a Passion Play in a dramatic, rather than strictly devotional, context sparked intense controversy. The director, a German Jewish immigrant named Salmi Morse, was arrested in San Francisco in 1879 and encountered repeated obstacles when he attempted to relocate the production to New York City (Musser 1993; Sponsler 2004: 124; Bial 2015: 18).

By the early twentieth century, the strict divide was shifting. A 1906 *New York Times* story lauded the unique potential of biblically based productions, anticipating *Job*'s spectacle dimensions:

> A Biblical subject offers exceptional opportunities for spectacular display. The reverence with which Biblical personages are regarded invests the characters with a half-mystical grandeur that seems to call for a ponderous setting. Moreover, the age of the Old Testament, with its barbaric splendor, affords a wonderful field for the ambitious producer.[28]

Broadway, at least, followed this advice; between 1899 and 2014 more than 120 different biblically based plays were staged (Bial 2015). Still, ideologies of theatre as secular and/or as morally questionable lingered, especially among Protestants. The circulation of this tension prompted qualifications, and a labor to ease skeptics, when non-church theatre staged religious drama. Consider, for example, this 1952 announcement from Georgetown College about an early iteration of *Job*:

> The concept of drama belonging in the churches may appear incongruous at first thought, but reflection will reveal the naturalness of the combination. . . . In troublous times men and women are groping for security. Christian drama can help them find a new star by which to steer.[29]

As for the Coreys, they strategically appealed to the conflicting sides of this tension. In his script preface, Orlin notes: "*Job* is a poem of both traditional piety and religious revolt of no comfort to any orthodoxy. It has secular and religious advocates of all varieties." In nearly the same breath, he invited audiences to engage the production in a devotional register. The short prelude he spoke before each performance concluded with this call: "If the Players remind us of [God's] glory, if they sing our faith, if they stir our hope, then the purpose of this play will have been fulfilled. The Word of God, through the book of Job will live anew in our lives tonight. Watch then and pray. Listen. Wonder. Worship."[30]

Recall that the Corey's attraction to the story of Job was grounded in an assertion of its universality. They sought to dislodge the story's moral and existential lessons from any particular theology, to treat *Job* as a reflection on the human condition rather than a doctrinal mouthpiece. Orlin returns to this theme throughout his autobiography of the Players. Early on, he claimed: "We were not committed to agendas—religious, social, or political."[31] And, near the end, he clarified that they engaged religion "in the universal sense of reverence and mystery."[32]

This kind of secularizing existed uneasily alongside the play's origins. Georgetown is a historically Baptist college and the original 1957 playbill presents the production in unambiguously Christian terms:

> Job is presented because of three basic beliefs: Christian faith should be revealed in action (drama) in this age of the Eye; Christian faith in action needs to be performed in the churches and the world; Churches must be stimulated by such performances to employ the drama as a tool of teaching and the highest type of evangelism.

This tension, coupled with the facts that the troupe performed plays ranging from *Job* to *The Tempest* and performed in settings ranging from local churches to World's Fairs, placed audiences in an ambiguous experiential frame. At the beginning of his autobiography, Orlin reflects that "reviewers seldom know where to have us."[33] The production received a series of negative reviews during the 1964 South Africa run, such as a Johannesburg critic who opined that *Job* belonged exclusively in churches and not on dramatic stages.[34] Quite the opposite, a 1962 reviewer for the *Knoxville News-Sentinel* described a Pineville performance in decidedly devotional terms: "A spell is cast. Many persons believe they have had a religious experience. For nearly everyone, 'The Book of Job' has a cleansing effect as a good sermon does." Audiences, too, were often uncertain of how to understand the production. Orlin recalls "hundreds of nights" when minor variations on the same exchange occurred following performances:

"Are you preachers?"

"No sir, actors."[35]

Curtain Call

Was the book of Job a "religious" performance? Neither critics nor audiences settled on a definitive answer to this question. The Coreys, clearly, hoped the production would inspire diverse audiences, and in turn they invoked divergent frames. The ambiguity of *Job*'s experiential frame—devotional? evangelistic? just good theatre?—may have confused audiences, but it did not dissuade them. Apart from its difficult reception on the 1964 South Africa run, published reviews were nearly uniform in glowing praise. A 1971 *Cincinnati Enquirer* critic summarized well the response of many audiences: "However you slice it, it's powerful stuff."[36]

In light of *Job*'s ambiguous framing, I want to close with a story relayed by Orlin Corey in a 1958 report about *Job*'s first tour.[37] I find the story suggestive because it highlights an ambition that can exist across experiential frames. The ambition is to generate renewed interest in the value of biblical texts. This certainly takes on different inflections if deployed theologically, historically, or morally, but that is part of its power: it is a flexible ambition, adaptable to multiple frames.

In this report, Corey details *Job*'s run in England and Wales. They were transported by bus, led by the same driver throughout. Corey described the man as, "A quiet, pipe-smoking, ex-navy bachelor, in his mid-thirties. . . . He was reluctant to see the play because he was dubious about churches and religion." Spending time with the troupe prompted the driver to view a performance, which prompted him to attend every subsequent show remaining on the itinerary. By tour's end, he shared with the Players that he had read and reread the biblical book of Job, though he had not "converted" and did not expect to. "Proud as the players were of their reviews, audiences, and renewed invitations, this was their finest compliment."

Figure 4 Ark Encounter, exterior view (Williamstown, Kentucky). Photo credit: James S. Bielo.

4

Imagineering

Ark Encounter is a Christian theme park in central Kentucky, about halfway between the urban centers of Cincinnati and Lexington.[1] The park was announced to the public in December 2010, and its first phase, costing roughly $92 million, opened in July 2016. Ark Encounter circulates the theo-politics of its affiliate ministry, Answers in Genesis: a biblical literalism that teaches young earth creationism, including a hostile rejection of evolutionary science, and vitalizes the touchstones of fundamentalist public culture, such as Christian nationalism and the denial of anthropogenic climate change.

The centerpiece of the park is a "full-scale" replica of Noah's ark: built of timber and iron, measuring 510 feet in length, 85 feet in width, and 51 feet in height. Inside the replicated ark, visitors roam throughout three decks filled with 100,000 square feet of themed space: sculpted animals, Noah and his seven family members in static and animatronic form, mural art, didactic signage, interactive displays, multimedia exhibits, food and souvenir vendors, restrooms, short films, and children's play areas.

Each deck is organized by a particular affective experience. Deck One highlights the emotional drama of Noah and his family after the closing of the ark's door. They are relieved to have escaped a terrifying storm, just witnessed mass death, and are anxious about the weeks ahead. Ark Encounter's creative team always talked about Deck One as the "darkest" of the decks, indexed sensorially by low levels of lighting. The storm is audible, as visitors hear sounds of wind, rain, thunder, and debris banging against the ark's sides. The first exhibit of Noah and his family portrays them in the middle of praise and thanksgiving for their deliverance, with the auditory cacophony of a raging storm and agitated animals in the background.

Deck Two extends a vision of everyday life onboard the ark. Noah and his family are settled, going about their liminal living. Exhibits include a library, workshops demonstrating woodworking and blacksmithing, and animal feeding. For the team, Deck Two was the primary "how-to" deck, addressing numerous "practical" issues from the Genesis story. How did they care for all the animals? What did they do with all the animal waste? How were air, water, and sunlight distributed? What did Noah's workshop and library look like? By addressing these questions, Deck Two presents the pivotal creationist claim that "ancient man" was "brilliant and capable."

Deck Three continues themes from the first two decks and introduces several new experiences. More exhibits teach about animal kinds. More exhibits address everyday conditions, such as what the passengers' living quarters might have been like. Deck Three also celebrates the salvific realization that God's wrath has been expended, the storm is over, the waters have receded, the eight passengers spared, and the whole world is now theirs.

As visitors move through these decks, 132 exhibit bays combine to tell an immersive story about the plausibility of a literalist ark, the creationist rejection of evolutionary science, the steadfast faithfulness of Noah and his family, and ultimately the fundamentalist gospel of salvation. The iconicity of moving from darkness to light, from judgment to salvation, was always a self-conscious strategy for the creative team; they wanted visitors to experience this embodied progression.

Creationist Imagineers

Ark Encounter is, among other things, a $92 million testimony. It is missionization, massively materialized, performed in the key of biblical literalism. But the creative team understood their task as much more complicated than merely presenting the creationist message. First, they needed to address the historical plausibility of this biblical story and demonstrate that Noah could have built the ark described in the book of Genesis. Using the exact dimensions detailed in Genesis and using only building materials that would have been available to Noah were vital. Exhibits at the park illustrate building tools and techniques that might have been used by Noah, but the project's publicity materials repeatedly explain that contemporary construction technology (e.g., cranes) was unavoidable (e.g., to complete construction within the timeframe required by building permits). This plausibility imperative captures a key cultural fact about creationists: they practice a literalist scriptural hermeneutic, which is shaped dialogically by the historical challenges of both Darwinian science and biblical textual criticism.

For the creative team, plausibility alone was deeply insufficient. Noah's story cannot merely be told; it must be felt. Their goal was to create an affective consumer experience, one that works on and through the sensory channels of visitors. What was it like to hear the fierce storm outside? The chorus of animals? To live on the ark day after day? And what was it like when the dove did not return? To see the rainbow and be the center of God's saving grace? An immersive experience promises to bridge the gap between the plausibility and believability of a creationist past, and the logic of immersion was the primary engine of the team's creative labor.

From the team's trust in immersion as an effective strategy to Ark Encounter's reliance on "theme park" as the primary self-identification, we see the robust influence of Disney on this project of religious public culture. The message is Protestant fundamentalism, and the medium is immersive entertainment. In the tradition of Disney, a creationist theme park operates according to the same consumerist logic: "the carefully controlled sale of goods (souvenirs) and experiences (architecture, rides, and performances) [is] 'themed' to the corporate owner's proprietary image" (Davis 1996: 401–2). If we sub ministry brand for corporate brand and theo-politics for proprietary image, then Ark Encounter exemplifies the theme park genre (cf. Paine 2019).

Disney not only is present in the actualized product but also was present throughout the design process as a creative and professional exemplar. This was always evident with Emily, an artist hired by the ministry in 2005 and one of four core artists who led the design of Ark Encounter. Emily completed a master's degree in theatre design from the California Institute of the Arts, the private university founded by Walt Disney in 1961, and her training focused on spatial, building, and set design. Throughout my fieldwork with the creative team, a short, rectangular placard sat atop a file cabinet in her cubicle: "It's kind of fun to do the impossible," followed by the name "Walt Disney." During an interview, I asked Emily how she would describe her role in the creative process:

> My role on the team is, I, if you know what an imagineer is at Disney. That's what we do.... We dream up, conceptualize an experience where we're trying to either one, tell the story, or two, teach something. Where we're concerned, we are wanting people to understand the Word of God in a simple and fun way so that it's not overwhelming or it's not something that they sort of turn away from because they can't understand it. Do you know what I mean? So, here, we're trying to create fun atmospheres.

Creationist imagineers: this is the disposition the design team brought to their creative labor. With this disposition playing an organizing role, Ark Encounter appeals to the cultural capital of entertainment to stake a bid for the cultural legitimacy and authority of creationism.

Evolution of a Film

The imagineering of Ark Encounter took place over a six-year period. When I first visited the park in August 2016, I walked the three decks with my senses alert for where and how the in-progress designs I had documented during fieldwork with the creative team might be present onboard the actualized ark. Much was familiar; I recognized many of Emily's "fun atmospheres" from concept art, storyboards, and preliminary sketches. One notable exception was the absence of a film the team had devoted significant labor to. In six visits to Ark Encounter over the course of three years, it became clear what happened to that initial idea. Here, I present the evolution of this film as an example of the imagineering process.

My fieldwork with the creative team ran from October 2011 through June 2014. From early on, the team developed design concepts for an animated film that visitors would view before entering the ark. Accompanying concept art in a promotional/fundraising booklet, the creative director described the film as a "dramatic, fast-paced, 5-minute film [that] will pitch guests into the tense fallen world before the Flood, introduce them to the character of Noah and experience the last few moments before the Flood." The team always talked about the film as brief, but important: it would be the first major display, establishing an experiential frame for the visitors' journey through the three decks to come.

In April 2012, I sat with Tyler, the team's lead illustrator, as he worked on storyboarding the film. He worked in pencil on a small pad of white paper and puzzled over one of the final scenes. In three vertical panes, he sketched three potential scenarios. In the first, the ark door is shut, ready to be lifted by rising waters. The second places Noah in an open doorway, standing still and surveying the world poised for destruction. The third also places Noah in the doorway, this time with one hand extended to catch in his palm the storm's first drops of rain.

Ultimately, Tyler's concept art followed Noah through several scenes in the final pre-Flood days: meeting with Methuselah before his death, Methuselah passing scrolls to Noah, Noah being tempted by three "prostitutes," Noah preaching his final sermon, and the start of the rain. This rough script exists almost entirely in an intertextual gap. All of these events are possible given the text of Genesis 5, but none are explicitly named. Methuselah was Noah's grandfather and one translation of the biblical Hebrew name Methuselah can be glossed as "his death will bring judgment." The presence of scrolls functions indexically to mark the claim of direct scriptural transmission (the content is not revealed, but the scrolls are presumably a proto-text for the first chapters of Genesis). The women function symbolically to mark Noah's righteousness (resisting sexual advances as a sign of moral purity). The rain would have had to start at some point, but portraying Noah catching the first drops is much more about dramatic, multisensory effect than it is stating a pivotal literalist claim.

A month later, I was eating lunch with Tyler in the design studio's kitchen. We talked candidly about the working script for the animated film. He thought the current approach was "good," but he was feeling discontent and certain that a "better, more creative" idea could still be discovered. I asked what he meant. Depicting Noah's final pre-Flood days would "work just fine," but he thought it was "too event-driven." The "so-what" was being lost. Without any further prompting, Tyler began talking about a film he recently saw that he thought could work beautifully as a model.

Remember Me is a romance drama set in New York City. He walked me through the film without much attention to plot details. When I read the film's synopsis later that day, it was clear his retelling was partial. But, a play-by-play plot summary was less important for Tyler; what he really cared about was the film's ending. While viewers are aware the film is set in contemporary times, no exact date is provided. It could be a recent past, the viewer's present, or a near future. In the final scene, the main character stares out the window of one of the World Trade Center towers. The camera zooms out to set the towers against a clear blue sky. What follows are a series of street-level scenes: it is the morning of September 11, 2001. Ash is floating. Another central character, a policeman, is barely managing chaotic traffic. Other major characters stare upward. The object of their stare is not revealed. It would be unnecessary, gratuitous to do so. Tyler "loved" how this dramatic ending "totally changed" his viewing of the entire film. He wanted to share the film with the team and use this same logic of a surprise reveal at the end to revise the script. In its current form, he reflected, they were "giving everything away up front."

I don't know if Tyler ever showed *Remember Me* to the rest of the team, but despite his hesitations the script was not revised in this direction. In fact, the entire script concept was scrapped and the team contracted with an evangelical media company to produce a twenty-minute live action film. Initially, this film was shown on screens placed throughout the queue line where visitors board the ark, but it was soon relocated to an open area with benches midway through

Deck Two. Whatever the relocation sacrificed in establishing a desired frame, it gained in sustaining visitors' attention. Most visitors on most operating days are likely to move relatively quickly through the queue line, mostly bypassing the film. They are far more likely to pause on Deck Two to take a restful sit and watch the film in its entirety without any pressure to continue moving forward.

The film, titled *The Noah Interview*, depicts Noah at the ark construction site with his family, nearing completion and anticipating the deluge. Most of the film is a dialogue between Noah and a "tabloid-style" journalist.[2] The film's director describes its premise and framing role onboard the ark in his online portfolio:

> The short film features Noah and his family as a pre-historic tabloid news team interrupts the final stages of building to interview—and mock—Noah about the project. Full of colorful characters and slapstick comedy for all ages, the exchange between Noah and the reporters also highlights intriguing details about the ancient world and gives a taste of some of the fascinating material presented at the Ark Encounter.[3]

In a scathing review of Ark Encounter, the president of the Kentucky Paleontological Society interprets the film as an expression of creationists' anxious and angry feeling of cultural embattlement: "I suspect the video is Ken Ham's swipe at reporters who have asked him uncomfortable questions about the Ark and tax rebate incentives."[4] Perhaps. But, it is also more than this. The semiotic reach of this dramatization exceeds Ham (the ministry CEO) as an individual and Ark Encounter as a project. Whatever aesthetic evaluations creationist visitors might conclude about the filming, characterization, or storyline, they are poised to recognize the "snide" reporter as illustrative of a familiar cultural symbol: skeptics who mock "Bible-believing Christians" and who are part of a secular conspiracy to undermine the authority of a literal Bible and, in turn, the public legitimacy of fundamentalism (Toumey 1994; Harding 2000; Butler 2010).

The film begins with Noah and his wife making final preparations before the impending storm, the ark set on a hill in the backdrop. She reminds Noah that today is the day of his interview with "The Pangea Independent Tabloids, the PITS," the first of many gibes taken at the *fake news* of *liberal media*. The interviewer is written and acted as utterly sardonic and dislikable; she could not seem more bored or annoyed with her interviewing assignment. Noah's wife encourages him: "You're doing the work of God, maybe they'll be fair with you."

The exchange between Noah and the interviewer is thoroughly dialogical, replete with winks and nods toward multiple creationist discourses. At one point, one of the journalist's two assistants challenges Noah's reference to God's judgment of "sin and wickedness." "What you call sin, I call freedom, you bigot": calling up creationist antagonists and hot button culture war issues such as abortion rights and marriage equality. The character of the journalist and the format of a media interview are used to voice some of the historical plausibility questions that are integral to Ark Encounter's argumentation. For example, she asks Noah why the ship has three keels instead of one and why it has no rudder. There are also callouts to debates among creationists about the finer points of the ark's design—for example, when the journalist questions Noah's choice of one hull design over another. Their exchange, in true fundamentalist form, closes with an act of witnessing. Noah calls the journalist to "turn from your sin and seek God so that you may be spared."

The closing scene presents Noah and his wife, standing side-by-side, watching the crew depart as lightning and thunder begin to crack across the sky. She asks, "How'd it go?" and he responds unsurprised, "About as bad as I thought it would." She replies with one more intertextual nod, this time to lingo appropriated from hip-hop pop culture, "Well, scoffers gonna scoff." The film's final word is soberer, as Noah sounds dismayed: "I do wish they would listen. I wish they would all listen." Like this closing couplet, the film is designed to be both silly and serious; recalling the director's terms, it is a mix of "intriguing details" and "slapstick comedy for all ages." It operates simultaneously as a creationist satire of a mainstream culture they feel embattled by and a creationist performance of theo-political commitment.

I do not know the extent to which the creative team informed the making of *The Noah Interview*. The team's creative director is named as a cowriter, and the film credits include several team members. Certainly, though, the actualized film at Ark Encounter evolved markedly from the team's original concept. While it is set in a biblical frame and the aesthetics of costuming, set design, and green screen backdrop maintain the park's theme, this moment of imagineering is more ideological then atmospheric, drawing visitors into the creationist present more so than the creationist past.

Coda

Ark Encounter exemplifies the modern idea of a "biblical theme park" and, in turn, the integration of Disney with Protestant fundamentalism. This Kentucky tourist attraction illustrates well what can materialize when biblically themed worlds are not just imagined but imagineered. Ultimately, one lesson to glean from Ark Encounter is that in this project of public culture, legitimacy is distributed among biblical literalism and the imperatives of immersive entertainment. Strategies such as immersion are leveraged to solidify and enliven creationist support, convert non-creationists, and make a claim for social viability. Attractions like Ark Encounter do not simply teach creationist theo-politics. They teach creationists to be proud of creationism and demand that non-creationist audiences take notice. As forms of religious publicity and public culture, they mobilize the cultural capital of entertainment to claim and proclaim cultural authority.

Figure 5 Biblical Sand Sculpture by Randy Hofman (Ocean City, Maryland). Photo credit: Randy Hofman.

5

Plastic Jesus

In 1962, the folk duo the Goldcoast Singers first recorded "Plastic Jesus". The song's eponymous object is a mass-produced figurine designed to perch on car dashboards. The song is satire, originating amid the broader Americana folk music revival. But, is it poking good-natured fun at the commercialized devotional stuff that circulated widely among US Christians, especially Catholics? (Orsi 2005: 48; Morgan 2017: 26). Or, is the song more biting, mocking devotion for resorting to mass-produced icons?

Irrespective of the band's intent, the figure of Plastic Jesus became a trope that still circulates widely among US Christians to signify religion gone wrong. *Good Old Plastic Jesus* is a Beatnik-style long-form poem written by a Roman Catholic priest and set in New York City (Larsen 1968). It mixes prayer and proclamation, citing the dashboard figurine (and the song's performance in the 1967 film *Cool Hand Luke*) as the epitome of true devotion's opposite. A book—*Plastic Jesus: Exposing the Hollowness of Comfortable Christianity* (Sandras 2006)—picks up the trope decades later, exchanging Beat poetry for the genre of pastoral memoir. For the author, a charismatic Protestant, Plastic Jesus crystallizes how middle-class suburban life corrupts "authentic" faith. "I had been living in a spiritual suburbia with nice sidewalks and picket fences around my Christianity.... Yet as my faith became more neat and tidy on the outside, on the inside it grew more and more superficial" (15–16).

This trope orbits around negative evaluations assigned to plastic as a form of materiality: connotations of being nondurable and cheap, designed for discard. Such a theology of plastic calls attention to a fundamental problem animating Christianity (Bialecki 2012). Christians everywhere wrestle with how to classify, semiotically and ideologically, different material forms. Why is it that some forms are designated as normatively acceptable, even special, while others are deemed less legitimate, even dangerous? (Engelke 2007). Such classifications can figure in broader projects of claiming who is or is not a Christian and what is or is not proper Christian activity (Garriot and O'Neill 2008). For example, the thirteenth-century Cistercian monk St. Bernard "worried about the power of fine materials and images that might distract Christians from their reflections on the word of God" (Oliphant 2015: 356). From Plastic Jesus to the spiritual anxieties of "fine materials," the materiality of things became a theological question for Christians, a way to police boundaries and engage ethical self-making.

How might an attention to material theologies help illuminate our understanding of materializing the Bible? Across traditions (from Catholic to Reformed Protestant to Charismatic), we find a wide diversity of material forms put to use in projects of replication. Wood, sand, fiberglass and wax, biblical landscape materials (e.g., botanicals, soil, stone, water), terracotta, bronze, adobe bricks, reclaimed refuse, rebar and cement, marble, gemstones, and—yes—plastic: all have served as construction materials to render scripturally themed environments.

Of course, different makers prefer different materials. Sifting through who chooses what material and why it is not as simple as aligning a theology of a thing with the choice of a thing. The situation is more dynamic (and more interesting!) than that. It is more useful to think in terms of an interplay between theologies and the "affordances" of material forms. This term, derived from environmental psychology (Gibson 1977), has been elaborated by Keane (2014) to explore how and why religious actors make use of the materials they do (cf. Morgan 2017). Put simply, affordances refer to "the properties of something in light of what those properties offer to someone who perceives them" (s315). A single thing can be mobilized for variable uses, "an indeterminate number of possibilities depending on which aspect is brought into focus by a practice or reflection" (s317).

An instructive example comes from Promey (2019) and her analysis of Elijah Pierce's woodcarving art. Pierce was a self-taught artist, active from the 1920s through the early 1980s. He depicted a variety of subjects, but biblical themes were his most prominent source material: Noah's ark, Jesus's Crucifixion, and many others. Promey observes that wood, Pierce's exclusive media, "naturally appears in a range of beiges and browns." Pierce capitalized on this visual affordance for his representations of skin color, using it to call attention to regimes of racial inequality and a theology of racial equality. As a concept, affordances help us think about the structuring of both limitation and possibility. It is about the ways in which humans engage bits of the world in ways that are full of potential but not completely unbridled. If we learn that x number of uses of a thing are physically possible given the media, and y number of those are legible or valued in a local context, then we are primed to understand how people discern and select among those uses. Why are some uses prohibited, while others concealed, and still others attractive? Consider, then, three cases of materializing the Bible: site builders who mobilized the physical and symbolic affordances of construction materials to express and advance material theologies.

Imperishable

The Grotto of the Redemption is a Roman Catholic shrine in north-central Iowa.[1] The Grotto emerged from the better part of a life's work by Paul Dobberstein: a German-born priest who immigrated to the United States in 1892 at the age of twenty and was called to lead a rural Iowa parish in 1897. As the story goes, Dobberstein fell ill and promised Mother Mary that he would build a shrine in her honor if she delivered him back into good health. He recovered and began gathering construction materials. In 1912, those materials became the beginnings of the Grotto. The project consumed "the waking hours of his earthly existence" until his death in 1954.

The Grotto is comprised of cement, Italian marble, and thousands of "precious and semi-precious stones": jade, sapphire, and at least forty other kinds collected by Dobberstein and donated to the project from around the world. Nine core scenes materialize "the story of the Redemption . . . Man lost the friendship of God and regained it through the Incarnation, Passion, Death and Resurrection of Jesus." It begins with the Garden of Eden, then moves to the stable of Bethlehem, home of Nazareth, the Trinity, the Ten Commandments, Garden of Gethsemane, thirteen Stations of the Cross, burial of Jesus, and finally the Resurrection.

Unlike many Catholic shrine sites such as Lourdes in France and Fatima in Portugal, the Grotto claims no history of divine intervention into local lives: "There have never been miraculous apparitions of any kind connected to the Grotto. No claim for cures or miracles have been made." The devotional power of the site, instead, testifies to the devotional labor of Dobberstein—a material witness to what is borne of dedicated faith and work. Like so many sites that materialize the Bible, the Grotto's stated ambition is to make the stories of scripture newly real, to collapse the distance of space-time between a scriptural then and there and a present here and now. "To bring people of today, who live centuries removed from those blessed [biblical] days into closer touch with the things of God, is the aim and effort of the builder of the Grotto of the Redemption."

In its self-presentation, the Grotto maintains a self-conscious sense that its method and media are perfectly suited to human faculties. "It is the aim of the Grotto to present, in palpable form, this reunion of Man and God, the reconciliation between fallen human nature and offended Divine Justice; because truth reaches the mind most easily by way of the senses." The Grotto promises to mainline truth through its physical qualities—a somatically rich environment where visitors can walk, touch, and be immersed. This promise is extended by the builder's reflections on the affordances of precious stones as construction materials. I first observed the following as a guidebook epigraph, a recontextualized quote from Dobberstein on why these geologic finds were his media of choice:

> Spoken words are ephemeral: written words remain, but their durability depends upon the material upon which they are written: but if carved into bronze or sculpted into stone they are well nigh imperishable. This *imperishableness* is the outstanding feature of the Grotto. Thus the story of the *redemption* will continue to tell its edifying story long after the builder has laid down his trowel, and will be a silent sermon expressing in permanently enduring precious stones, the fundamental truths of Christianity [emphasis in original].

Dobberstein begins critically, drawing legitimacy away from oral discourse, the media associated most directly with homilies and sermons. He sizes up print culture more favorably, but not without immediate pause. Facts of materiality separate the perishable from the imperishable. Facts of years separate the wheat from the chaff. Imperishability is prized for its durability into the unforeseen future, its capacity to withstand the pelting storm of time in ways more fragile media cannot: human, human-made, and natural alike.

Ephemeral

If imperishability organizes the Grotto of Redemption, impermanence organizes the Biblical Sand Sculptures of Ocean City, Maryland.[2] Since 1974, born-again evangelist Randy Hofman has used the oceanfront setting of local beaches to craft scenes and stories from Christian scripture. His subjects range across favorites of the evangelical imagination: Daniel in the lion's den, David and Goliath, Noah's ark, Jesus's baptism, the Last Supper, and Jesus's crucifixion, ascension, and Second Coming.

Born in 1951 into a Catholic household, Randy entered art school in New York City in the late 1960s with hopes of doing visual communication work in advertising. This ambition faded as he explored the industry; he describes a moral repulsion to a "skanky" business. In the early 1970s he became a born-again evangelical, prompted by reading Hal Lindsey's 1970 *The Late Great Planet Earth*, a best seller that popularized dispensational theology. When he first arrived in Ocean City, he apprenticed with another evangelical sand sculptor and divided his time between oil paintings of local nature scenes, sand sculpting with his mentor, and chalk drawings of biblical scenes on city sidewalks. He continued oil painting for money to live on, but he abandoned the chalk. While this transformed a long-standing technique of Sunday school pedagogy (Lindquist 2019) into a tool of public evangelism, he decided it lacked the "indigenous" feel afforded by working with sand. For Hofman, one attraction of sand as a media is its attachment to place, an indexical marker of belonging and local experience.

Randy works throughout summer tourist seasons, and his sculptures are viewed by as many as 10,000 visitors every day for two months. Each sculpture requires roughly fourteen hours of construction, from digging out the sand to completing the artwork to finishing it with a mixture of water and Elmer's glue. The latter has proven to be a particularly important innovation, one he learned on a visit to California to work with sand sculptors there. By spraying the sculptures with this mixture, their lifespan is extended from a single day to at least a week and as long as a month. Still, even the occasional month-long display is defined by temporariness and tenuousness; interventions of weather, passersby, and animals are ever-present destructive agents.

When I asked Randy why he favored the media of sand, he reflected on two motivating interests. First, he noted the widespread popularity and affectively charged nature of "playing in the sand," an activity many in the US associate with play, childhood, and summer vacations. By capitalizing on this powerful familiarity of sand, he likened his work to Jesus's use of agricultural imagery in parables, "he knew just what would resonate [with his audience]." Second, Randy observed a "delicious little spiritual parallel" between a sand sculpture and our mortal lives on earth. Both, he said, were defined by ephemerality, "here today and gone tomorrow," as the proverbial saying goes.

Hofman's biblical sand sculptures mix devotional labor, attachment to place, and the temporality of materiality. Perhaps in spite of, perhaps because of, the hours he invests in a single sculpture, it is the quality of temporariness that defines his material theology. Each sculpture's short-lived tenure is inextricable from sand's physical affordances, which Hofman treats as an iconic sign for human earthly existence. Our earthly lives will disappear as quickly, as easily, and as unpredictably as his sculptures on the beach.

Indexical

In July 2014, more than 15,000 people gathered in Sao Paulo, Brazil, for the public unveiling of the Temple of Solomon.[3] The event included Brazilian pop culture celebrities and heads of state—such as the Republic's then president Dilma Rouseff and the general consul of Israel Yoel Barnea. The main attraction is an oversized replica of the temple described in the Book of 1 Kings of the Hebrew Bible/Old Testament, but the site also features a "life-sized" replica of the Tabernacle described in the book of Exodus and a museum that houses a miniaturized Tabernacle as well as other biblically themed items. After four years of construction, at a rumored cost of US$300 million, the Brazilian Temple covers nearly 100,000 square meters of built space. The Temple of Solomon functions simultaneously as a pilgrimage and tourist destination, a house of worship, conference center, and world headquarters for a neo-Pentecostal denomination, the Universal Church of the Kingdom of God (UCKG).[4]

The UCKG's Temple of Solomon mobilizes the promises of materializing the Bible according to a Christian Zionist logic, constructing an indexical relationship to the scriptural past and the nationhood of Israel. Bits of landscape are woven into the attraction's physical structures, conjuring a relation of direct connection to Bible lands. Eight million dollars' worth of "Jerusalem stone" was flown in from Israel-Palestine to integrate into the temple's exterior construction. The materiality of the stone is not claimed to have magical properties. Rather, it creates an aesthetic bridge to the Holy Land and a claim to memory; the stones are described in guiding performances as "witnesses" to an ancient Israelite past. Four date-palm trees, also flown in from Israel-Palestine, are planted by the front entrance to "represent strength." The museum area includes a dried bush, flown in from the Mt. Sinai region, as a natural link to the Exodus story of Moses and the burning bush.

The Tabernacle replica is replete with further indexical links to biblical stories and lands. Like the examples featured in Chapter 1, this replica was built from the instructions detailed in the book of Exodus, including the physical measurements and tricolor woven exterior. The ritual implements inside the Tabernacle are presented as "exact size" and arranged spatially according to

Exodus. In the "holy of holies" area visitors view an Ark of the Covenant replica, built from acacia wood and covered with gold. This logic of literalist replication extends to the sacrificial pyre outside the Tabernacle, which features sculpted models of burnt animal offerings atop an acacia wood altar.

Through geological and botanical media, the Temple of Solomon promises visitors special access to the biblical past. The promise goes something like this: experience contact with the awe and aura of the Holy Land by physically contacting and being copresent with indexical fragments of nature. As we learn more thoroughly in Section II of this book, biblical landscape items are often mobilized to transform the expansive and ungraspable "land" of the Bible into a conceivable thing that one can experience more directly. Pieces of biblical nature entwine place, story, memory, materiality, imagination, and sensory experience. As physical objects, they act as empirical proof: testimonies that the mundane and miraculous events of scripture happened at an earthly somewhere and share a relation of direct proximity to the very object being engaged. Stones and wood and plants are mobilized as material channels for accessing the biblical past and all its divine mystery.

Coda

The materialities used to create biblically themed environments and provoke scriptural imaginations are not incidental. Precious stones, sand, and biblical landscape items: all are mobilized to express and advance theological projects. Engaging with the concept of affordances, I hope to have illustrated here that there is a revealing interplay between materiality and theology. The physical properties and symbolic associations of materials guide how they are mobilized. All media abide by this certain truth; no media lacks physical form and, in turn, all media must negotiate the relationship between their material constitution and their range of possible uses. To materialize the Bible is to perform a particular theology, and the actual materiality of things always works to limit and enable how performances unfold.

Figure 6 Inside the World of Jesus of Nazareth at the Museum of the Bible (Washington, DC). Photo credit: James S. Bielo.

6

Ways of Remaining

Collier Township is nestled in the Allegheny Plateau's rolling, forested hills, southwest of Pittsburgh, Pennsylvania. In 2020, the township's Parks and Recreation department lists eleven public areas for outdoor leisure, including "Neville Woods—Bible Walk." Several sites in the region bear the Neville name, US Revolutionary War commanders who settled nearby. But, Bible Walk? The township website explains no history, just a mention in passing: "Formerly known as the Bible Walk, trails on the Collier land now provide the perfect 'Nature Walk' for area residents."[1] All that survives in public view is a name without a story, a curious signifier emptied of reference.

The story is one of ecstatic vision and legal dispute. In 1977, a lifelong Catholic and born-again charismatic named Bill Warren received a "very strong prompting by the Holy Spirit" to create a park in a forest filled with biblical statues.[2] At the time he did not understand what to do, but he and his wife Gail committed themselves to pursuing this vision. They found a fiberglass artisan in the Bronx, New York, and commissioned 105 figures. In 1979, they purchased 42 acres of undeveloped land in Collier. They clothed the figures in "biblical dress" and arranged them along an oval, quarter-mile pathway: thirty scenes, from the Garden of Eden to Jesus's crucifixion.

For Bill and Gail, "Bible Walk" was always a divinely anointed project. Remembering across four decades, he told me multiple miracle stories. In New York, a worker helping to craft the figures experienced a physical healing while making one of the Jesus statues. In Pennsylvania, Bill was "woken up at 5am by God" and directed to leave that instant for the pathway and bring his Bible. He arrived onsite to find a Vietnam veteran "crying his heart out." The man was suicidal and said that Bible Walk was the only place he "could have a decent feeling about himself." They prayed together, and Bill led him through a born-again confession.

Bill and Gail operated Bible Walk in Collier for nearly two years, though they never received the requisite township permits to do so. In 1981, the site was forced to close because local officials contended that the land was not zoned for tourism. Bill recalled the dispute in both secular and spiritual registers. He said that the owners of a golf club planned for nearby did not want tour buses coming and going, and they bribed local officials to close Bible Walk. But, this was not mere greed. Written as an annotation on a scanned newspaper story that he mailed to me, Bill detailed his explanation: "Whenever someone has something to spiritually help the Lord's people, they can experience tremendous obstacles set up against it by Satan & his demons."

Today, "Bible Walk" remains only as a name with no story, and the Collier woods have no fiberglass figures in "biblical dress." But, the figures do remain. Bill donated a large portion to a friend in West Virginia who ran a Friary, and in 1983 Bill donated the remaining twenty-two to a nondenominational, charismatic pastor in Mansfield, Ohio, who was seeking to build a biblical wax museum.[3] When the Friary closed in the mid-1980s, Bill arranged for this set of figures to rejoin the others in Mansfield. In 1987, Bible Walk was born again, housed in a building adjacent to the Mansfield church (cf. Eyl 2019).

Recontextualizing

The history of biblical tourism sites is, in part, a history of closure. Sites become nonextant for a host of reasons: energetic founders die, legal challenges arise, property is vandalized or stolen, land is sold, and finances become unsustainable. For some sites, whatever was there slowly deteriorates in place—an eroding remainder to a failed or concluded endeavor. The material for other sites become refuse, discarded and erased from existence save what documentation might remain in photographs, film, or writing. Others are declared heritage objects and the preservation of their materiality is legally ensured. Bible Walk tells a different story: the material items that existed in one place (Collier Township, Pennsylvania) are relocated to a new place (Mansfield, Ohio). Remaining is achieved through physical recontextualization.

The story of Bible Walk is not anomalous in the historical record of materializing the Bible. To name just a few other examples:

- The Biblical Gardens in the Wisconsin Dells was also an outdoor statue park. When it closed in 1997 after thirty-six years, the biblical figures were purchased by the Wisconsin Evangelical Lutheran Synod for use in films and then donated to one of the denomination's summer camps. The camp

director uses them as object lessons for devotional activities with youth and hopes to create his own indoor museum to redisplay the whole set.[4]
- From 1935 until 1989, the Musee Historique Canadienne in Montreal displayed dozens of wax figures composed as biblical scenes. When the museum closed, the collection was acquired by the Musee de la Civilisation in Quebec City and assigned value as provincial heritage. They have been redisplayed as a temporary exhibition and selected figures are displayed online.[5]
- Christus Gardens—a series of life-size biblical dioramas displayed in Gatlinburg, Tennessee, for forty-eight years—closed in 2008. The collection remains intact, now on display at the Holy Land Experience in Orlando. Though, it has been reframed in its recontextualization. The original owner widely advertised the clothing to be historically authentic, created "by the same company that did costume design for such famous motion pictures as *Quo Vadis* and *Ben Hur*."[6] When entering the Holy Land Experience display, a small placard guides visitors: "You are now entering Christus Gardens Wax Museum. The figure are antiques, the costumes are art pieces. They do not portray authentic biblical attire. Please enjoy this rare and beautiful collection as art and museum pieces."[7]
- For five years, a Baptist pastor in St. Petersburg, Florida, worked to build a replica of Moses's "Tabernacle in the Wilderness." In 1948, the replica opened as a teaching and devotional device for the church and a tourist attraction. The pastor died in 1955, and after two years of maintaining the replica, his family sold it to a local Mennonite church in 1959. The whole assemblage was sold again to the Eastern Mennonite Board of Missions and relocated in 1975 to the Mennonite Information Center in Lancaster, Pennsylvania, where it still welcomes visitors.[8]

Some materials wither in place, and some are physically recontextualized to new places. To explore this range of trajectories, this chapter could compare closed sites that erode and those that endure. Instead, I pivot from this direction and use the pattern of physically recontextualizing biblical tourism materials to highlight a broader issue. All materiality has a dynamic tension between fixity and contingency. Objects endure until they do not, moving from physical existence to disappearance. Processes of endurance and erosion are an intersection of temporality (how much time), substance (which physical properties), and inter-agentiality (exchanges shared with other actors in the world) (Colloredo-Mansfield 2003). I mean no existential or theological insight, but it is true that all things eventually pass. The labor, technology, and infrastructure used to keep materiality intact, transform it, or destroy it is always part and parcel with the relative durability and ephemerality of things.

This tension informs a range of questions in the study of material religion: from how sacralized objects are ritually disposed (Myrvold, ed. 2010) to how technologies mediate divine presence (Wojcik 1996; Blanton 2015), relations between mass-produced religious commodities and heritage-ization (Meyer 2019), landscape presence as an assertion of power (Promey 2018), alterations of infrastructure (Farinacci 2017), the labor of memorialization (DeConinck 2019), and the iconicity of architecture (Irvine 2011).

The tension of fixity and contingency helps illuminate a great deal about the social and material life of biblical tourism sites. For example, it might help us think through practices of maintenance: from the necessary seasonal cultivation of biblical gardens to caretaking outdoor statues exposed to changing weather, the preservationist labor of protecting heritage-ized objects, and the computerized updating of digitized museum exhibitions. Here, I look to this tension to reflect on the ways in which material forms remain in circulation. The example of Bible Walk presents a case of physical recontextualization, of relocating materiality into a new context. Objects persist while the original location bears little to no trace of its ties to biblical tourism. If physical movement is one way to remain, then another is through aesthetic recontextualization. This shifts the focus from particular material objects to how a patterned material style remains in circulation through intertextual borrowing. To illustrate, we move between multiple Nazareths: in Israel and Washington, DC.

DC's Nazareth

The World of Jesus of Nazareth is a 7,000-square-foot exhibit on the third floor of the Museum of the Bible (MOTB) in Washington, DC.[9] *Nazareth* is designed to be an immersive environment, a multisensory conjuring of quotidian scenes in a first-century Galilean village. Painted wall murals visualize landscape and agrarian scenes. Individual areas branch off from a central corridor: a kitchen, construction area, *mikveh*, olive mill, and synagogue. The soundscape shifts from scene to scene: birdsong, sheep, goats, ironworking tools in action, and water droplets hitting the ritual bath. Actors portray first-century villagers, always in character as they greet you, asking and answering questions. Archaeological objects in several areas are enclosed by glass panes, but most of the exhibit consists of fabrications. Hand-crafted stones, olive trees, foods, and technologies (e.g., an olive press) constitute much of the scenery—visitors are encouraged to touch, but not climb. Ethereal lighting bathes the entire area, rotating among shades of amethyst, marigold, and rose to mimic atmospheres of dawn, midday, and dusk.

Nazareth was designed and produced by Jonathan Martin Creative (JMC), an experiential design firm based near Nashville, Tennessee. Their production of the exhibit emerged from a diverse intertextual matrix: scriptural references, archaeological records of agrarian technology in the first-century Levant, Holy Land representations from popular and evangelical culture, and the JMC creative director's Holy Land travels. The latter included an influential intertextual source: a themed attraction in Israel called *Nazareth Village* (*NV*).

Since opening in 2000, *NV* has been a collaborative project between local Arab Protestants; (primarily) North American-based Mennonite donors, advisers, and volunteers; and Christian archaeologists (Ron and Feldman 2009; Rose 2020). From its inception, *NV* has been a Protestant alternative to the Roman Catholic and Eastern Orthodox structures that are prevalent throughout Israel-Palestine. Preferring an outdoor, scripturalized landscape over indoor ritual materiality reproduces a historically durable Protestant gaze, which values biblical nature over liturgical culture (Kaell 2014; Feldman 2016).

A detailed guidebook—*The Nazareth Jesus Knew* (2005), written by Joel Kauffmann, one of the early Mennonite advisers—describes *NV* with this experiential promise:

> Guests encounter hillside farm terraces growing olive trees, grape arbors, and other crops typical of Jesus' day. Donkeys, goats, and a flock of sheep roam the land. Visits continue in a fully reconstructed village that includes homes, shops, a synagogue, and a working olive press. Villagers in first-century costumes demonstrate the farm practices and daily life Jesus knew. (80)

Conjuring the everyday lifeworld of Jesus is referenced twice and connected with nature (landscape, flora, fauna), architecture ("homes, synagogue"), technology ("olive press"), and agrarian culture ("farm practices"). This rural biblical past is sought amid a contemporary urban center of nearly 80,000 residents. The attraction is situated on an elevated rise, just 500 meters from the densely packed Old City area. In her ethnographic work onsite, Rose (2020) observes that tour guides routinely draw the attention of visitors toward the immediate materiality of olive trees and first-century replicas and away from the surrounding city in the backdrop.

NV draws together multiple authoritative sources: namely, a location indexically tied to scripture and archaeological science. Several features onsite were discovered through excavation and have been dated to antiquity: the agricultural terraces, the wine press, and some building cornerstones. Kauffmann writes in his guidebook that "Nazareth Village preserves the last remaining fields worked by Jesus's friends, family, and fellow villagers" (7), enticing visitors that the land at *NV* is not merely a generic scriptural location but a direct scriptural witness. Describing the wine press, he makes the promise more explicit: "For visitors to the Holy Land who long to have their feet fall in the same imprints as Jesus', they can do no better than here" (36).

Just outside the entrance to MOTB's *Nazareth* there is a small dedication plaque on the wall:

> In memory of:
> Joel Kauffmann
> we are thankful for the creative genius
> he brought to the museum of the Bible

The same Mennonite adviser and guidebook author for *NV* played an instrumental role in the design process at MOTB. Up until his unexpected death in 2015, Kauffmann worked closely with JMC, using his experience with *NV* to inform *Nazareth*. Kauffmann, Martin, and other design principals for MOTB spent several weeks touring the Holy Land in 2012. During this trip, they spent time at *NV*, an especially formative experience for Martin. He took hundreds of photographs, which were used throughout the design process for *Nazareth*. In short, *NV* is a key intertextual reference for *Nazareth*. And, the Protestant gaze that structures *NV* is aesthetically recontextualized at MOTB.

Parables

When MOTB opened, it was touted in its own and others' publicity as one of the "most technologically advanced" museums in the world.[10] According to its lead architectural firm, the museum uses 384 monitors, 93 projectors, 83 interactive elements, and 12 theaters to engage visitors' bodies and attention. With its interest in conjuring a first-century lifeworld, *Nazareth* breaks from the rest of the museum. The art director recalled that the design team's "primary mandate" was to produce a "low tech, high touch" environment.

There is only one digital projection inside *Nazareth*: a ~10-minute recording, playing on a loop and projected onto a fabricated stone wall. The recording features an actor in first-century dress reading parables from the New Testament Gospels. He stares directly into the camera, bringing visitors face-to-face with an auditory performance of scriptural stories. Spliced throughout each recording are clips of reenactments. This footage was filmed at *NV*, intensifying the intertextual bond between the sites.

Gospel parables are an integral part of *NV*. Guided tours are organized by nine teachings, which they call the "Parable Walk" (Rose 2020). For example, one tour stop presents a sheep pen, which is used to materialize Jesus's parable of the Good Shepherd (Jn 10:10). Early in the *NV* guidebook (2005), Kauffmann reflects on the fundamental aim of *NV*: "From the beginning, the purpose of Nazareth Village was to help religious pilgrims see the Nazareth Jesus knew and hear Jesus's words, especially the parables, with first century ears" (4). Later in the book, this takes a more critical edge. He argues that a materialized environment can counter false or misleading imagery inherited from European art. He presents the example of how an unnamed "drawing from the Middle Ages" misrepresents the parable of the wheat and tares (Matt. 13:24-30). The critique claims that details of the artwork are wrong (e.g., the size and location of the agricultural field), which in turn has hermeneutic consequences: "Jesus, then, is not chastising his followers for being lazy, but encouraging patience and trust in God that in good time, the unwanted weeds will be separated from the spiritually-fruitful wheat" (64).

At MOTB, the parable room is the first space visitors can move into, departing from the main pathway that runs throughout the exhibit. If visitors take this spatial cue, then this room plays a framing role for the other displays. Apart from an inscribed scriptural verse when you first enter *Nazareth*—"Jesus went through cities and villages proclaiming the good news of the kingdom of god" (Lk. 8:1)—the parable room also contains the first signage for visitors to read. One of eleven signs posted throughout the exhibit, the first is titled "Teaching in Parables" and reads:

> Realities of work and home life were ripe for teaching lessons, especially through parables. Teachers often told simple stories that reflected familiar scenarios from village farms and flocks to urban merchants and royal subjects. Like the still-familiar "Good Samaritan" story (Luke 10:25-37) parables often drew listeners into common topics of debate. They mixed familiar images with a vivid twist of detail.

References to ordinariness—"work," "home," "simple," "familiar," "common"—reflect and recreate the organizing aesthetic of this materialized environment: a quotidian first-century lifeworld.

Sensory Indexicality

Nazareth's art director emphasized that the exhibit is designed to be immersive. The ambition is to transport visitors away from the here and now of a twenty-first-century museum to the there and then of a scriptural place where Jesus lived. One experiential strategy present throughout the space is the choreographed integration of sight and sound. The use of auditory visuality echoes a key dynamic of religious visual culture, what Morgan (2012) describes as the "embodied eye": "Seeing is not disembodied or immaterial and vision should not be isolated from other forms of sensation and the social life of feeling" (xvii).

Visitors see any number of scenes inside *Nazareth*: archaeological artifacts, fabricated olive trees, technology replicas, a digital projection of a man reading parables. But, the visual form that occupies the most space is a series of wall-sized murals. The scenes—all hand-painted by Jonathan Martin, based largely on his *NV* photographs—depict landscapes (e.g., Galilean hills stretching into the distance) and agrarian activities (e.g., harvesting olives). All are painted two-dimensionally, engendering the illusion of spatial distance inside a confined environment. Each mural is accompanied by a soundtrack, emitting from speakers built into fabricated rocks nearby. Most of these sounds are nature recordings: sheep, goats, and a birdsong mix of species native to the Galilee region.

The emphasis on nature (landscape, animals) and cultivated nature (farming) uses the ideology of sensory indexicality to express the organizing aesthetic of the Protestant gaze (Feldman 2016). Much like the biblical gardens, biblical meals, and collecting of biblical landscape items featured in Section II of this book, *Nazareth*'s choreography of auditory visuality mobilizes the senses to claim a direct, unmediated connection between humans and nature, undisturbed by time, history, or culture. The animating logic is that we are linked to biblical characters because the human sensorium and the natural world have not changed. Their natural world is our natural world; their embodied experience is our embodied experience. While the lifeworld of first-century Nazareth may be distant to us in many ways, we can best access it through a shared experience of nature.

Intertextual Gaps

Linguistic anthropologists Bauman and Briggs (1992) observe that intertextual performances always produce interpretive gaps, resulting from a necessarily imperfect fit between a text that has been decontextualized from its original context and recontextualized in a new context. Minimizing or maximizing intertextual gaps become agentive opportunities. For example, minimizing a gap can be a way to construct fidelity to the original text/context, and maximizing can be a way to claim virtuosic authority for the performer through "individual creativity and innovation" (149). In the case of *Nazareth*, intertextual gaps are filled in ways that gesture toward the figure of Jesus and that elaborate the exhibit's broader ambition of immersing visitors into an imagineered and Protestant scriptural past.

One technique for filling gaps is the wall signage, which prompts visitors to attend to selected features as teaching displays. In the building technology area, a plaque entitled "Under Construction" reads:

> Builders in first-century Nazareth were experts in blending stone, wood, earth, and plaster. The backbreaking work often began by revealing the bedrock, establishing the foundation, and placing carefully hewn cornerstones to support the structure. Later, they shaped wood into rafters and crafted doors and furniture. While family members commonly labored to build their own homes, they occasionally needed assistance from a master builder.

The closing reference to "a master builder" is most operative here. Visitors are called to draw Jesus into the scene, perhaps by recalling specific scriptural references to Jesus's trade (Mk 6:3; Matt. 13:54-55) or perhaps other cultural references to Jesus as a "carpenter."[11]

The gap between materialized environment and imagined first-century referent is filled more vividly by the series of actors (or, "living history interpreters," as the museum's job posting terms the position) who roam the exhibit as first-century Jewish Nazarenes. *Nazareth*'s art director confirmed that from its inception the design process assumed the presence of live actors. Their presence impacted decisions about directing traffic flow and ensuring that the actors would have enough space to move and talk with visitors. At any given time of day, there is typically at least one actor onsite and as many as four.

Actors mark their identity as first-century living history interpreters—not docents or tour guides—by greeting visitors in Aramaic (*sh'lam*) before switching to English. They also rely heavily on spatial and pronominal deictics to mark their location in a different space-time: "here in Nazareth," "our village," "we speak Aramaic." The actors also draw visitors into their performance to bolster the play frame. For example, in a visitor recording from December 2017, an actor in the synagogue area begins his explanation with a description of Nazareth as a rural village. He asks if anyone else is from a "small town." When a willing visitor volunteers a place name, he puts on a confused look and responds: "I'm sorry, I've not heard of this place. Is it near the Sea of Galilee?"[12] Much like the signage, the actors find ways to bring Jesus into the scene (cf. Hicks-Keeton and Concannon 2018). In the same visitor recording, the actor describes the synagogue as a village gathering place and the place where boys can learn Torah. He then asks the crowd if they have heard of a man named Jesus and noted that "Jesus learned and memorized the Torah here, and with Joseph."

The actors also reinforce the exhibit's quotidian aesthetic, emphasizing features of everyday life such as farming and food preparation. On my first visit to the museum in November 2017, I recorded a performance by a female interpreter in the kitchen area. She explained the fabricated food items on the table and placed her hand on a fabricated jug:

> Right here we have some water. So, every morning before the sun comes in, my daughters and I go get water from the well. When we're going to the well, the jugs are light. When we are coming back, they are heaVY [elongated "ea" and amplified "vy" for emphasis]. But, it is the one time we get to see our friends, so it is our favorite time of the day [smiling].

Here, the actor seeks to minimize the intertextual gap by conjuring an imagined scene of first-century life. In performances like this, actors build connections between everyday activities likely unfamiliar to visitors (gathering water from a community well) and sensations visitors can attach to: the physical struggle of hauling something heavy, the joy of conviviality, and the capacity of friendship to lighten the difficulty of work.

Coda

This chapter has explored an animating tension in the study of material religion: the capacity of material forms to be relatively fixed and relatively contingent. Lived religious practice, memory, and religious publicity all intersect with processes of material endurance and erosion. I have presented two ways in which material forms remain in circulation: the physical recontextualization of materiality and the recontextualization of a particular aesthetic style. In the former, specific objects (Bible Walk's fiberglass statues in "biblical dress") are preserved through new owners and a new spatial setting. In the latter, a specific aesthetic (*Nazareth's* Protestant Holy Land gaze emphasizing nature and a quotidian lifeworld tied closely to nature) is preserved through intertextual reference and the cultural production of an imagineered biblical past.

Section II

The Power of Nature

In four chapters, Section II explores ways in which the natural world associated with and depicted by the Bible is mobilized as a privileged media. Respectively, the chapters in this section examine: (7) flora referenced in biblical texts, in particular their cultivation outside Israel-Palestine in themed botanical gardens; (8) fauna mentioned in biblical texts, from their presence in nature to themed zoological gardens; (9) food items named in biblical texts and related culinary practices, in particular the production of biblically themed cookbooks; and, (10) the historical circulation of biblical landscape items—flower, soil, water, stone—and their incorporation into modern sites of biblical tourism.

This set of materializing the Bible performances resonates with the Christian tradition of "natural theology," which posited that God gifted humanity two revelations: scripture and the natural world (e.g., Paley 1802). If early proponents of natural theology explored physical environments to experience God's presence, makers of biblical gardens, zoos, and cookbooks create sensory encounters with recontextualized pieces of nature in order to foster a sense of divine presence and an intimacy with the biblical past.

Particular moments in Section I anticipated these chapters' engagements with biblical nature, such as the World of Jesus of Nazareth's use of agrarian sounds and scenes, and the Temple of Solomon's integration of Jerusalem stone, date palms, acacia wood, and a dried bush from Mt. Sinai. What is glimpsed in these examples, and what is elaborated in the coming chapters, is the treatment of biblical nature as a common sensory ground, an experiential territory that can traverse borders of time, space, and culture.

The materialities at play in this section are closely associated with nature, and, in turn, the attempt to create an experiential access to the past is mediated by an ideology of sensory indexicality. This term refers to the ways in which sensory experiences are used to claim a direct connection between humans and nature, undisturbed by history. Visitors to biblical gardens, for example, are encouraged to remember biblical stories and imagine themselves alongside biblical characters, as sharing the same botanical world and embodied experience of that world. The power of nature is that it promises to provide an un-mediated access to the biblical past: lavender smells as sweet as it always has, and the sandpaper texture of a fig leaf feels the same. To encounter biblical nature is to enter the biblical lifeworld. It is through this ideology that gardens, zoos, cookbooks, and the handling of landscape items enliven relationships with the biblical past and intensify scriptural intimacy.

Figure 7 Entry to Biblical Garden at Paradise Valley United Methodist Church (Paradise Valley, Arizona). Photo credit: James S. Bielo.

7

Flora

In 1865, the Methodist Episcopal denomination began publishing the *Sunday School Journal for Teachers and Young People*. This monthly periodical featured theological and historical essays, write-in proposals for biblical teaching, and promoted a uniform lesson plan. John Heyl Vincent, a central figure in the Methodist Sunday School movement and in the US history of materializing the Bible, began editing the journal in 1869 (Boylan 1988: 90). It was Vincent who envisioned Chautauqua's Palestine Park in 1874, a scaled topographic model of the Holy Land used to teach biblical geography and encourage virtual pilgrimage (Long 2000). One of the journal's regular features, "The Months in Palestine," echoed Palestine Park's emphasis on the natural setting of biblical history. Each month, this column called readers to imagine what seasonal changes were taking place in the Holy Land. For example, in February 1871:

> Adar, "magnificent," from the profusion of flowers everywhere. Lebanon covered with snow. Chiefly remarkable for rains, though they do not continue many days. Barley may still be sown. Snap-beans begin to mature sufficiently for table use. Apple-trees in bloom; peach-trees also. Hyacinths, daffodils, tulips, ranunculuses, lilies, narcissus, geraniums, scarlet poppies, anemones, daisies, and many other familiar flowers in bloom, spreading themselves over the country in rich carpets; besides vast numbers of unknown herbs, springing everything in the fields. Cauliflowers, onions, carrots, beets, radishes; orange-trees, too, laden with ripe fruit.[1]

"The Months in Palestine" sought to create a sensual connection between readers and the land of the Bible, and *flora* was its primary media for doing so. This reflected and fueled an already robust practice of using the flowers, trees, plants, and herbs named in biblical texts to teach biblical lessons and build intimacy with the biblical past. This chapter explores such sensory mobilizations of nature, wild and cultivated, from its origins in botanical science to the global phenomenon of creating biblical gardens.[2]

"Through two thousand springtimes"

In a 1747 public lecture, Carl Linneaus identified Palestine as the kind of place that needed empirical exploration and that would advance the emerging field of botany. Fredrik Hasselquist—a fellow Swedish Lutheran and student of Linneaus—was in the audience and took the call seriously. At the age of twenty-six, he began a four-year expedition throughout the Levant, collecting botanical samples and overseeing their transport back to Sweden. The journey claimed his life, but his work was not lost. The Queen of Sweden ordered his travelogue to be published, and Linneaus arranged for the 1757 printing of *Voyages and Travels in the Levant in the Years 1749, 50, 51, 52: Containing Observations in Natural History, Physick, Agriculture, and Commerce: Particularly on the Holy Land, and the Natural History of Scriptures*.

Hasselquist's writing is not saturated with devotional reflection and is dismissive of Catholic piety. He was amused, even exasperated, by the ever-present assertion of sacredness: "Every thing, even to the table on which we supped, was holy. The wine we drank came from the holy desart where St. John dwelt; and the olives grew on the Mountain of Olives near Jerusalem" (117). Hasselquist preferred a scientific register, though he ultimately wed this to his Christian commitments. Consider this sensory-rich description of *paliurus athenai*, in which he uses the details of flora to reflect on the history and meaning of biblical texts:

> In all probability this is the tree which afforded the crown of thorns put on the head of Christ; it grows very common in the East. This plant was very fit for the purpose, for it has many small and sharp spines, which are well adapted to give pain; the crown might be easily made of these soft, round, and pliant branches, and what in my opinion seems to be the greatest proof, is, that the leaves much resemble those of ivy, as they are of a very deep green. Perhaps the enemies of Christ, would have a plant somewhat resembling that, with which emperors and generals were used to be crowned, that there might be calumny even in the punishment. (289)

The 1766 reprinting of Hasselquist's volume in English sparked a lively tradition among Anglophone scholars, beginning with *Natural History of the Bible: Or, a Description of All the Quadrupeds, Birds, Fishes, Reptiles, and Insects, Trees, Plants, Flowers, Gums, and Precious Stones, Mentioned in the Sacred Scriptures* (1820). Thaddeus Mason Harris, a New England librarian and Unitarian minister, played up the relation between scriptural literacy and proper scientific knowledge. Inadequate understanding of natural history, he writes in the

Preface, "prevents us from discovering the propriety of many allusions to their nature and habits, and conceals from us the beauty of many similies [*sic*] which are founded on their characteristic qualities" (iii).

In 1835, the American Sunday School Union published a similar volume by Francis Ewing: *Bible Natural History: Or, a Description of the Animals, Plants, and Minerals Mentioned in the Sacred Scriptures, with Copious References and Explanation of Texts*. One reviewer, writing in the *Princeton Review*, congratulated Ewing and revived Harris's commitment that botanical education enhances biblical literacy: "The darkest texts have had no obscurity except from the ignorance of facts in [natural history]. Some of the most startling objections urged by infidels lose all force, when the natural history of the subjects is cleared up" (author unknown, 1835: 560).

Biblical botany entered the popular consciousness through magazine periodicals, expanding beyond niche scholarly interest. In 1850, *The Gardeners' Magazine of Botany, Horticulture, Floriculture, and Natural Science* included entries for "Sacred Botany," such as hyssop and tamarisk, which combined scientific details with nods to how the varietals evidence scriptural historicity. Similar entries continued in the 1874 inaugural publication of *The Gardeners' Chronicle: a weekly illustrated journal*. The popular resonance of biblical botany was cemented through association with a related attraction, the public botanical garden. The Missouri Botanical Gardens opened to the public in 1859. As early as 1884, the Missouri Gardens published *Plants of the Bible*, a self-guiding pamphlet that identified thirty-four biblical varieties housed on the grounds. The guiding text is minimal, providing only a basic list that includes the common name for each variety, scientific classification, and a linked scriptural verse:

> The Bay-Tree (*Laurus nobilis.*)
> I have seen the wicked in great power and spreading himself like a green bay-tree. (Ps. 37:35)

Another public institution, Chicago's Field Museum, maintained a "plants of the Bible" display as part of its broader botanical exhibits beginning in 1908. A similar exhibition ran briefly at the New York Botanical Gardens in the 1930s, and around the same time, a California flower show exhibited plants that were native to both Palestine and the American Southwest. A local newspaper praised the exhibit, echoing writers like Thaddeus Harris: "It somehow makes the Bible stories seem more real, more intimate, to realize that they were enacted against a background in many respects so similar to California."[3]

These public exhibitions inspired popular books that instructed gardeners to cultivate biblical flora in their home and churchyards. Eleanor Anthony King, once editor of *Audubon Magazine*, published *Bible Plants for American Gardens* in 1941. The book begins with a sharp juxtaposition, grounded in themes of historical authenticity and sensory touch. She describes a New York museum display of the Great Chalice of Antioch, a disputed artifact housed in protective glass, "carefully guarded from the fingers of those who would touch" (ix). She contrasts this with "a sidewalk vendor [who] is selling anemones," highlighting themes of ready accessibility and sensorial access to the past: "For a few cents you may hold a handful of ruby and amethyst chalices, glowing like the jeweled Grail of legend. Yet there is no doubt that these are the flowers of the field which Jesus saw and touched, which he used to make his teaching clear to the people" (ibid).

Mobilizing biblical flora for sensory pleasure and scriptural study is fully realized in modern biblical gardens, which exclusively or primarily cultivate varieties of flora named in biblical texts. The earliest garden I have verified dates to 1940—located at a Methodist church near California's Monterey coast and perhaps was inspired by the 1930s flower exhibition.[4] In 2020, there were at least 148 extant Christian biblical gardens in 25 countries.[5] They range widely in size and internal organization. There are small congregational gardens that measure only a few square meters, and there is an 80-acre garden in Myczkowce, Poland.[6] Some are a jumble, with botanical varieties arranged in no apparent order. Others follow scriptural logics. Some separate Old and New Testament varieties, while others are more exacting. For example, the Bangor Cathedral garden in Wales arranges plants sequentially by their mention from Genesis to Revelation. The Warsaw Biblical Gardens in northern Indiana implements yet another approach, divided into six "micro-climates" of biblical lands: Forest, Desert, Orchard, Meadow, Brook, and Crops.

Biblical gardens use the sensory engagement with nature to integrate devotion and scriptural instruction. Caretakers, tour guides, guiding pamphlets, and websites consistently describe gardens as prayerful spaces. Founded in 2008, a Canberra, Australia garden frames its devotional capacity as an intimate connection with biblical people:

> The Bible Garden is a sacred place: for solitude, personal reflection and learning. It is made holy by: the source of its inspiration, the dedication of those who made it, by our thoughtful presence. The Bible is the story of seekers just like us thousands of years ago. Here for a moment we can feel united to them in quiet wonder. Through these common garden plants we reach out to our long-ago

spiritual brothers and sisters. We admire their courage in holding fast to truth as it was unfolded before them; we are uplifted by the beautiful expression of their relationship with the Divine.[7]

Biblical gardens are also designed to teach. They proclaim themselves to be a unique channel for reencountering the stories, places, and figures of scripture. The garden's pedagogy is fundamentally experiential. They call to visitors: learn the text of scripture better through a physical encounter with cultivated nature. Like other religious projects that hone sensory attunement, the garden mobilizes bodily experience to foster an intimate relationship with tradition (e.g., Blanton 2015).

The instructional dimension of gardens is often used to attract visitors. An Oklahoma garden, founded by a born-again Christian, offers tours for Bible study groups, school groups, home school groups, and Sunday school classes.[8] On guided tours of gardens in Arizona and Indiana, caretakers explained that they arrange visits from both Sunday school and public school science classes. Eleanor King closes her 1941 popular book with a call to integrate biblical gardens into Sunday school curricula: "This would prove an inspiration to the whole church community; for children, like plants, grow toward the light. And they will have no difficulty in entering the spirit of the Bible teaching by way of the study of plants" (198).

Most gardens focus on a twofold aim: teaching how flora were used in the biblical past, and how botanical knowledge heightens the meaning of scriptural content. To achieve this, biblical gardens immerse visitors into the natural world of scripture. This immersive imperative is illustrated well by the guiding pamphlet of an American Baptist congregation in eastern Connecticut:

> Welcome members, friends and visitors to a special garden to *rest your senses* by the simplicity of *rewinding time*—to Biblical time! *Sit* under the Tamarix; let the *coolness* of its shade and gentle breeze *touch* your face *just as Jesus* and his disciples did during their travels. As you *watch* the bees bounce among the Hyssop, *imagine* the *taste* of honey they make for you *just as* they made honey for Jesus. *Enjoy the smell* of Juniper sage mint *as enjoyed by Jesus* as he visited many gardens. In the sunlit renewal of spring, *look upon* the colorful bulbs in bloom *just as Jesus* did when he spoke of the "lilies of the field." Do this and comfort and joy will come.[9] (Emphasis added)

This framing text uses a poetic device, the parallelism of "just as," to perform an immersive imperative that is decidedly sensual: sit, touch, watch, imagine the taste, enjoy the smell.

Irrespective of their size and organization, every garden I have observed includes two common elements: walkways and benches. While these elements pose as mundane, in reality they are anything but mundane because they work as experiential invitations. They insist that the garden is not designed to be gazed on from the outside or hastily consumed. The garden is designed to be moved through, lingered in, and experienced from the inside. In this way, the biblical garden follows a principle of cultivated landscapes more generally: "[They] build in a mobile, participatory aesthetic that emphasizes movement and continuing hands-on engagement in all dimensions" (Gundaker 2016: 46). As visitors move through and linger in biblical gardens, they are encouraged to get caught up in sensory immersion. Smell the fragrant rosemary. Touch the gnarly olive trunk. Pinch off a bay leaf, rub it between your fingers, and inhale. See the vibrant red skin of a pomegranate fruit. Hear the sound of leaves jostled by breeze. Enter scripture via flora.

The promise of sensory immersion rests on the ideology of sensory indexicality, inviting visitors to imagine that they are gaining unmediated access to the biblical past.[10] The herbs smell as they always have, the leaves and fruits feel the same: you are linked to biblical characters because the human sensorium and the natural world have not changed. Their botanical world is your botanical world. Your embodied experience was their embodied experience. This promise continues unaltered from early instructional guides: "Plants mentioned in the Bible are the living link between us and the people of these hallowed and distant times. . . . We can reach back to Bible days, through two thousand springtimes, when we plant a garden" (King 1941: xi–xii).

During my tour of Indiana's Warsaw Biblical Gardens, the caretaker and I shared a few moments of such sensory engagement. At one point, we lingered awhile in the "Herbs and Crops" section, and I noticed a sign for wormwood. I asked why this plant was included, and he answered without pause that the book of Revelation uses wormwood to describe the taste of bitter waters. Intending a light-hearted moment, I asked if he ever uses his green thumb to tempt the green fairy (i.e., absinthe). I received only a confused look and a curious question. I stumbled through a description of the wormwood-based alcohol, and he nodded in appreciation; we were both learning a little. He described wormwood as "really invasive," pointing out its rising between cracks in the concrete pathway several meters away from where it was planted. I knelt down to pinch a bit off, and he did the same. We rubbed it between our fingers, inhaled the fennel-like herbaceous aroma, and agreed the smell was pleasing. He seized this moment to reiterate that the whole garden should be interactive for visitors, an invitation he repeats during group tours. He explained that most people come to the garden with a keep-off-the-grass ethic, which he wants to disrupt.

The pedagogical promise of biblical gardens can only be fulfilled by engaging the full sensorium.

From Eleanor King to the Warsaw Gardens, biblical gardens cultivate a commitment that the sensory encounter with scriptural nature is transformative. While the Warsaw gardener wanted to disrupt a cautious no-touch disposition among visitors, others mobilize biblical flora to make other challenges. In our final example, we go to the Biblical History Center (BHC) in southwestern Georgia. Founded in 2006, the BHC is not strictly a biblical garden, though one section of its primary teaching space is dedicated to growing biblical plants and showing how they were integrated into "first century [i.e., biblical] life."

In a 2012 televised tour for a fundamentalist media network, the founder (Jim Fleming) walks the host and viewers through the biblical plant section.[11] For a few minutes, they linger in the vineyard. In the transcript below, note how Fleming uses botanical knowledge to critique authorized Bible translators. In doing so, he claims legitimacy for himself, the BHC as a biblical tourist site, and biblical botany as a tradition. He begins by explaining to the host that "in antiquity [i.e., Jesus's lifeworld]" grapes were grown on the ground not on elevated wire.

> Host (H): They just let the grapes grow on the ground?
>
> Fleming (F): Yep, but, every vine has a couple of rocks next to it.
>
> H: That's right.
>
> F: That we do have. Anyways.
>
> H: Okay, so, what's the purpose of that, to keep 'em off the ground?
>
> F: Now, here's the thing. You have to keep lifting the branches up on the rock, as they get further away, because if it touches the ground it will make a root at that point.
>
> H: Oh.
>
> F: And then, what will happen it will wither its connection with the deeper root of the mother vine.
>
> H: Ah.
>
> F: And then, we get five months of no rain: May, June, July, August, September. In Judea, grapes come out August, September and it will wither. Now, let's go back to Jesus' saying at the Last Supper. I am the vine. You are the branches. Abide in me. Everybody knows if you don't keep a vine off the ground it will make its own nourishment.
>
> H: Except twentieth century people don't know that.

F: Well, we gotta work on that.

H: {laughs}

F: But, isn't it interesting, Jesus' last saying for his disciple was keep your nourishment in life based upon my deeper root.

H: Your deeper root, yes.

F: That will hold you through the droughts. And, did you know the same word "take away" in Greek is "lift up"? In fact, three out of four times it's translated "lift up." Instead of understanding any branch that bear not fruit I will take away.

H: Mhm.

F: Three out of four times that word is "I will lift up." And, if you're all the time stacking branches up onto rocks, it's a very different feeling isn't it, between "take away" and "lift up"?

H: Yes.

F: I'll help you keep your nourishment based on my deeper root.

H: Once again, understanding the culture, farming methods and whatever helps us to better understand the Bible.

F: I think if more translators would see an ancient vineyard.

H: Yes.

F: Without branches already up on wire, they may have thought of putting "lift up" instead of "take away."

H: Okay, well, what's our next stop in this tour?

Conclusion

To be in a biblical garden is to be in designed space: emplaced, exposed to, and engulfed by sensory experience. Sensuality—the united affect of visuality, tactility, physical movement, taste, smell, and aurality—is integral to their effectiveness. Biblical gardens promise visitors intimate access to the biblical past, and an enlivened relationship with the biblical lifeworld. Garden visitors are encouraged to remember biblical stories and imagine themselves alongside biblical characters, sharing the same botanical world and embodied experience.

The sensual pedagogy of biblical gardens is revealing with respect to how the history of the senses is narrated in the study of religion. In *Hearing Things* (2000), Leigh Schmidt explored how post-Reformation Christian traditions arranged and rearranged sensory hierarchies. "Christian devotion has always been deeply bound up with the refusal and deflection of the senses, whether plugging the ears, averting the eyes, or avoiding the touch, constantly negotiating the temptations of the body through the body" (viii). These traditions had to reckon with a dominant modern sensory ideology that elevated sight as authoritative and treated other sensory modes as either suspicious or overly subjective. The "visual piety" that came to dominate US Christianity has been expressed through a wide array of objects, such as portrait images of Jesus (McDannell 1995), the design of children's Bibles (Lindquist 2014), touring biblical panoramas (Morgan 2007), and popular devotional commodities (Morgan 1999).

Biblical gardens resist the modern ideology that elevates vision atop a sensory hierarchy. Visuality is important, from the vibrancy of plant color to the size and form of biblical botanicals. But, the optical is not endowed with special importance. If anything, smell, taste, and touch are elevated because they signify a more intimate encounter with nature and, in turn, a more intimate performance of sensual indexicality. The garden promises a tandem sensory experience, in which our tactile, aromatic, audible, and visual capacities are entangled. In this way, biblical gardens echo the comparative insight that visuality is always an embodied experience (Morgan 2012). These gardens leverage the weight of a combined sensorium to trust the promises of sensual indexicality, to be immersed into the sacred past through biblical flora, and learn the scriptures anew. Rather than overturning or inverting a modern sensory hierarchy, perhaps the garden can best be said to flatten it. The gaze, the touch, the sniff, and the attuned ear are mutually reliant and equally enhanced.

Figure 8 Sign at Creation Museum Petting Zoo (Petersburg, Kentucky). Photo credit: James S. Bielo.

8

Fauna

The "Eden Animal Experience" is what the Answers in Genesis Creation Museum in northern Kentucky calls its zoo. This small collection, home to a dozen or so animals, is located near the lush botanical gardens outside the main building. On fieldwork visits between 2009 and 2017, animals were available to view, some to pet and, in one case, ride. For $5, anyone taller than 36 inches can ride a Dromedary camel. Signage details the animal's morphological and behavioral traits and notes for visitors that "the word 'camel' is found 62 times in the King James Version of the Bible spread throughout 21 different books."[1]

Donkeys, alpacas, coatis, goats, sheep, and wallabies keep the camel company. Two final animals round out the zoo's roster, and they make a particular contribution to the site's teaching of creationist theology. As signage explains, the "zorse" and "zedonk" are "interspecific hybrids" born of zebra-horse parentage. These animals are used to reiterate one of the Creation Museum's central teaching points, that a literal Noah as described in Genesis filled a literal ark with animal "kinds," not modern species. In this creationist spin on speciation, zebras and horses are descendants of an ancestral "horse kind," which is why they are able to still produce viable offspring. The Eden Animal Experience presents "zebroids" as living examples of creationist truth claims, theology proofed zoologically.

A petting zoo at a creationist site is unsurprising for a few reasons. Generally, for tourist attractions that have sufficient acreage and operating expenses, a petting zoo is a common installation. It offers outdoor activity; appeals to interests in an "up close," sensory encounter with animals; helps attractions market themselves as multipurpose family destinations; and, per the $5 camel ride, creates additional monetized possibilities. There is also a more creationist-specific reason. Given the scriptural and theological centrality of the Noah's ark story for creationists, animals are potent figures for creationist teaching and are widely represented in their aesthetic productions.

A petting zoo at a biblical tourism site makes sense for another reason as well. The Creation Museum's camel sign notes the numerous biblical references, setting a frame for visitors to associate the living animal in their immediate sensory orbit with distant biblical lifeworlds. Here, animals are transformed into yet another media for materializing the Bible. At least since the seventeenth century, biblical commentators have read scriptural texts with a zoological lens, using the theme of "animals of the bible" as a way to claim hermeneutic insight, knowledge of Holy Land geography, and enhance scriptural intimacy. The Eden Animal Experience is, then, a distinctly creationist expression of a broader phenomenon: mobilizing zoological nature to create sensorial access to a scriptural past.

A Biblical Aviary

The first modern effort to catalogue the "animals of the Bible" appeared in 1663 from a French Protestant biblical scholar, Samuel Bochart (Sheehan 2005: 203). Attempts to provide encyclopedic accounts of biblical fauna proliferated in the nineteenth century alongside other projects of Holy Land mapping: topographic, botanical, and archaeological. Writers of biblical zoology sounded a refrain familiar to biblical botanists, claiming that the intricate study of biblical animals would yield new insight into scriptural understanding. For example, a Church of England clergyman, J. G. Wood, introduced his 1888 *Story of the Bible Animals* with this declaration:

> The importance of understanding the nature, habits, and uses of the animals which are constantly mentioned in the Bible, cannot be overrated as a means of elucidating the Scriptures, and without this knowledge we shall not only miss the point of innumerable passages of the Old and New Testaments, but the words of our Lord Himself will often be totally misinterpreted, or at least lose part of their significance. (v)

A popular expression within the biblical zoology tradition is a focus on biblical birds. Thaddeus Mason Harris, a New England librarian and Unitarian minister, included several bird entries in his 1820 *Natural History of the Bible*. The first bird-focused volume, *The Birds of the Bible*, was published in 1854 by a German Reformed minister, Henry Harbaugh. He identified twenty-six bird varieties, discussing their appearance in scriptural stories, their symbolism, and how a zoological understanding of bird behavior sharpens scriptural knowledge.

"Why birds?" is a useful question. Harbaugh poses two answers. The first asserts a symbolic meaning that birds are "of the earth or not, just as they please" (25). Grounded in a Platonic cosmology that locates heaven as up above the earth, birds are endowed with a liminal quality of existing between heaven and earth, connecting human and divine realms. The second answer shifts the orientation to human sensory engagements with nature, as Harbaugh highlights the auditory pleasure of birdsong:

> They are the birds which sang in Paradise—which hovered around the tents of the Patriarchs—which cheered the Prophets in the desert—and which gave sweet response to the shepherd's song amid the pastoral scenes of peace and pleasure in the rural regions of the Holy Land. (27)

In celebrating the sounds of birds in nature, he draws his readers into a pair of interlaced processes. Readers are invited to imagine a direct continuity between biblical and contemporary lifeworlds, with birdsong as a sonic bridge across space-time. Readers are also invited to attend anew to the birdsong of their local environment, to find a moment of biblical presence breaking into a local lifeworld. As he writes elsewhere in the volume, "The Bible we cannot have always open before us; but, wherever we are, the world around us speaks to us through all our senses" (23).

Singling out birds proved a rich vein for many others. Several volumes followed in the nineteenth century also pitched as studies in biblical scholarship. In 1909, the American transcendentalist writer Gene Stratton-Porter published *The Birds of the Bible* for a more popular audience. Stratton-Porter veered from the strategy of encyclopedic cataloguing but also made sensory encounters with nature central to her work. "The Bible makes it quite evident that even in those early days people so loved the graceful motion and cheery songs of the birds that they constructed rude cages of peeled willow wands and confined beautiful feathered creatures for pets" (38). For some readers, her detachment from detailed scriptural study was refreshing, as evidenced by a book reviewer for the *San Francisco Call* in 1910: "When the student who seeks is tired of the long arguments as to the real meaning of an obscure word and tired of the volume of 'higher criticism' he may take down this very human book and let the birds tell their story."

Stratton-Porter instigated a more devotional register for reflecting on biblical birds, one taken up numerous times in the century that followed. In 1959, the popular Christian writer Alice Parmelee published *All the Birds of the Bible*, a collection of twenty-five short essays. Parmelee presents her readers with much the same promise of sensorial access to the biblical past as Harbaugh did a century earlier: "[Birds] infuse life into ancient stories and bring us close to the Hebrews who, centuries ago, watched the lively actions of the same species of birds that fly in Palestine today" (19). In 2013, a progressive Christian pastor and author, Debbie Blue, published *Consider the Birds: A Provocative Guide to*

Birds of the Bible. Like Parmelee and those before her, Blue's conceit was that a concentrated reflection on the birds in our world and the birds in our Bible would yield precious spiritual insight. As she writes in her introduction, "People identify with birds. We watch them, research them, tell stories about them, and in the process we explore our humanity and inhumanity—mystery and manners. They're funny and dirty, nobly and shifty—much like us" (xiii).

In researching this chapter I did not discover any tourism sites focused on birds of the Bible and no biblical aviaries in the landscape of biblical tourism (at least, not yet). The closest analogue is bird watching tours of Israel-Palestine, which some Holy Land travelers integrate into pilgrimage itineraries.[2] What did turn up were Christian birdwatching websites, blogs, and books. Written from a range of theological perspectives, from fundamentalist Protestant to Dominican friars, Christian birdwatching operates primarily in a devotional register, celebrating the ways in which birding reveals the "wonder of God's creation."

Much like the published books about biblical birds, those who articulate the spiritual virtues of birdwatching highlight the importance of an attuned sensoria. For example, writing for an InterVarsity campus ministry blog, an Iowa pastor reflects on the links between birdwatching and contemplative prayer.[3] He begins with "seeing" and how both birdwatching and a healthy prayer life require mindful adjustment: "Unless I consciously choose to alter my pace and pay attention, I miss much of what is all around me." Echoing the charged experience of embodied visuality (Morgan 2012), he continues by extolling "hearing" as a companion sense:

> I find that my ears, when alert, are the best tools I have for locating a bird in the first place. A call, the rustle of leaves, or the whirr of wings gets my attention and turns my eyes in the right direction. Seeing and hearing work together. In contemplative prayer, to hear requires not only slowing down and paying attention, but also stillness.

A Biblical Zoo

Given the widespread adoption of themed, immersive environments in modern zoos (Grazian 2012), we might expect biblically themed zoos to be an established kind of tourist attraction. In fact, there are relatively few on record. Since 1998, four have appeared in three nations: two creationist zoos, one in southwestern Virginia, and one in western England; and, two Hasidic zoos focused on animals named in the Torah, one in Brooklyn and one in

Beit Shemesh, Israel.[4] The oldest example is in Jerusalem: initially called the Jerusalem Biblical Zoo and renamed in 1993 as the Tisch Family Zoological Gardens.[5]

The Jerusalem Biblical Zoo was started in 1940 by Aharon Shulov: a Hebrew University biologist who migrated to Palestine in 1926 from the Soviet Union. Started in Shulov's home, the zoo moved twice before settling on 13 acres in a northern Jerusalem neighborhood in 1950. From its inception, the zoo had two orienting values.

First, Shulov wanted to bring visitors face-to-face with biblical fauna. In a 1961 profile of the zoo for the *New Scientist*, he wrote: "Its declared aim is to exhibit all the animals and birds mentioned in the Bible, accompanied by plaques inscribed with suitable Biblical quotations."[6] For decades, reviewers delighted in the idea of a biblical menagerie. Susan Nevil, an American children's book author, published an illustrated volume about the zoo in 1960. The book fictionalizes a set of Jewish twins, Michael and Deborah, as guides. Throughout, the children are used to depict an exclusively Jewish Israel and an intimacy between contemporary nature and the scriptural past:

> The places and their names are the same now as they were then. The modern child in Israel treads the same paths and climbs the same hills as did the child of Bible times. He sees farmers drawing water from the same rivers and tilling the same fields and harvesting the same crops. The flowers he picks in the fields, the trees in the woods, the grandeur or softness of the scenery are a joy to him as they were to the people of the Bible. And the animals, too, are the same as they were in those far-off days.[7]

Other reviewers, while not so thoroughly Zionist, retain the fascination with a biblically themed zoo. Writing for the *Negro History Bulletin* in 1962, famed African American diplomat Marguerite Cartwright lauded her experience at the zoo: "all enjoy this wonderland of the scriptures and pages of living Bible history."[8] A decade later, a journalist writing in the *Chicago Tribune* applauds the zoo's commitment to its theme: "Jerusalem's unique collection of fauna houses all but one of the 130 creatures mentioned in the Good Book."[9] And, another decade on, a retired Cornell University professor writing for the *New York Times* celebrates again the idea of space-time collapse: "[The zoo] can help any visitor to Jerusalem to acquire some sense of the fauna that lived there 2,000 years ago, in the age of the patriarchs."[10]

Shulov expanded the biblical theming to a series of staged animal scenes. Reviewers frequently commented on the zoo's materialization of Isa. 11:6, a prophetic text about a future kingdom of peace: "The wolf shall live with the lamb, the leopard shall lie down with the kid" (NRSV). In 1977, London's *Sunday Times* reported on this planned exhibit, noting the precautions being put in place: the carnivores would be cubs; the animals would be trained from birth to interact together; they would be separated during non-visitor hours; and "before being put together the carnivores will be fed to bursting point."[11] The 1983 *New York Times* review noted the same exhibit, and its eventual closing: "prophecy must give way to reality, because the young lions of Judah, unaware of their own strength, begin to play too rough."[12]

The second value was a zoological expression, and extension, of ethnic Zionism. The interest in biblical animals could also be articulated as a "repatriation of animals that once lived in the Holy Land."[13] Shulov's return of animals to the land was designed to parallel the return of Jewish people to a biblically defined homeland. Similar to other Zionist projects, such as tree planting, the zoo engaged the global Jewish diaspora to acquire animals. For example, the Philadelphia Zoo sent gray squirrels in 1958 "at the request of [Shulov] . . . who reported that the little animal, whose name appears in the Scriptures, had disappeared from Israel and its vicinity."[14]

In 1991, the Jerusalem Biblical Zoo closed for relocation. The previous property was no longer suitable for its size, and the zoo wanted an updated facility with naturalistic environments rather than enclosed cages. Buoyed by a $5 million donation from the New York-based Tisch family, the zoo reopened in 1993 under a new name, a new location, and a reframed mission. The zoo now resides on 62 acres in southwestern Jerusalem, just north of the 1949 partition boundary.

Still known by many as the "biblical zoo," the new Tisch Family Zoological Gardens presents itself more in conservationist than scriptural terms. As a curator phrased it during an interview with legal scholar Irus Braverman (2013), "you can call them biblical animals, but in fact they are local animals" (128). A prime example is the Persian Fallow Deer. The zoo makes the biblical link, citing it in Deuteronomy and 1 Kings, but instead of focusing on any kind of scriptural recreation they highlight the animal's gradual decline from the Levant and presumed extinction by the 1950s. A small remaining population was discovered in Iran and a male-female pair was smuggled to Israel in 1979 just before the Iranian Revolution. This project aligned with Shulov's zoological Zionism and the Jerusalem zoo became a center for the deer's repopulation. This effort continues into the present, as zoo scientists wrestle with reintroducing the deer into local habitats amid human-caused environmental changes.[15]

With respect to visitors, the zoo's shift from biblical theming to indigenous nature conservation has been successful. It consistently ranks among the city's most popular sites, attracting nearly a million visitors annually (Braverman 2013). The zoo is not an established stop for Christian Holy Land tours; its traffic comes primarily from local tourism and Jerusalemites seeking leisure.[16] The zoo markets itself as one of the rare spots in Jerusalem where the city's cultural diversity is not thoroughly segregated—a place where, for example, ultraorthodox Jewish families are copresent with East Jerusalem Palestinians. This was partially borne out in Braverman's analysis of the zoo; she concluded that while this diversity does exist side-by-side, it does not translate to meaningful social exchange (2013: 134).

Coda

This chapter draws together some of the ways in which biblical fauna have been used as a theme for materializing the Bible. Examples range widely and find expression with multiple theological and ideological agendas. We began with Protestant creationists who present "zebroids" as living proof for their biblical literalism, then moved to educational and devotional treatments of "birds of the Bible," and concluded with the mutable identity of a biblical zoo in Jerusalem.

The organizing insight is that animals are mobilized as a zoological encounter with biblical nature. Using biblical fauna in this way transforms animals into a living media for scriptural teaching, devotion, and history-making. In some cases, this is about designing sensory experiences around the theme of "animals of the Bible," such as the creationist Eden Animal Experience and the Jerusalem Zoo's early experiments in staging biblical scenes. In other cases, this is performed by choreographing a Bible-centric encounter with nature, as Christian birdwatchers do. And, in other cases, this is performed more indirectly, using the biblical link to assert other claims, such as the zoo's Zionist-inflected conservation. Ultimately, much like flora and other landscape items, mobilizing biblical fauna helps us think closely about the ways in which diverse media are used to generate sensorial access to a scriptural past.

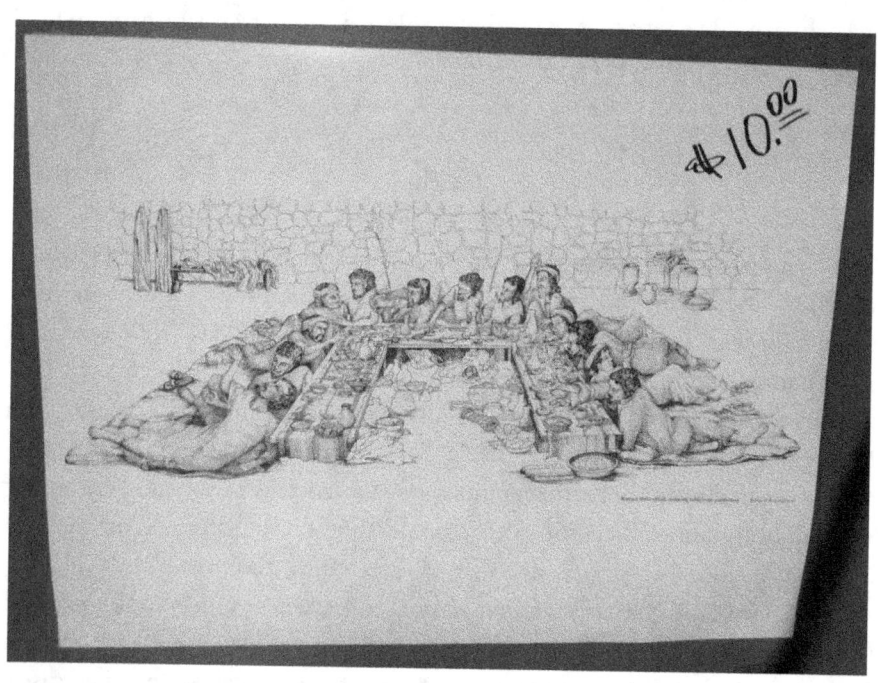

Figure 9 Print for sale at Biblical History Center gift shop (La Grange, Georgia). Photo credit: James S. Bielo.

9

Ingesting the Word

Olives, dates, almonds, figs, grapes, garlic-infused olive oil, fresh baked bread, hard-boiled eggs, bitter herbs, lentil soup. When visitors sit for their "biblical meal" at the Biblical History Center (BHC) in La Grange, Georgia, these are a few foods they consume. The meal is part of BHC's broader ambition to "help people encounter the ancient biblical world through its history and culture."[1] Along with their meal, visitors explore an object-centered museum with 250 archaeological items on loan from the Israel Antiquities Authority and an "archaeological garden," the site's largest exhibition. The garden stages household and agricultural replications of first-century life in Palestine, including a goat hair tent, grape stomping vat, sheepfold tombs, threshing materials, olive press, watchtower, underground grain silo, and vineyard. Whether they eat before or after touring, the meal is contextualized within the site's material performance of biblically themed cultivated nature.

BHC opened in 2006, located in southwestern Georgia, near the Alabama border and an hour's drive from Atlanta. Funded by the Callaway family, immensely wealthy philanthropists with a long history of building development in the state (Minchew 2014), BHC was designed by Jim Fleming—an amateur archaeologist, biblical teacher, and entrepreneur. Fleming earned a doctorate in education at a conservative Southern Baptist seminary in Dallas, though his claim to authority owes as much to the fact that he lived in Jerusalem for three decades. Starting in the 1990s, he opened several predecessors to BHC, all of which closed and he settled in Georgia because of the Callaway's financial commitment (Ron and Timothy 2013).

BHC sits on the small city's western edge, nestled amid an industrial corridor, and receives around 12,000 visitors annually. Many of those visitors pay extra for the ninety-minute biblical meal. There are two meal rooms onsite, both designed as replicas of first-century Italian archaeological sites that were preserved in volcanic ash. This geographic reference might seem to disrupt the desired Holy Land immersion, but the claim to authenticity is resumed by the idea of a uniquely preserved first-century context that was, like Jerusalem, within the Roman Empire. The meal mixes modern accommodations, such as upright seating around a triclinium-like arrangement, with more historically immersive practices, such as eating without utensils from communal platters. The rooms also include a life-size triclinium replica that displays for visitors how first-century diners would have been positioned: leaning on their left elbow while eating with the right hand. Why not extend the immersion and ask visitors to comport their bodies in first-century style? At least in this moment, valuing touristic comfort outstrips biblical role play.

Visitors eat while listening to a tour guide presentation, focused on first-century food and dining practices. Some of this teaching references activities in the archaeological garden, but the core framing is pitched as cultural critique. Highlighting Da Vinci's famous Last Supper painting from the late fifteenth century, guides explain that this imagery is full of historical errors. The shape of the table, how people are seated, where figures are sitting: all are factually incorrect. Drawing on the cultural authority of archaeological science, BHC reimagines the scene for visitors. While historically accurate, this strategy for engaging visitors resonates in a distinctly fundamentalist register: the claim that dominant culture has concealed a truth, producing a malformed biblical understanding, which BHC will reveal and correct. Much like creationists and Christian nationalists who ritually recite such conspiratorial claims, BHC's biblical meal is presented as a reclamation of fact from secular misinformation (Kerby 2020). Interested visitors can preserve this reimagined biblical scene with a gift shop souvenir: a matted print of a pencil drawing depicting how Jesus and his disciples might "actually" have been arranged at the Last Supper.

* * *

The biblical meal promises visitors that they will develop a more intimate, more robust biblical knowledge through a culinary experience. If Holy Land pilgrimage is about walking where Jesus walked, the biblical meal is about eating what Jesus ate. This promise is partly grounded in the scientifically framed explanation of historical foodways and first-century cultural patterns, but it is more centrally a matter of bodily sensation. The immersive potential of the biblical meal rests on the sensory indexicality of taste, touch, and smell.[2] BHC and other biblical tourism sites have been serving visitors for a few decades, but their performances resonate with a much longer history of ingesting sacred scripture. Holy Land pilgrims from the fifth century onward consumed and transported "edible or ingestible substances such as bread, dew, dust, earth, hair, manna, poil, water, and frequently fruit" (Flood 2014: 463). In the seventeen and eighteenth centuries, German-speaking Catholics mass-produced *Schluckbildchen*, printed sheets with small biblical figures that were dissolved in water or baked into foodstuffs (484). And, biblical cookbooks have circulated among Christian readers since at least 1958. The biblical meal at contemporary tourism sites like BHC join this tradition, all geared toward reproducing the authority and intimacy of scripture via gustatory pleasure.

The Joy of Biblical Cooking

Between 1958 and 2019, at least thirty-three books have been mass-produced that collect recipes of "biblical foods" for readers.[3] While there is an organizing conceit—namely, that modern people can share a gustatory experience with "the people of the Bible"—this genre is not totally uniform. Here, five biblical cookbooks are analyzed, and each performs this organizing conceit in a way that reflects cultural and theological priorities. None have become especially influential, nothing akin to the way Jewish people in the United States valorized *The Settlement Cook Book* as a distinctly Jewish culinary guide (Rubel 2015). What does unite them is a relocation of religious authority from the usually ratified set of actors—preachers and priests, congregational and movement leaders—to otherwise unknown Christians (cf. Gross 2019).

The earliest biblical cookbook dates to 1958, published by a Missouri-based Christian publisher. Authored by Marian Maeve O'Brien, *The Bible Cookbook* integrates foods named in biblical texts with non-biblical ingredients to present over 500 recipes. The book's primary interpretive frame draws on sensory indexicality to claim a direct intimacy between a scriptural past and a modern present. For example, when introducing a series of bread recipes, O'Brien writes: "Bread is the one food which you may reproduce today exactly as it was in biblical times. How long has it been since you sniffed the good earthy scent of yeast dissolving in warm milk?" (209).

What really distinguishes this text within the genre of biblical cookbooks is the way it genders its audience through a normative 1950s femininity. Throughout, O'Brien addresses "housewives" as the presumed reader and scriptural connections are drawn with "biblical housewives." Much of the book reads less like a culinary devotional and more like a pious *Good Housekeeping*, mixing biblical trivia and verse quotations with suggested meal time prayers and recommendations for hosting and table settings. This extends to its scriptural appeals, as when she analogizes dried milk powder to leben: "It gives me a warm feeling of being not so different, after all, from Mary and Martha and all the other wise women of the biblical stories. I hope that you, too, will experience this feeling of kinship as you go through these pages" (104).

In contrast, *Cookbook of Foods from Bible Days* shifts the register away from how women can integrate biblical foods into happy homemaking and toward dietary health. Published in 1971 by a Pennsylvania-based Christian publisher, this text is less ambitious and more food focused: there are no table setting recommendations and about 100 recipes. The authors, Jean and Frank McKibben, were a married couple, and much of the book emerged from a weekly column Frank wrote for a southern California newspaper: "food from Bible days." Like O'Brien, the McKibben's regularly use a sensory indexical frame to appeal to readers. For example, when introducing a section on using nuts in recipes, they write: "to walk through a California almond orchard in February or March is to understand the delight of the people of Bible times" (55). The book's distinction, though, is its emphasis on the health benefits of a biblical diet. There are general claims—"many of the ancient foods were highly nutritious" (5)—but more striking is that nearly every discussion of biblical foods works in the register of nutritional science. For example, when recommending brain meat as a lost culinary delicacy they note: "Brains, for instance, have over twice as much phosphorus as T-bone steak, four times as much vitamin B1. In fact, brains are an excellent source of several members of the vitamin B complex like B1, B2 (riboflavin) and cholin" (24).

The third text, *Cooking for the Lord: A Nutritional Guide Based on the Scriptures*, elaborates the nutritional frame and integrates it with a fundamentalist critique of the industrialized food system. Self-published in 1981 by Mary June and Burgess Parks, the book reflects the authors' charismatic Christianity identity. The famed televangelist Robert Schuller wrote a foreword for the book, and Mary June promoted their approach to eating on Schuller's "Hour of Power" broadcast. The book was inspired by Burgess's cancer diagnosis, and they attribute his healing to a combination of modern medicine, "born again" faith, and the adoption of a biblical food diet.

The book has comparably fewer recipes (roughly fifty), which are preceded by an extensive narrative that contrasts biblical and modern foods. Unlike some contemporaries that used foodways to reflect on the structural conditions of global inequality, such as the Mennonite *More-With-Less* cookbook (Rose 2019), the Parks presented their critique in more immediately present spiritual and moral terms. Consider a prime example: "Expounding the poisons masquerading on the shelves of the supermarket could make a book in itself.... In the beginning we defined natural foods as those that God made and are untampered by man. When food and deadly chemicals are merged, the results are devastating" (39). The Burgess' would almost certainly reject books like O'Brien's and the McKibbens' because they break from recipes that exclusively adhere to "natural foods" derived from the pages of scripture.

Other texts in the genre maintain a strict emphasis on biblical ingredients, but shift away from the Parks' ideological critique. For example, *Biblical Garden Cookery* (1976) and *A Biblical Feast* (1998) were both written by established gourmands: the former by Eileen Gaden, an editor of *Gourmet Magazine*, and the latter by Kitty Morse, a widely celebrated cookbook author. Gaden's book compiles several hundred recipes and is, compared to the others, most detailed in discussing how ancient flora and fauna indigenous to Palestine compare with modern varieties. Morse's book features about fifty recipes, but is the only text to provide a glossary of eighty-five "foodstuffs" (97) named in biblical stories. Emphasizing authenticity, simplicity, and nutritional health, Morse states a purpose in the introduction that neatly matches Gaden: "My purpose was not to invent a biblical *haute cuisine*, but rather to recreate dishes that the ancient Hebrews and early Christians might have prepared, always keeping in mind that they were, for the most part, common people who ate simple, uncomplicated, yet wholesome food" (15).

The five biblical cookbooks discussed here highlight some of the diversity within this genre of Christian literature. While not exactly isomorphic, there is much that makes them easily identifiable within a shared genre. As noted earlier, they make regular appeals that food provides a shared experience with biblical people. From O'Brien's olfactory pleasure of yeast dissolving in milk to the McKibben's orchard stroll, the idea of a universal and timeless sensing body is the media that enables shared experience. This sensory connection to the biblical past is also used to promise a newly illuminated intimacy with Bible stories. Gaden is most prolific in this regard, as she uses food experiences to reflect on biblical quotations. When referencing the escape from Egypt, she quotes Num. 11:5 and muses: "The cool, moist, green cucumber must have been especially hard for the thirsty Hebrews to forget" (45). Each in their own way, these texts are also thoroughly romantic about "life in biblical times." The "simplicity" of ingredients and cooking methods is often celebrated, often pitched against modern lifestyles and foodways. Some are more wistful about learning from a lost authenticity, while the Parks are more strident that biblical food is our only salvation from a deadly system. By celebrating biblical people through food, this is ultimately a devotional genre. The authors promise not only better health but intensified spiritual intimacy. The copy of *A Biblical Feast* that I purchased on eBay was previously owned and the first page bears an inscription. Exchanged as a gift, the giver of this cookbook highlighted its non-culinary potential: "May this be a joyful and nourishing journey that brings you ever closer to the heart and love of our King. Merry Christmas!"

Digestif

Much like biblical gardens, biblical meals are a materializing the Bible phenomenon with diverse resonances. We focused here on at-home cookbooks as an immediate predecessor to the biblical meal as a tourist-pilgrim attraction. But, there are certainly other nodes that circulate the idea of biblical foods as a compelling experience. We've noted throughout how other discourses are woven into biblical cooking and eating, such as Protestant fundamentalist critiques of mainstream culture and natural food critiques of industrialized food. And, we began by noting that there is a long tradition of ingesting materialized scripture, from *Schluckbildchen* to Holy Land collectibles and, of course, the Eucharist as a paramount ritual in Christian tradition.

To close, consider a few further resonances in the historical accumulation that informs biblical meal performances like that of Georgia's BHC. As Ron and Timothy (2013) observe, biblical meals cannot be disentangled from a broader increase in food tourism and are well poised to benefit from this increase. Just as discourses of terroir work indexically to link place, history, and sensory experience for commodities such as wine and cheese, so do appeals to the direct connection of edible flora and fauna to Holy Land nature.

In all of the cookbooks discussed earlier, and the McKibbens especially, the value of biblical food is framed in the register of nutritional science. This attachment to scientific authority also appears elsewhere. For example, in February 2020 several news media outlets (e.g., *National Public Radio*, *Science*, *Medium*) profiled the collaboration of an Israeli medical doctor and an Israeli botanist. The story detailed their work to cultivate date palms grown from seeds excavated at first-century archaeological sites. Ultimately, *National Public Radio* invokes the same logic of sensory indexicality, noting for readers that fruit born of these trees would be "dates just like the one that people in the Bible ate."[4]

If biblical cookbooks bring scriptural foods to home cooks in domestic contexts, we also see biblical gastronomy reframed as haute cuisine. One example comes from a biblical tourism site, Washington, DC's Museum of the Bible. The primary onsite dining option for visitors is Manna, a restaurant under the direction of Todd Gray, a renowned chef in the city. Styled more as "Israeli/Mediterranean-inspired" cuisine than the kind of biblical meal one receives at the BHC, Manna does make constant appeal to the use of "ancient" ingredients, methods, and gustatory experiences. For example, in an interview with a Texas-based Holy Land food tourism company, Gray cites one of his menu influences as a "3,000-year-old braised lamb recipe" he learned while visiting Israel.[5] And, in an August 2018 *Washington Post* profile of the restaurant, Gray discusses his search to replicate the taste and textural sensations of "manna," a resin imported from Iran and claimed to be the edible named in Exodus 16.[6]

From tourist meals to cookbooks, this chapter observes how a particular media—food—is mobilized as a device for biblical immersion. By promising that we can eat what Jesus ate, this gustatory tradition draws on the sensory indexicality of food to conjure scriptural intimacy and recreate scriptural authority. For Christian eaters visiting Gray's Manna or the BHC, eating the foods that biblical people ate is about breaking down experiential boundaries. From basic fruits and nuts to date palms grown from millennia-old seeds and replicated manna, the biblical meal is about collapsing the distance between a modern now and a scriptural then, between the quotidian and the eternal.

Figure 10 Holy Land stone on display at the Garden of Hope (Covington, Kentucky). Photo credit: James S. Bielo.

10

How Stones Do Things

The Garden of Hope is a 2.5-acre site in Covington, Kentucky—set atop a hill overlooking the city of Cincinnati to the north. The Garden was envisioned by a Southern Baptist pastor, Morris Coers. After two terms in the Indiana state legislature and clergy positions in Indiana, Illinois, and Michigan, Coers accepted the Covington pastorate. When the Garden opened on Palm Sunday 1958, it realized a twenty-year vision. It was in 1938 when Coers made a pilgrimage to British Palestine and was inspired to create a place back home for anyone who could never make the trip themselves. During the Garden's construction, the site was first profiled by *The Cincinnati Post*, and Coers described his ambition in a distinctly sensory register. He wanted to recreate "a bit of the fragrance of that holy place."[1]

Coers began at Covington's Immanuel Baptist Church in 1945 and quickly developed a visible public persona. He first appeared in Cincinnati newspapers in June 1949, profiled as a "dynamic" preacher known throughout the city for his daily radio ministry. In 1950, Coers added a television ministry, "Chapel of Dreams," to his media repertoire. The program aired every morning from 9:45 to 10am, Monday through Friday, and mixed reports of local citizens, gospel hymns, and a short sermon. A 1951 *Billboard* review lauded the program, including this summary:

> In a sermonette with organ background music, Reverend Coers uses an inspirational approach, with some down-to-earth, visual object and its practical application to life as the basis of his message. On this program, *the object was a bottle containing water from the Sea of Galilee*, obtained by Mr. Coers on a visit there some years ago. Reverend Coers told the story of Christ walking on Galilee's stormy waves, and explained that its shallowness is the reason for frequent storms. Shallowness of human character, he pointed out, often is the cause of human suffering, and told his audience that much anguish could be alleviated if people lived in accordance with spiritual teachings (emphasis added).[2]

Coers's affinity for biblical landscape items carried into the Garden of Hope. The centerpiece of the site is a 1:1 scale replica of Jerusalem's Garden Tomb, and the claim of architectural precision was grounded in a relationship Coers built with the tomb's warden in Jerusalem. A Palestinian Christian named Solomon Mattar cared for the tomb and guided pilgrims from 1953 until his untimely death in 1967. Like so many families, the Mattars were displaced from their land during the 1948 Arab-Israeli war. After resettling in Jerusalem, Solomon's only son Samuel decided to pursue a college degree in the United States. Samuel lost his immigration sponsor after withdrawing from an initial college, prompting Solomon to ask the Kentucky pastor who he had been corresponding with if he would sponsor his son. Coers agreed, and Samuel relocated to Kentucky to attend a nearby Catholic college. As a thank you, Solomon agreed to send Coers a series of landscape materials for the Garden.[3]

Solomon's shipment included 5,000 seeds and seedlings of flowers, trees, and shrubs, all botanical species indigenous to Palestine. By featuring the sight, feel, and aroma of biblical flora, Coers mobilized the idea of biblical nature to help transport visitors from Kentucky to Jerusalem. Coers passed away in 1960, and without his devotional labor these varietals did not last. Today, the botanical dimension of the experience is lost from Coers's original vision. Flora, however, was not all that Mattar sent.

Scattered throughout the Garden are four stones, still residing where Coers placed them. Two are set in decorative wrought-iron cages near a grassy welcome area. Signage explains the first stone as "from Good Samaritan Inn, over 2,000 years old from Jerusalem" and the second as "from Jordan River where Jesus was baptized over 2,000 years ago." The third stone is positioned differently; embedded into the floor inside the Garden's chapel. The chapel was created primarily for weddings, a practice Coers initiated in 1958 and that continues today. During the ceremony couples stand atop a pink stone, which signage explains "is from the Horns of Hatton where Jesus delivered the Sermon on the Mount." The final stone, also set in an ornate iron cage, is located just beyond the chapel, at the end of a small downhill path. Signage presents it as, "from Solomon's Temple, 500-pound block from Wailing Wall."

By teaching with water from the Sea of Galilee and recontextualizing Holy Land stones into a devotional park, Morris Coers conjoined durable traditions of Christian materiality. In one sense, biblical landscape items have long been valued for their "metonymic" quality, ideologically linked to the biblical past as indexical fragments of nature (Kaell 2012: 139). In another sense, these items resonate with the object lesson, which proliferated in Christian pedagogical contexts beginning in the mid-nineteenth century (Morgan 1999: 245; cf. Boylan 1988; Hasinoff 2011; Blanton 2019). This chapter explores these traditions of Christian materiality and, ultimately, argues that to properly understand them we must attend to the agency of nonhuman objects.

Portable Landscape

At least since the fourth century, travelers to the "lands of the Bible" have extracted and transported pieces of those lands: water from the Sea of Galilee, Jordan River, and Dead Sea; stones, soil, and flora from innumerable locations narrated as the spots where biblical history unfolded (Bartal, Bodner, and Kuhnel, eds. 2017).[4] Biblical landscape fragments function as *loca sancta* relics: a material connection to the Holy Land that is informed by an ideology of enduring nature, fostering a bond to history via physical presence and tactile intimacy (Bartal, Bodner, and Kuhnel 2017: xxiv). As Harries (2017) observes in a different context, "the act of touching extends beyond the thing in the hand to a sensation of something or someone else" (116). At the Garden of Hope, for example, touching the stones onsite is a media for channeling scriptural people and events. These fragments transform the expansive and ungraspable "land of the Bible" into an easily conceivable thing to hold, give, trade, keep, pray with, read with, use for proclaiming sacred truths, and be in the presence of. They are material conduits for engaging the sacred. Like any object, their capacity to function in this way is contingent on the social relations and contexts of their use. As we trace later, how biblical landscape items are mobilized is subject to change, ranging from architectural and burial materials to gifts, mementos, devotional relics, immersive media, and object lessons.

Ways of Circulating

As long as there have been Holy Land travelers, biblical landscape items have circulated beyond the land itself. This began in the fourth century when Empress Helena traveled to Jerusalem and proclaimed particular sites as authentic biblical locations: "Jerusalem first circulated in the West in the form of its physical fragments—pieces of stone, drops of oil, bits of bone, particles of wood" (Wharton 2006: 45). The nature of this appetite morphed over time, but it did not wane. Mark Twain famously mocked this appetite in *The Innocents Abroad* (1869):

> We find a piece of the true cross in every old church we go into, and some of the nails that held it together. I would not like to be positive, but I think we have seen as much as a keg of these nails. Then there is the crown of thorns; they have part of one in Sainte Chapelle, in Paris, and part of one also in Notre Dame. (165)

One enduring use for biblical landscape items has been to integrate them into building projects. Beginning with Rome's Church of Santa Croce in the fourth century, the practice of consecrating new sites with fragments of Holy Land nature lasted for more than a millennium (Bartal, Bodner, and Kuhnel 2017; Donkin 2017; Gertsman and Mittman 2017; Bartal 2018). For example, the Italian Camposanto of Pisa is a monumental cemetery begun in 1278. The cemetery is said to be built atop soil brought back from Jerusalem in 1188 by an archbishop. The earliest surviving written versions of this legend date to the fourteenth century, and reports disagree whether the earthen source was Golgotha or Akeldama (Bodner 2015). In either case, the soil was said to possess miraculous properties, such as the ability to decompose bodies in three days and eliminate all foul odor. A similar story exists for the Sedlec Monastery, located east of Prague. A Cistercian abbot returned from the Holy Land in 1278 with a small jar of Golgotha soil, which he spread atop the cemetery grounds. This generated widespread attention, and tens of thousands of Catholic bodies from all over Europe were brought to the site for burial.

This practice continued over time, but purposes shifted. Enchantment remained, but a new interest cohered: heightening an immersive sense of virtual pilgrimage through atmospheric, affective, and sensory engagements with biblical landscape items. At Chautauqua's Palestine Park, a daughter of the Institute's president returned from Palestine in the 1920s with a vial of Dead Sea water, which she placed in the park's replica equivalent (Long 2003: 37). Morris Coers arranged for plants and stones to be sent from Palestine to Kentucky as a way to forge a material and aesthetic bond between his replica and the biblical past. At Holy Land, USA in southwestern Virginia, United States, a 250-acre biblically themed park that closed in 2009, a map on the Welcome Center wall was "constituted of materials from the regions it depicts—sand from the Negev, soil from Jerusalem, earth from the Dead Sea basin" (Wharton 2006: 233). Recall the Temple of Solomon in Sao Paulo, Brazil, from Chapter 5. When it opened in 2014, it boasted landscape items flown in from Christian Holy Lands: eight million dollars' worth of Jerusalem stone as part of the exterior construction; four date-palm trees; and, a dried bush from Mt. Sinai. When the Museum of the Bible opened in Washington, DC, in 2017, the structural pillars throughout the lobby area were covered with Jerusalem stone and other landscape items were interspersed throughout the building. When first entering a permanent exhibit curated by the Israel Antiquities Authority on the fifth floor, you encounter a massive stone with an invitation to "please touch" and a description that places the tactile experience in a biblical temporality: "This stone was part of the enclosure walls of the Temple Mount built by Herod. . . . The heavy damage on the stone's surface is clear evidence of the dramatic destruction of the temple in Jerusalem in 70 CE."

Biblical landscape fragments have also circulated as a way to manage social relations. In the nineteenth century, a popular expression of this was the inclusion of dried flowers with correspondence cards. In March 2017, I stumbled on an extraordinary example at the Amherst College Library Archives and Special Collections. While inquiring about a different item, one of the archivists smartly remembered a piece from their Emily Dickinson collection. Written neatly in pencil across the top edge of a folder was the following:

"A Flower Message from the Holy Land," n.d.
(thought to be sent to ED by Abby Wood Bliss, wife
of Daniel Bliss (AC 1852), from Jerusalem)

Inside the folder was a stack of identical pocket-sized paper cards. The script on the front was attractive, but not overly elegant: "A Flower Message from the Holy Land. Collection of Natural Flowers which grow in the Holy Land." On the inside left, a beautifully preserved dried flower was accompanied by a more decorative script: "Flowers from the Holy Land." On the inside right were music notes and lyrics for "Song of Galilee, which is sung by tourists on the Lake of Tiberias." The back cover included the remaining lyrics and a Christmas greeting.

It took a moment to fully register. I was holding a pre-Hallmark Season's Greetings card once held by Emily Dickinson. Abby Bliss was a lifelong friend of the renowned poet; they were born the same year and progressed through school together. Their friendship strained when Wood experienced a born-again conversion and Dickinson, famously, resisted the fervent Calvinist revival that was dominating New England. In 1855, Wood married Daniel Bliss and the following year they left for missionary work in Lebanon. Daniel and Abby Bliss lived in the Middle East for the remainder of their lives, helping to found the American University of Beirut. Despite the geographic and spiritual distance between them, Abby and Emily remained friends. At some point between 1856 and Emily's death in 1886, Abby sent her friend these Flower Messages from the Holy Land.

The cards likely served several functions in their relationship. Abby used them to keep communication open with her lifelong friend. The cards fed their shared love of botany, conjuring youthful excursions in the woods to collect plant specimens. She may also have intended for them to bring a glimpse of a faraway place to the increasingly reclusive Dickinson. As much or more, Abby's flower message from the Holy Land served as an evangelistic outreach to a friend whose soul she feared for. In an 1850 letter, soon after her conversion, Abby expressed concern to a mutual friend following a visit with Emily: "She ridicules and opposes us, and shuts her own heart against the truth. . . . Let us pray for her that she may not 'grieve the Holy Spirit' to depart from her" (quoted in Longsworth 2009: 343). Abby used the flower as a testimony of and from the land of the Bible, material evidence that the scriptural landscape was a real landscape, a botanical witness to the life of Jesus.

The hundreds of thousands of US tourist-pilgrims who travel to the Holy Land continue this practice, bringing home landscape souvenirs as gifts and mementos. Tourist-pilgrims collect found objects (e.g., bags of sand from Sea of Galilee shores) and make purchases among ubiquitous commodified forms (e.g., olive wood carvings). In her ethnography of US Holy Land pilgrims, Kaell (2012) discovered that travelers invest significant time and emotional energy in matching people at home with particular Holy Land gifts (143). In similar stories, an evangelical grandmother brought "rocks, water, and sand" in the hopes of sparking her grandchildren's interest in biblical history (144) and a Catholic grandmother gave a stone necklace from the Sea of Galilee to her granddaughter (146). For the latter, the child's delighted reception of the gift was cherished as a highlight of the woman's entire pilgrimage experience.

Object Lessons

In the nineteenth century, another use for biblical landscape items developed in dialogue with a significant movement in the Sunday School institution. The use was theological education and the movement was the refinement of object lesson teaching. The practice of the object lesson is relatively straightforward: use a material culture item, ideally something relatively simple and/or familiar to the learner, as a way to understand abstract ideas and values. Object lesson pedagogy was widely practiced in US public schools by the 1860s and soon after was made an integral part of Sunday School curricula (Carter 2018; Morgan 1999: 242).

Pitched as a critique of rote memorization and verbal-centric explanation, the object lesson entailed several promises for teachers and students. This concrete, tactile mode of engagement would make a more lasting impression because it focused not only on the knowledge to be gained but on the process of understanding. It would also work to train the senses of pupils, instilling a desire for them to more closely and more intimately engage with the material worlds they inhabit (Carter 2018). Blanton (2019) observes how prominent Sunday School leaders celebrated the object lesson "as a pious technique of the body that attuned the sense faculties and 'vivified' the moral and spiritual character through a process of manual training" (408). His prime example, Patterson Du Bois, published an influential treatise in 1896 on the Christian applications of the object lesson. Du Bois analogized this pedagogy with Jesus's teachings (12), imploring Sunday School instructors to always work within students' "plane of experience" (21)—that is, the sensory and material worlds they were familiar with.

By the early 1900s, the value of object lessons was taken for granted in Sunday Schools, fully integrated into Christian and secular mainstreams. Several early adopters who helped establish the pedagogy in Christian contexts made substantial use of biblical landscape items. For example, John Heyl Vincent, the influential Methodist Sunday School leader, developed a "Palestine class" in the 1950s (Vincent 1861). With a primary emphasis on the "sacred geography" of biblical lands, Vincent used *loca sancta* relics to help students imagine and build an experiential intimacy with scriptural stories (Kimball 1913).

In tandem with increasing pilgrimage to the Holy Land, Vincent's Palestine Class helped kindle an interest among Sunday Schools for the stones, soil, water, and flora that indexed the land of the Bible. Religious entrepreneurs like Robert Morris capitalized on this desire. A Freemason, Morris popularized the "Holy Land cabinet" in the 1870s as a teaching tool and a conduit for virtual pilgrimage. As a fundraising strategy to enable his own Holy Land trip, Morris sold "ten-dollar subscriptions for 'Holy Land Cabinets,' each to be equipped with 150 sacred objects" (Davis 1996: 50). He returned in 1868 and immediately set about fulfilling subscriptions, eventually circulating several hundred thousand samples. Morris reframed landscape materials from devotional relics with transformative properties into scriptural object lessons that could enliven the imagination of Bible readers, connecting sensory intimacy with biblical learning. Regarding a soil specimen from the Garden of Gethsemane, he wrote: "an honest portion of Gethsemane; a portion upon which the Divine *feet* may have trodden, the Divine knees pressed, the Divine *tears* and *sweat* moistened" (quoted in Davis 1996: 51; emphasis in original).

Inspired by the success of his cabinets, Morris aspired to open a museum in LaGrange, Kentucky, near Louisville. His plans were disrupted, though, when his massive stock of Holy Land materials stored in Chicago burned in the city's 1871 fire (Mitchell 1887). Morris's innovation prompted others to create similar products. For example, Paul Iskiyan of the Protestant School for Christian Workers in Massachusetts developed a "Biblical Museum" to teach scriptural history. An 1890 example (available on eBay for US$999.99 as of December 2020) features samples of anise, boxwood, brayed wheat, camphire, cassia, cumin, fitches, ground corn, husk, hyssop, incense, lentils, lentils split, manna, mint, mustard seed, myrrh, olive leaves, olive wood, oriental nuts, pulse, reed pen, rue, sackcloth, saffron, tares, the powder, and "the most interesting coins of the bible." The description of the powder, for instance, explains that "the practice of painting the eyelids to make the eyes look large, lustrous and languishing is often alluded to in the Old Testament," then directs readers to the story of Jezebel in 2 Kings.

When Morris Coers presented viewers with a bottle of Sea of Galilee water, he joined this tradition of using biblical landscape items as theological object lessons. There is a seeming tension, though, between this tradition and the prescriptive training circulated by Du Bois. In his 1896 treatise, Du Bois insists that for an object to be efficacious it must resonate with the student's plane of experience. At one point, perhaps as a coded critique of Vincent, he argues that "the bass drum and the brass horn" are what have value when doing urban ministry, not "a map of Palestine" (64). For most people at this time, biblical landscape items were not everyday objects that could resonate with the immediate sensory and material worlds of students. For Vincent, for scores of people who purchased Morris's cabinets, and later for Coers, this was no trouble in practice. I suspect this is because of the ideology of sensory indexicality, which presumes that nature has a universal quality and that the tactile encounter with soil, stone, water, and flora is unchanged from the scriptural past to the present. Remembering Harries (2017), if "the thing in the hand" extends to the sensation of others and elsewhere, then there is a place for biblical landscape items in everyone's plane of experience.

The Agency of Things

Biblical landscape fragments are geologic stone, earthen soil, salt and freshwater, and botanical flora. As they circulate through various hands and contexts, they become healing and protective relics, sacred architectural material, enchanted burial matter, gifts, commodities, personal keepsakes, immersive media, and pedagogical object lessons. Through this social life, these fragments make things happen for their users: namely, they intensify bonds with biblical texts, with the Holy Land as a real and imagined place, with sensory ideologies that authorize nature, and with non-scriptural places that are asserted as sacred.

One way to understand this proliferation of uses and affects is as a case of human and religious creativity, the expressive imagination of people working to experience the holy, transcendent, and miraculous. To close, I recommend a complementary perspective, one that recognizes the agency of materiality. As an analytical framework, "new materialism" understands objects and places as capable of making things happen in the world (Hazard 2013; cf. Bialecki 2014; Mitchell 2020).[5] Here, materiality is not merely props or stages for human creativity, "not passive and pliable instruments of human intention" (Hazard 2013: 65). Rather, objects and places act. They do so because they exist as part of broader assemblages, networks of diverse human and nonhuman entities.

Assemblages function as generative hives of actors (animate and inanimate), creating and recreating the worlds we inhabit, from durable conditions to contingent affects. In this approach, the global circulation and diverse mobilizations of biblical landscape items are not detached from human creativity, but they position that creativity alongside the agentive capacity of the items themselves. In turn, the agency of landscape items traces to their position in assemblages that are historically, socially, and materially dense and dynamic (cf. Morgan 2014).

To say that materiality is agentive in this way calls attention to the ways in which materiality operates in tandem with various human and nonhuman actors. What, then, is the assemblage giving life to biblical landscape items? Any analysis is partial, but a few of the actors include the broader geographies they are extracted from; the scriptural texts that provide a narrative frame for their identity; other media they interact with (e.g., places, such as the Garden of Hope; mass media performances, such as fifteen-minute televised ministries); ecclesiological structures that authorize their efficacy; institutional structures that foster their circulation and use; other Holy Land engagements, such as imperialistic and scientific mapping; and, of course, the various human actors who surround them with ambitions and performative scenes. When we encounter a stone "from Jordan River where Jesus was baptized over 2,000 years ago" on a Kentucky hillside, we are encountering an object that is enlivened by this kind of assemblage. We are encountering an object that acts on us, as much as we might act on it.

Section III

Choreographing Experience

Circulation

Section III examines the theme of "choreographing experience"—that is, the ways in which physical engagements with materializing the Bible are oriented and engineered. Choreographing elements are incredibly diverse, from landscapes to ritual traditions, objects, planned routes, sound, lighting, and narrative storytelling. We will encounter human and nonhuman actors activating select experiential possibilities and eliding or erasing others. Choreography should not be mistaken as an overdetermined process. Visitors to biblical tourism sites certainly respond in different ways, at times in ways not anticipated by the site's design or overtly contrary to the site's intentions.

Scholarship in ritual studies and material religion are especially attuned to processes of choreography and the ways in which materialities are configured to foster subject formation. In their seminal analysis of Catholic pilgrimage, Victor and Edith Turner observe how shrine environments engineer ritual sequences and interactions with local landscapes in order to help pilgrims get caught up in the experience (1978: 138). Choreography continues to be an organizing theme for recent scholarship. For example, Katja Rakow (2020a) explores the exacting coordination of light and sound in structuring the primary worship ritual of a premier US megachurch. As works like these illustrate, choreography is not about predicting or delimiting visitor responses; it is about understanding the lived interactions with material affordances.

The first set of chapters in this section approaches choreography by way of "circulation"—that is, the movement of materiality, discourse, ideology, and ritual form through space-time and across contexts of performance (Morgan 2017; Handman 2018). By understanding circulation, we better understand how social worlds are "infused with the communicative norms and material forms" of religious traditions (Handman 2018: 158; cf. Engelke 2013). Processes of circulation constitute pivotal dynamics in the public life of religion, drawing attention to the trails of movement, the actors involved in making media move, the transformation of circulating media through its recontextualization, and the cultural conditions that structure movement.

Materializing the Bible performances are forged through varieties of circulation: the religious tourists who travel, the many promotional resources produced by biblical tourism sites, purchased and collected souvenirs, and stories of experience. All of these circulating elements attached to places are embedded within authorizing assemblages, in which the promised power of a site is cultivated and performed through a network of technologies, actors, and relations (Morgan 2014). In turn, forms of materializing the Bible are part of infrastructures that circulate enchantment, promising visitors something special, be it access to divine presence, miraculous healing, enriched sociality, or ideological claims to physical space, tradition, or legitimacy.

Each of the three chapters in this set considers a particular media of circulation: (11) guiding brochures, (12) picture postcards, and (13) Instagram posts. Each of these technologies plays a role in the process of choreography, helping to orient expectations, experiences, and memories. They do so in tandem with their respective genres, material affordances, and uses. Ultimately, they expand our understanding of how biblical tourism sites are composed, how they seek to exist in public life, and what kinds of practices and experiences are authorized.

Figure 11 Brochure for Saint-Anne-de-Beaupré shrine (Quebec, Canada) (author's collection).

11

Miracles and Lavatories

Pilgrims have visited the Shrine of Sainte-Anne-de-Beaupré since the late seventeenth century when stories began circulating of a miraculous healing onsite. Pilgrims to the site in 1928 interacted with a souvenir brochure—perhaps to help guide their way while visiting, perhaps to share with others after leaving, perhaps to stoke their own memories years later. I acquired a copy in May 2019 through eBay, and in my hands today it feels slight. The four-paneled text begins with a brief history, informing visitors that the "Breton Sailors" who built the original chapel had been "MIRACULOUSLY saved from shipwreck by St. Anne" (CAPS included). It tells of the "FIRST MIRACLE" in 1658 and the "countless MIRACLES and favors" in the centuries that followed. It estimates that "no less than 9 million have visited" and proclaims the shrine, with no equivocation, as "the most HALLOWED SPOT in all America."

The second and third panels provide a site map with twenty-five numbered attractions. These include devotional spots, like a Scala Sancta replica completed in 1891, as well as information for travelers arriving by different modes of transport: an "Auto Park" that "can accommodate 1,000 autos" and where the railroad station "lavatories" are located. The back panel details thirteen main points of interest as well as the cost of items "on sale in the CHURCH STORES and BUREAU": a detailed guidebook for .25 cents, an 18 x 24 "Colored picture of the Shrine" for .50 cents, and others.

This chapter examines the souvenir brochure as an important textual genre in the circulating media that flow from sites of biblical tourism. I analyzed fifty brochures produced between 1928 and 2019.[1] The Beaupré text is the earliest brochure in the sample, and its integration of miracles, lavatories, and items for purchase performs a defining element of religious tourism. Strict separations between sacred and secular, devotional and commercial are untenable; in reality, these classifications and discourses are blended (Badone and Roseman 2004; Timothy and Olsen 2006; Stausberg 2011; Giumbelli 2018). I analyze this genre from a linguistic anthropology perspective, highlighting how these texts use multiple voices to construct a sense of legitimation for the sites they detail and promote.

Brochure as Genre

The souvenir brochure is a commonplace object in modern tourism and has been analyzed as a text that mediates the traveler's experience, especially through its use of visual imagery (e.g., Buck 1977; Dann 1996; Scarles 2004; Vanolo 2017). A useful way to think about the brochure is as a textual genre. Linguistic anthropologists, inspired by the work of Bakhtin (1934), understand genres as "historically specific conventions and ideals according to which authors compose discourse and audiences receive it" (Hanks 1987: 670). Producing texts within a discourse genre and engaging texts as emerging from a particular genre means that we activate an established set of understandings and frameworks. In short, genres inform how we interpret by orienting expectations. Genres are not immutable over time; interpretive expectations are reflected, recreated, and challenged through our continual performance and reception of them. Textual producers may abide closely to established conventions, and they may work outside those conventions, playing with their formulaic nature to surprise audiences and transgress norms.

The primary expectation set by the brochures in this analysis is that visitors can anticipate a biblical tourism experience that is both exceptional and accessible. As Kaufman (2005) observed for the related genre of pilgrimage guidebooks, brochures signify both "pilgrimage" as sacred travel and "tourism" as leisure travel. Through elements such as hours of operation, transportation directions, location maps, and entry cost (if any), these texts situate themselves within the universe of mass travel. At the same time, these texts use descriptions, stories, iconography, and images to conjure the promise of a special, set apart experience. The travel represented by these texts is designed to be equally recognizable as extraordinary and familiar, powerful and practical. In this genre, miracles and lavatories are equally at home.

Three conventions defining this genre emerged from the analysis. First, they are informational. They provide logistical details such as how to locate the site and what kinds of attractions travelers will find when visiting. Second, they are promotional. Their fundamental aim is to stimulate interest, to draw people in, to instigate a desire to go. To pursue this aim, brochures perform in a hyperbolic register. The more I read these texts, the more I came to expect bold claims of uniqueness and awe, worthy of however long a distance one might need to travel. For example, a 1989 brochure for Christus Gardens (Gatlinburg, Tennessee) proclaims the site as "America's #1 religious attraction." A c. 1970 brochure for Ave Maria Grotto (Cullman, Alabama) reports "some of the greatest edifices of all time." A 1965 brochure for the Shrine of Our Lady of La Leche (Ft. Lauderdale, Florida) advertises "America's Most Sacred Acre." And, perhaps my favorite for its spiritual specificity, a 1956 brochure for Fields of the Wood (Murphy, North Caroline) promises: "a place where you find refuge for thought and concentration on things of the Bible that will lift you from the cares of this life and from the throes that assail us as wayfaring pilgrims." Third, while brochures do not shy away from bold promises, they also engage in a play of strategic concealment. They tempt as well as boast. For example, a c. 1960 brochure for Bibleland (Orlando, Florida) teases visitors' curiosity with this description: "We have a new scene showing Moses approaching the burning bush which was not consumed. We use actual fire but the bush is unharmed."

These conventions are not unique to biblical tourism; they closely mirror the broader tourist industry. The same is true for their social life, as they move from production to circulation. They are designed (primarily, written and illustrated) by site personnel and produced either in-house or contracted out to professional publishers (several in the sample bore the logo of local or regional printing houses). They are given to visitors upon entry (usually free of charge); displayed in traveler kiosks at hotels, gas stations, and airports; and, more recently, they are made available online as a downloadable digital copy. They might be read before visiting, perhaps as part of the decision-making process of whether or not to go, fueling anticipation and shaping expectations. They might be read onsite, helping to make decisions about how to navigate different attractions, where to go first, how to manage time. And, they might be read afterward: as a way to inform others, as a way to remember. Some are lost or discarded, while others are kept in photo albums or with other travel memorabilia. Some are donated to museum collections, while others are sold to collectors.

Hiipala (2014) observes that the brochure's production is tailored for ease, not longevity: "mass produced for a relatively short lifespan and sized for easy distribution and use" (3). Most brochures I collected fit easily in my pant pockets, and all slide easily into a folder or the pages of a book. Like postcards and other souvenir objects, brochures are classed as tourist "ephemera." But, like postcards they are often preserved as a valued collectible and can outlast the sites they were produced to advertise. Six brochures in this collection are from nonextant sites, preserving details that are otherwise lost or difficult to access.

Voices

It is easy to dismiss the hyperbole of biblical tourism brochures as a register overdetermined by the imperatives of modern advertising. While brochures are certainly an expression of advertising as a broader cultural form, there is more to say about them. These brochures are extensions of the sites they advertise, and, in turn, they communicate a message that sites themselves constantly work to generate and sustain: legitimacy. Biblical tourism sites seek legitimation, as authoritative for religious visitors and as quality tourist experiences, worthwhile for nonreligious visitors. Hyperbolic promises—"America's #1 religious attraction" and "America's Most Sacred Acre"—are a discourse strategy for constructing legitimation. Another strategy is the interweaving of multiple "voices" in the text—that is, performing different social institutions, identities, and stances through direct and indirect reference.

Everyday visitors are one such voice. Several brochures integrate quotes from travelers, but none more robustly than a c. 1970 brochure for the Cyclorama that resided adjacent to the Sainte-Anne-de-Beaupré shrine until its closure in 2018. Installed in 1895, the Cyclorama features a panoramic painting of Jerusalem on the Day of the Crucifixion, "162,000 square feet of amazing illusion." In many ways, it is a standard brochure: images from the attraction, a brief history, and hyperbolic promises of amazingness. But, whereas other brochures quote from just a handful of travelers, this text includes forty guest-book type reports. All are from the United States and Canada, a few are in French, and all are, no surprise, laudatory. Visitors are identified by name and residence and awe-struck is the collective sentiment. Many frame their experience as being beyond description. Mr. and Mrs. J. Hargrett and son from Tampa, Florida, mused: "Another word should be added to the dictionary, wonderful cannot express the beauty of perfection." A few compared this display to other cyclorama productions. John Bernick of Milton, Massachusetts, reflected: "One of the finest Cycloramas I have seen, surpassing the two I have recently seen—The Battle of Atlanta and the Battle of Gettysburg." Others favored brevity. Armand from Montreal reflected concisely: "*simplement merveilleux*."

Bibleland was an indoor attraction located just south of Orlando, Florida, from *c*. 1955 to *c*. 1970. Its brochures cast the visitor voice in more formal, authoritative terms. Two brochures from successive years, both *c*. 1960, include a bold-print heading, "Endorsed by Pastors," noting the support of organizations representing "over 50 churches." One panel on each is devoted to "What Others Say," citing the credentials of the quoted voices. In the earlier brochure, a "President Emeritus—Chicago Evangelistic Institute" predicts, "the time is not far distant when Bibleland will be known across the nation as one of Florida's great attractions," and President of the Ohio-based Bible Meditation League reflects, "One of the most thrilling hours I have yet experienced in traveling through Florida." The later brochure adds a blurb from the local Orange County Ministerial Association, forecasting that the site "will stimulate an interest in the Bible and the growth of righteousness and good will on earth."

Some brochures integrate secular voices, seeking to broaden the reach of legitimation. A 2015 brochure for the Biblical History Center (La Grange, Georgia) references a *Time* magazine description of one exhibit as "a world class experience." A 2013 brochure for Passages, a traveling exhibit that anticipated the 2017 opening of the Museum of the Bible in Washington, DC, includes a *CNN* quote: "These rare biblical texts and artifacts would make Indiana Jones salivate." Three sites—Ave Maria Grotto, Christus Gardens, and the Shrine of Our Lady of the Snows (Belleville, Illinois)—integrate the logos of tourist organizations they were members of. For example, a 1989 Christus Gardens brochure includes logos from the American Automobile Association, the American Bus Association, National Tour Association, Inc., Discover America, and the Southern Highland Attraction Group. All are non-faith-based networks, designed to advance regional, state, and national tourist economies.

Ordinary travelers, religious authorities, and secular organizations are all voiced directly to legitimize sites. Other voices are present indirectly, registered through allusion and inference and reliant on presumed background knowledge. One such voice is that of historical veracity. Authenticity is constructed by claiming intimacy or verisimilitude with biblical history. For example, a 1965 brochure for Christus Gardens notes this about the clothing used to dress its biblical characters: "Each figure's garment is a faithful reproduction from Biblical times and was woven in the land from whence its wearer came." A 1970 brochure adjusts the description but is geared toward the same affect, exchanging material indigeneity for a connection to Hollywood quality production: "The figures are dressed in costumes designed by the same company that did costume design for such famous motion pictures as *Quo Vadis* and *Ben Hur*." A 2016 brochure for the Shrine of Christ's Passion (St. John, Indiana) shifts the frame more explicitly toward pilgrimage: "You don't have to go to the Holy Land!"

Another voice is dialogically engaged with critics of biblical tourism, those who would be dismissive or suspicious of the promises sites proclaim so boldly. A 1962 brochure for Biblical Gardens in the Wisconsin Dells notes in a short description of the site that it is "MORE than 'just a tourist attraction'" (CAPS and quotes included). The c. 1960 Bibleland brochures anticipate critiques of religious profiteering multiples times. When introducing the founders, the earlier brochure assures visitors: "They will receive no profit from [Bibleland]." On the same panel, explaining the free admission and voluntary donation: "None of these offerings go to Mr. and Mrs. Fay Morse, the founders. Surplus after expenses will be used for missions." The later brochure performs this voice amid a quotation from one of the religious organizations, which assures visitors: "this attraction will in no way exploit our visitors, but will give them something good to remember about their visit to our state." A c. 1980 brochure for the National Historical and Bible History Wax Museum (Washington, DC) offers an example that made me laugh, perhaps intentionally. Demonstrating a keen awareness that life like wax figures are often considered creepy or eerie, the brochure includes a note at the very top of the inside panel: "*Historical—NOT a Chamber of Horrors*" (CAPS and *italics* included).

Conclusion

The visitor brochure is an important media of circulation for biblical tourism and a revealing textual artifact, offering a rich data source for understanding religious tourism and pilgrimage. A brochure is often the first contact potential visitors have with a site before experiencing it firsthand and a material souvenir that travelers and sites themselves keep as treasured mementos (MacCannell 1976: 110; Scarles 2004: 45). Much like postcards, guidebooks, and other texts, brochures help mediate how visitors experience a site. These texts can play an integral role in shaping the imagination, expectations, and memories of what it meant to travel there, be there, and talk about having been there.

The emphasis here has been on how brochures operate as genres of self-representation. How do sites use this media to say something about themselves to the traveling public? And, in the course of doing so, what do they say about the phenomenon of biblical tourism? The primary observation that emerged from this analysis is that brochures perform multiple strategies geared toward constructing legitimacy. In step with modern advertising, brochures tend to work in a hyperbolic register, never shy about promising visitors a memorable, even unforgettable experience. This common register is complemented by an ensemble of other voices, which are drawn together to authorize the site as a special place.

In the Web 2.0 era, various forms of print, digital, and user generated promotional media now circulate parallel to the visitor brochure. Truth be told, the functional value of the brochure as a necessary marketing device has been outstripped. And yet, they persist; still a standard feature of sites—offered freely upon entry, waiting in stacks at hotels, airports, and other nodes of tourist infrastructure. Their continued production and use likely has something to do with the increasing ease of designing and printing attractive texts, but it also reflects this genre's established position in the traveler's world. The value of the brochure is not reducible to its marketing potential; it is souvenir, gift, collectible, guide, and, ultimately, part of the complex work of crafting identity and authority.

Figure 12 Postcard for Tabernacle replica (St. Petersburg, Florida) (author's collection).

12

Greetings From . . .

We just went to This & it's a pretty good production of light Through the painting with clear music. You might be interested in catching it. Rte 45/75 North to Park Lane Exit Left to Boedeker & Park Lane.[1]

Sent to a friend in Waco in 1977, this postcard inscription describes a scene from the Biblical Arts Center in Dallas, Texas. The card's front looks down the length of a panorama painting, with a piece of the biblical scene in view as well as the auditorium seating. The inscription combines familiar elements of postcard writing ("we were here," "it's worth seeing if you can go"), a pre-internet practice of providing driving directions, and a nod to sensory excitement (the theatricality of lighting and sound).

The picture postcard, a seemingly simple object, does a great deal in minimal space and few words: a greeting, a recommendation, a souvenir, and a media of circulation. One of modernity's most ubiquitous commodities, postcards have been a central technology for promoting travel, including pilgrimage and religious tourism. They have circulated globally since appearing in the 1860s, exploding in popularity in the first decades of the 1900s and enduring amid a digital age (Woody 1998). In this chapter, we examine the picture postcard as a multimodal media of circulation for biblical tourism sites.[2]

Tentacles

The postcard was born of technology, infrastructure, capitalism, and global mobility. After a failed attempt in Germany, the first card was mailed in Austria in 1869.[3] The original correspondence card did not include images and was adopted in the United States in 1872. With the innovation of the halftone screen in 1888, higher resolution images could be printed on cards. This change was well received, as evidenced by the popularity of cards produced and purchased for the Paris World's Fair in 1889 and the Chicago Exhibition in 1893. The new capacity for imagery coupled with industrial production and one cent postal rates created an "international post card craze" (Smith 2001: 229). Between 1895 and 1920, 200–300 billion cards were sold worldwide, including over 700 million in the United States in 1906 (Rogan 2005).

Another innovation also fueled the craze and led to what is, essentially, the modern postcard form that still endures. First in England in 1902, followed by France in 1903, and the United States in 1907, the card's backside was divided: one side designated as a space for inscribing messages and the other for postage and address. As Gillen (2013) observes, this change entailed material affordances, an increased emphasis on the visual front (no longer distracted by squeezed-in writing) and a space where messages had to be contained. In this way, the postcard challenged elite norms of communication by circulating an alternative to the longer and more formal letter.

The incredible use of early postcards was due, in part, to the fact that they were not solely tied to travel. Given the affordable postal rate and multiple daily deliveries, people used them to trade messages across relatively short distances (Gillen and Hall 2010). This began to change by 1915 with the widespread adoption of telephone technology, at which point the postcard became primarily a tourist media.

As a material testimony of having been somewhere, postcards are collected by travelers for display and for remembrance, and given as gifts. Like all souvenirs, they help "locate, define, and freeze in time a fleeting, transitory experience, and bring back into ordinary experience something of the quality of an extraordinary experience" (Gordon 1986: 135). Along with these socially and affectively rich expressive capacities, the postcard has also circulated ideologically saturated ways of seeing and imagining people and places. From exoticizing non-Western others to reproducing de-humanizing racialized stereotypes, postcard imagery has reflected and recreated various structural inequalities (e.g., Mellinger 1992).

Often classed as ephemera, the actual social life of the postcard is far more expansive (Kopytoff 1986). Among other possible pathways, it moves from mass produced object to commodity, tourist souvenir, mailed gift, keepsake, estate sale item, re-commodified object via internet sales, archival acquisition, and museum exhibit. As part of its robust social life, the popular resonance of the postcard is evidenced by its use in marketing frames: clothing, advertisements, and music album covers (think: Bruce Springsteen's 1973 album "Greetings from Asbury Park, N.J."), to name but a few. In short, the picture postcard is a potent visual-linguistic commodity.

Postcards and other media of circulation are especially valuable because sites of tourism-pilgrimage face a particular challenge as destinations fixed-in-place. Being highly localized and decidedly emplaced are key to the identity and spiritual capital of these sites, but this also means that the extent of their reach is tied to their use of circulating media. Sites of biblical tourism rely heavily on networks of circulation to attract visitors, to spread the word, to spread the Word, and to establish a broader public presence outside their localized environment. Kaufman (2005) illustrates this in her analysis of postcards from the French Catholic shrine of Lourdes. Purchased, written, and sent primarily by women, Lourdes postcards were used to legitimize the site's healing efficacy, divine presence, miraculous possibilities, and promote continued pilgrimage (55). Lourdes postcards became vital to the site's ongoing circulation in French public life and global Catholic networks. As media of circulation, postcards are like tentacles extending out from localized places. They go into the world as an invitation: "come here, come experience."

Postcard Views

In her analysis of American Jewish New Year's postcards from the early twentieth century, Smith (2001) emphasizes the visual posing of postcard imagery. In her case, cards "conveyed a clear message of belonging and intimacy" by placing viewers "on the same platform as the actors in the card" (237). Smith's observation raises a key question about postcard imagery, one that recalibrates the focus from *what* is being viewed to *how* viewing is configured (Morgan 2012). How are postcard viewers positioned by the posed view? Or, put differently, what stance vis-à-vis the scene are viewers encouraged to take up as they interact with the card?

For the data analyzed here—302 postcard views representing 48 sites—the relation between viewer and image oscillates between distance and proximity, from majesty to intimacy. Across the data set, I observed seven analytical codes that mark distinct viewing stances:

1. *Up close* ($N = 134$, 44 percent). The viewer is situated in front of a single-site feature, zoomed in so that other site features are not discernible. This is often a way to showcase artistry, such as the detail of a sculpture. Many sites are jumbles of distinct features, which creates numerous photographic opportunities and, in turn, numerous postcard views.

2. *Feature profile* ($N = 86$, 28 percent). The viewer is situated in front of a single-site feature, zoomed out so that the feature is visible in the surrounding context of other features or landscape elements.
3. *Peopled* ($N = 58$, 19 percent). The viewer is situated alongside other people in frame. The actors present range from other visitors to site creators. In fifteen cases, the people are in the midst of performing ritual action, typically a large worship gathering or individuals in prayer.
4. *Building exterior* ($N = 31$, 10 percent). The viewer is situated outside a building where one or more site features are housed.
5. *Panorama* ($N = 15$, 4 percent). The viewer is situated in an elevated position, affording a visual of the entire site from a distance. In some cases, the vantage point is likely a nearby topographic rise, while for others it is likely an airplane or helicopter.
6. *Entrance* ($N = 14$, 4 percent). The viewer is situated at a main or alternate entryway. Always photographed at ground level, this view perhaps most closely performs a visual tease: "this is where you enter, but come yourself to see what is inside."
7. *Midrange gaze* ($N = 5$, 1 percent). The viewer is situated at ground level, looking out onto a portion of the site. Numerous individual features are discernible, some more closely than others but none are especially near.

I encourage readers to consider this data analysis and explore your own insights about these codes (indeed, you may have coded the data differently), but I want to highlight two observations. First, these views suggest that sites of biblical tourism use the postcard to foster a desired intimacy. In other examples, such as Kaufman's analysis of Lourdes (2004), the *panorama* was among the most common postcard views. Here, the distanced, all-encompassing stance is exchanged for the *up close* and *feature profile* views. Second, while the scenes of ritual action are fascinating, it is striking that 81 percent of views are entirely absent of people. This, too, works toward a kind of intimacy via solitude rather than ritual sociality. The viewer is positioned as alone onsite (or, perhaps, alone with God), perhaps also feeding the tourist fantasy of having a place all to oneself.

Fields of the Wood

Located in North Carolina's far southwestern corner, Fields of the Wood is a 216-acre "biblical outdoor theme park" that opened in 1944.[4] Its name derives from the King James translation of Ps. 132:4-6: "I will not give sleep to mine eyes, or slumber to mine eyelids until I find out a place for the Lord, an habitation for the Mighty God of Jacob; Lo, we heard of it at Ephrathah, we found it in the fields of the wood." Its history is tethered to the Church of God of Prophecy, a Holiness Pentecostal denomination founded in 1923 and born out of a regional charismatic revival in the 1890s. The founder, A. J. Tomlinson, was an early convert of the revival and received a revealed prophecy in 1903 while praying at a spot now commemorated onsite (cf. Beal 2005).

Imagine turning right off a two-lane road, passing through an entry gate into a valley. If you find rolling hilltops densely covered with tall trees and steeply ascending hillsides appealing, then the landscape is gorgeous. There is no guided route through the park. Wandering around, you discover two Holy Land replicas: the Garden Tomb (with the stone rolled back to reveal an empty tomb) and Golgotha Hill (complete with three wooden crosses). Numerous monuments recontextualize scriptural verses, including sections from the Psalms and the New Testament Lord's Prayer. Written out across one of the steep hillsides is "the world's largest 10 Commandments." If you are able and inclined, you ascend 358 steps through the middle of the Commandments to reach a large monument displaying the text of Matt. 22:37-40. Ascending the other hill takes you up 321 steps to "Prayer Mountain" and the spot where Tomlinson prayed in 1903; 29 monuments spell out charismatic doctrine along the pathway up. Back in the valley a gated baptismal pool with a bilingual (English-Spanish) sign announces that entry is by appointment only. And, a small restaurant and shop features gifts and souvenirs for purchase, including contemporary postcards.

From its inception, Fields of the Wood has been a regular producer of postcards. The data analyzed here includes forty-two postcard views, twelve individual cards, and two postcard folders. Their dates range from just after the sites' opening in 1944 to the early 1970s, and the progression within this timeframe is instructive. Two early cards (*c.* 1945) were printed by a denominational publishing house, White Wing Press. While professionally done, these cards are of notably lesser quality than later versions: printed on thinner paper, grainier photo reproduction, and no identifying text on the postcard front. The rest of the cards in the project collection, two souvenir folders and ten cards ranging from 1947 to *c.* 1970, were printed by the Curt Teich Company. Teich was a premier postcard company based out of Chicago, influential in part for their innovation of linen card production and image manipulation (Meikle 2015). Given Teich's industry reputation and the thousands of different postcard views produced by the company at the time, this publishing shift marks a desire to both meet consumer expectations of quality and be part of a national phenomenon.

The individual views in our collection include aerial and topographic panoramas, numerous feature profiles, and sixteen peopled scenes. Taken together, not only do they provide a diverse visual representation of the site; they also perform key themes that define the kind of religious place Fields of the Wood is engineered to be. As Beal (2005) observes, Fields of the Wood is inseparable from the denomination's theological identity, namely its emphasis on charismatic revelation and the fulfillment of scriptural prophecy. A 1947 postcard folder makes this inseparability explicit, using language that would appear in various forms in later cards:

> The whole purpose in beautifying "Fields of the Wood," (the Place of His Sanctuary) is to write the vision of salvation and the Church and make it plain upon tables so that all people who visit it may see and understand God's promises and blessings provided for those who serve Him, thus fulfilling Habakkuk 2:2-3.

Fields of the Woods postcards represent a tourist site that is regularly visited, but also one that is used for religious ritual. Sixteen of the forty-two cards are peopled, double the percentage in the total data set. Among others, postcard views depict a baptismal service at the pool, a large gathering praying at the altar commemorating Tomlinson's 1903 revelation, and a swarm of people queued up at the main entrance with a long line of cars leading into the park. The latter is notable considering the site's organization: a roughly quarter-mile stretch of pavement separates the entrance from the spatial center. As the spiritual home place for the denomination, and certainly a pilgrimage destination, Fields of the Wood is central to its charismatic identity. The relatively pronounced presence of people in these cards reflects this fact, becoming not just a visual testimony to, but a contributing piece of, the sites' collective effervescence.

In his analysis of Teich's linen postcard era (1931–45), Meikle (2015) argues that postcards helped create an imagined sense of US nationhood. By investing in postcards, and especially the decision to contract with Teich, Fields of the Wood made the claim of being a destination that rightfully belongs as part of a national tourist experience. This is amplified by particular cards. For example, a 1955 postcard depicting the hillside Ten Commandments frames the scene as "America's Ten Commandment Mountain," a view and description that is reproduced for the backside of a souvenir folder. However, a curious element of the Fields of the Wood postcards is the regular presence of flags. Twenty-two of the cards feature different flags, which include the denomination's flag, the US national flag, and various state flags representing local denominational churches who sponsored features onsite. A closer look reveals a disruption to national belonging. Whenever the denominational flag and the national flag appear together, the former is either centered, foregrounded, or elevated. While these cards partake in the imagined community described by Meikle (2015), they are also part of the site's claim of alterity within the national context. Unlike national parks or other places of widely shared civil identity (Shaffer 2001), the embodied prophecy that is Fields of the Wood is self-consciously not representative of everyone or for everyone.

A final theme is the ways in which Fields of the Wood postcards connect the site to biblical Holy Lands. Two cards illustrate this best. A *c.* 1970 card depicts the Garden Tomb replica, one of two direct Holy Land replications onsite. The back description enhances the Holy Land connection by referencing the planting of botanicals indigenous to Palestine in front of the replica: "From such a sepulcher Jesus Christ arose from the dead more than nineteen centuries ago. In the flower garden before the tomb may be found plants peculiar to Palestine." An earlier card, part of a 1947 souvenir folder, depicts an older man and woman in front of the marker that explained these botanicals. Standing on either side of the marker, each are holding one end of an outstretch Israeli flag. Of course, this was the same year that the United Nations approved the formation of an Israeli state and the 1948 war was imminent. Here, the connection is not only to a biblical past but also to a political present and a scripturalized future in which the Second Coming anticipated by this stream of Pentecostalism was believed to be materializing.

PS

The picture postcard is a potent and enduring media of circulation. Important in the broader history of global travel, the postcard has been consistently mobilized by sites of biblical tourism. Through imagery, visual stance, and textual framing, postcards circulate the existence and message of these sites across public and private contexts. As they circulate, postcards participate in a networked infrastructure that creates, communicates, and intensifies the promise of sacrality (Morgan 2014). They invite viewers to "come and experience," and they also prime visitors that this place will deliver something special.

The assemblage of authorization that includes postcards ranges widely. Over time, this has encompassed technologies such as stereoscope cards, magic lantern slides, print advertisements, television and video recordings, and YouTube channels (to name a few). At times, technologies of circulation have taken more audacious form. Handman (2019) observes that for Lutheran missionaries working in Papua New Guinea in the first half of the twentieth century, aviation was a revolutionary technology. Beginning in 1935, missionaries started using airplanes to navigate (really, to bypass) the challenging physical landscape of the islands. In doing so, they transformed the space-time configuration of the missionary encounter.

Planes and postcards also intersected in Fields of the Wood's work of circulation. Beginning in 1943, a series of planes were commissioned as the "White Angel Fleet." One of the surviving planes is now exhibited onsite, and a sign describes their use: "Uniformed minister-aviators flew mainly within the United States and the Caribbean holding meetings, flyovers, and dropping tracts on cities and towns." Postcards have featured the Fleet in multiple ways. A 1955 card depicts a plane parked on the ground, and on the back cover of a 1947 postcard folder a Fleet member is depicted mid-flight above the park.

True to their charismatic identity, the denomination imbued missionary aviation with prophetic meaning. As part of the site description inside a 1955 postcard folder, Tomlinson's moment of revelation is linked with flight technology: "on the morning of June 13, 1903, just six months and four days before the Wright brothers made their successful airplane flight at Kill Devil Hills, North Carolina . . ." The onsite sign elaborates: "In the 1950s, Church leaders connected flying with Isaiah 60:8 and Ecclesiastes 10:20. These texts (as then understood) gave rise to the idea that modern inventions and travel methods were to be used to facilitate the Church's work of spreading the Gospel by the quickest possible means." The picture postcard worked in tandem with the White Angel Fleet. Though perhaps not at the same speed, both operated as technologies of circulation in spreading the denomination's theology of prophetic Christianity. Though not as quick or audacious, the postcard does continue to circulate while the plane sits stationary inside the park.

Figure 13 Instagram "selfie-spot" at Museum of the Bible (Washington, DC). Photo credit: James S. Bielo.

13

Like-able Me, Like-able There

Today, I decided to do something new & exciting. I visited the @ museumofbible for the very first time & I must say, I WAS VERY MUCH AMAZED at my experiences there. I will have to say, my most memorable highlights of my journey through the museum were, The Stories Of The Bible. • The Old Testament: The Hebrew Bible • The World Of Jesus Of Nazareth • The New Testament. These 3 Walk-Through video/exhibits were very intriguing, breathtaking, insightful & inspiring to know more about God's word & the stories behind it. But, the #1 showing that almost made me catch a Baptist Fit in there was, The Burning Bush!! When God Spoke to Moses, it was a wrap for me!! I'm glad I made this decision. It was well worth every coin I spent. Even the virtual tour I did of the Holy Land was amazing & gave me an insight of what I will experience & see for myself when I visit the actual Holy Land in 2021. #MuseumOfTheBible #ADayInDC #DC #SiteSeeingInDC #JustMe #LiveLaughLoveLife (<u>CAPS in original</u>)

Posted to Instagram in September 2019, this media act shares details from a visit to the Museum of the Bible (MOTB) in Washington, DC. The caption accompanies a series of eight images. Seven are selected spots from inside the museum, including images of entrances to the exhibits referenced. The first image in the series is different: a selfie, a picture taken by the visitor of himself standing on the city sidewalk in front of the building, with the museum's logo and iconic entrance gates as background. In this chapter, we examine the Instagram post as a multimodal media of circulation for biblical tourism sites.[1]

How might the practice of circulating self-posed images through Instagram advance the study of religious tourism as an expression of lived religion? This question organized my analysis of 500 Instagram self-poses at MOTB. The self-pose includes individual and group selfies as well as pictures taken by someone outside the frame (perhaps a fellow traveler, perhaps a stranger). Being spontaneous or planned, candid or staged is not the question, but rather how the body is being placed in selectively chosen space.

To focus on self-posing is to take a cue from Instagram's media ideologies and practices, such as the documentation of everyday life, the demand for like-able content, and the curation of a like-d life (Marwick 2015; Laestadius 2017; Ross 2019). In the visual economy of Instagram, a self-posed image is a particular communicative act: "I was here, I want my presence here known, this image performs a self I desire to circulate publicly, and I think it might secure desired likes." Instagram is impression management, maximally caffeinated (Goffman 1956).

The media act of self-posing suggests a provocative dynamic in the analysis of circulation: that there is a dialectical motion between representations of self and place, between personal and ideological brandings. The like-able me and the like-able there stimulate each other, mutually circulating through media networks.

From Postcard to Post

This chapter developed in tandem with Chapter 12's analysis of the picture postcard. While social media platforms may have eclipsed postcards, they did not displace them; they exist alongside one another as parallel media of circulation. As complementary forms of circulation, physical and digital media have shared and diverging affordances (Gillen 2017). For example, they both have material limits on textual annotations. Constrained space to write produces relatively short messages, "routines and conventions" that vary across media technology and emergent forms of creativity (e.g., abbreviations and shorthand on postcards, emojis, and hashtags on Instagram) (Gillen 2013: 505).

There are, of course, many differences. Exemplified by the self-posed image, visitors can place themselves onsite through digital media. The postcard is largely a one-to-one media of correspondence, sometimes achieving a limited collective audience through acts of display. Digital media enable something else: the synchronicity of mass readership, curated through the mechanism of followers yet also available to an immeasurably large audience because of the open nature of platforms (Gillen 2013). Digital media also afford multiple ways of sharing, creating multiple paths of circulation. Single posts enter the incalculable flood of new media acts occurring every minute of every day, but they can also remain in circulation through networked media acts (e.g., "likes," "shares," "retweets," "comments").

Ultimately, this analysis treats the picture postcard and platforms like Instagram as complementary because they both function as mobile tentacles of fixed places, circulating imagery and experiences across time and space (Handman 2018). The practice of acquiring, collecting, and/or sharing postcards has endured, emerging in the 1890s and still a reliable gift shop item in 2020. While the durability of Instagram's appeal is up for grabs, its social value in the historical moment of this chapter's analysis and writing is remarkable.

Launched in October 2010, Instagram immediately gained traction. Laestadius (2017) documented 500 million users as of mid-2016, a number that doubled to 1 billion in three years. It is a distinctly visual-centric platform. Users must include an image or video, nearly two-thirds of posts receive no comments, and the average caption is only 32 characters despite the affordance of a 2,200-character maximum (2017). Instagram is also a distinctly promotional platform: a media designed to elevate people, places, and brands (arguably, it is a tool used to transform selves and destinations into branded entities). In his analysis of college-aged female users in the United States, Ross (2019) finds that individual posts are often time-consuming, "carefully curated" (4) in search of "quintessential" (2) images that aspire to trend via "likes." In her analysis of celebrity Instagram practices, Marwick (2015) argues that Instagram reflects and recreates the "attention economy," where the goal is to attract and sustain "eyeballs" (138) in an always denser media world. Given these media ideologies and practices, Instagram presents a rich data source in the effort to understand the dynamics of circulation.

Self-Posing at MOTB

DC's MOTB opened in November 2017, receiving two million visitors in its first two years. Located two blocks south of the Washington Mall, the project cost roughly $1 billion dollars and boasts 430,000 square feet spread across seven public floors. Museum industry reviews have been mixed. On the one hand, individual exhibits have won design awards and *The Washington Post*'s art and architecture critic mused that its use of entertainment strategies to present a "master narrative" has the potential to fundamentally "change the museum business." On the other hand, MOTB has repeatedly courted controversy: from displaying modern forgeries to questionable acts of artifact acquisition and provenance tracing (Moss and Baden 2017).

When MOTB opened, a rush of news articles reviewed the museum, lauding its aesthetic success with superlative language for the sensory experience of exhibits, renovated space, and architecture: "high-tech," "state-of-the-art," "vivid," "gleaming," "cutting-edge," "stunning," "breath-taking," "captivating," "dynamic," "dazzling," "spectacular," "jaw-dropping," "ornate," "lively," "lavish," "glitzy," "ambitious," "experiential," "interactive," and "immersive."[2] Even MOTB's sharpest scholarly critics reserve a complimentary word for its material execution; for example, Hicks-Keeton and Concannon (2018) describe it as "glossy, prestigious, first class" (2). With its aesthetic appeal, MOTB is ripe for the attention economy. Its architects, designers, and planners were keen to the possibility that visitors would engage the place as hundreds of potential photo-op stages for the visual-centric possibilities of a platform like Instagram.

Given the data at hand—500 self-posed images from 263 Instagram accounts—what emerges from the analysis? There were 70 distinct backdrops altogether, though just 10 spots account for 250 images (50 percent). The single most popular spot was that chosen by our opening caption writer, the street entrance (83/500). Perhaps the MOTB logo paired with the iconic gates—40-feet high bronze replicas of Gutenberg Bible printing plates featuring the first 80 lines of the Book of Genesis in Latin—are an irresistible Instagram stage. Perhaps, though, there is also something overdetermined about this spot's popularity. It is a bottleneck where people regularly stand in queues, especially when waiting for the museum to open in the morning or when the line is backed up, and it is the best place for groups to gather onsite before dispersing inside.

Reframing from individual spots to exhibit areas, one area was clearly favored. One quarter of all self-poses (123/500) were taken within the *World of Jesus of Nazareth*, the first-century replica exhibit featured in Chapter 6. (The next most popular area had only 62/500.) Located on Floor Three's *Stories of the Bible* section, the exhibit includes several dozen artifacts housed in glass cases, but most of the space (and, every spot selected for self-posing) consists of fabricated nature (e.g., olive trees), technology (e.g., olive press), recreated spaces (e.g., *mikvah*), and painted wall murals of biblically themed landscapes and everyday activities. *Nazareth* is a 7,000-square foot space with several distinct rooms, but its Instagram appeal is even more striking considering its comparative size. The exhibit areas for the other two main floors are both 30,000 square feet, though their total self-poses were only 54/500 (Floor 2: Impact of the Bible) and 31/500 (Floor 4: History of the Bible).

The popularity of *Nazareth* makes sense in light of several patterns in the data, as well as some affordances of the space itself. An example of the latter is lighting. Throughout the space, the atmosphere of a recreated world is invoked by ethereal colors that rotate among amethyst, marigold, and rose to mimic dawn, midday, and dusk. Many of the self-posed images appear in spots where the lighting effects are most dramatic, acting as an environmental photo filter and lending a non-everyday (perhaps, transcendent) dimension to posts.

Nazareth also resonates with a broader promise MOTB makes to visitors, which is to offer a surrogate experience for Holy Land pilgrimage. In the lobby area visitors can take a nine-minute "Holy Land tour," a virtual reality headset film with footage collected on a 360-degree camera (cf. Chapter 17); Jerusalem stone encases lobby pillars; a touchable Western Wall stone opens a Floor Five exhibit (a spot for 9/500 self-poses); and, botanicals indigenous to Israel-Palestine adorn the Floor Six biblical garden (a spot for 19/500).

The single most popular self-posing spot within *Nazareth* was in front of a wall mural of the Sea of Galilee/Lake Tiberias (16/500). Rather than being a walk-through space that requires no doubling back, *Nazareth* ends in a cul-de-sac facing this mural. The painted vantage point is elevated, facing east at sunrise with seven biblical sites identified but no human presence. In other areas, overhead sounds match the activity represented (e.g., a sound of dripping water plays inside the *mikveh* replica), but the soundscape in front of the mural shifts to instrumental devotional music. This choreographed spot replicates evangelical Holy Land tours that prioritize the Galilee, mobilizing an ideology of timeless nature in order to "step back in time" to the lifeworld of Jesus (e.g., Kaell 2014; Feldman 2016). Some of the self-posing captions echoed this way of engaging the space, such as one user who announced to their Instagram public: "My inner geek came out in full form today . . . #biblehistory #israel #happyplace."

Another pattern performed by visitors and reflected in their engagement with *Nazareth* is posing with written out scripture. Throughout the museum there are spots where individual verses, or portions of verses, are inscribed or printed on walls and signage. For example, in the lobby area etched into a wall is a King James Version rendering of Ps. 119:105: "Thy word is a lamp unto my feet and a light unto my path." Twelve self-poses from twelve different posters are gathered around this spot. Just inside the entrance to *Nazareth*, next to a panoramic landscape mural and a fabricated olive tree, is a section from Luke 8:1, "Jesus went through cities and villages proclaiming the good news of the kingdom of God." This was the chosen spot for 12 of the 123 self-poses. It seems one way visitors seek to circulate their presence in a museum of the Bible is by seeking scripture in spelled out form, in addition to the many spots where scripture exists in atmospheric or replicated form.

If people seek out Holy Land representations and written out scripture to promote the Bible, they also find ways to connect their identities to the place. The exterior entry to Floor 4's "History of the Bible" exhibit features a lengthy map of the world with the word "Bible" spelled out in different languages. This was a popular spot, with 15/500 self-poses, and in most of those cases, individuals are either pointing to or standing next to their country of origin or first language (signified by captions). Throughout the museum there are numerous other world maps, several of which visitors used as an object to reference their personal, linguistic, or ethnic genealogy. In the lobby and on Floor 6 there are donor walls, which five visitors found, posing and pointing to their name. Other posters found another name wall and captured an eponymous pose. Inside Floor 2's "Impact of the Bible" is a lengthy wall display that identifies every name used in the Bible: most written in black, some in gold set against a cream backdrop. In August 2018, I participated in a guided tour led by the project manager from the design firm who created this exhibit. He stopped our group in front of the name wall to explain that it was one of several "Instagrammable moments" they had embedded throughout the space. While only 5/263 took this particular choreographed cue, visitors did take up the underlying design logic: an appealing strategy for self-posing is to pose with direct or indirect indices of one's self.

Any discussion of recurring patterns in the data should also reflect on what was (relatively) absent. That is, where people consistently do not place themselves onsite can be as revealing as the more favored spots and areas. In some cases, an absence can be misleading. For example, there are very few self-poses from inside Floor 3's Hebrew Bible Experience (only 3/263 posters). This seems odd given the exhibit's popularity, which won two industry-leading design awards.[3] It's not so odd when you consider that there are explicit directions before entering the exhibit to not use cameras, and each room includes a uniformed docent.

In other cases, the absences are telling. Many seemingly pose-worthy spots received little or no attention from visitors. For example, a de-commissioned jeep used to tour the Holy Land and featured in a short film sits outside the theatre's entry on Floor 4 next to the History exhibit. There are no physical barriers to touching or even climbing into the vehicle, and yet only 1/500 used it as a stage or a prop. Archaeological artifacts—a source of MOTB's controversy and for some the museum's bread-and-butter—were featured in only 3/500 poses. Returning to the first finding reported earlier, there were seventy distinct backdrops. Yet, with 430,000 square feet to work with and hundreds of potential self-posing stages, seventy actually covers very little of this ground.

If visitors are strategic about the stages they choose, and if only select areas are favored, then there is much to learn from tracking these self-posing decisions. This method cannot tell you necessarily why visitors chose the spots they chose or what the most memorable museum experiences were. What it can speak to are the aspects of the museum environment that visitors chose to use as a stage, or a prop. These decisions factor into their ongoing production of a "carefully curated" (Ross 2019: 4) Instagram self, always in search of "quintessential" (2) representations of an ideal self for current and potential followers to consume and, ideally, like.

Caption

An analysis of Instagram was prompted by an analysis of postcards. In the project's broader archival work, the picture postcard emerged as a revealing empirical object: offering insight into how sites marketed themselves, seeing images of sites that otherwise had little or no documentation, and in some cases learning that nonextant sites existed at all because postcards remained. They continue to strike me as immensely valuable for helping understand how sites of biblical tourism are part of broader Christian cultures of circulation (Handman 2018).

In working with postcards, I was increasingly compelled to consider how contemporary social media function in ways parallel and complementary to the picture postcard. Inspired by insightful work on the media ideologies and practices of Instagram (e.g., Marwick 2015; Ross 2019), I began experimenting with how best to leverage this data source in a comparative analysis of visual-linguistic nodes that help comprise the pathways of Christian circulation.

Focusing on the self-posed image emerged as I explored the presence of biblical tourism sites on Instagram. To circulate an image of one's self (perhaps in the company of others) is a key affordance of contemporary technology. For visitors to DC's MOTB, this media act performs multiple promotions at once. Posting a self-posed image onsite celebrates one's self, the place, and the Bible. The me in search of likes and the there in search of likes stimulate each other, bound up in the same attention economy, the same media game of staying in circulation.

Design

The second set of chapters in Section III approach the theme of choreographing experience by way of design—that is, the coordinated envisioning and production of technologies and places. To focus on design is to draw together interests in a product's formal properties, sensory engagements with those properties, the creative processes and labor that went into making the product, and the social consequences of that product's circulation (Murphy 2016).

Design is especially instructive for analyzing the assertion and negotiation of experiential frames. As outlined in this book's Introduction, frames such as devotion, education, evangelism, and entertainment establish structures of expectation, helping to guide how people interact with performances of materializing the Bible: what to do and how to be in relationship to the performance. By attending to design processes and practices, we are better poised to understand what experiences are anticipated, preferred, and authorized. Design draws our attention to the material expressions of those experiential ambitions, from how the senses are mobilized to the directing of kinetic and affective pathways.

The plan of design does not, of course, totally delimit the range of experiential possibilities. People challenge desired frames, introduce their own agendas, and unexpected outcomes emerge amid the lived encounter with frames, technologies, and places. What design attunes us to is the dynamic interplay between a maker's ambitions, the product itself, and the contexts of engagement. In short, understanding design is about understanding the affordances of any given performance.

Each of the four chapters in this set makes questions of design central to their analysis of materializing the Bible: (14) material replications of the Stations of the Cross, from handheld objects to themed outdoor parks; (15) how the industry of experiential design is shaping biblical tourist sites; and (16, 17), cyclorama exhibitions and Virtual Reality headsets as forms of immersion. In these chapters, I use design as a conceptual bridge to think across long-standing ritual traditions and an emerging industry and to consider how two technologies make similar experiential promises for their respective eras. I hope to demonstrate that design is integral for understanding how experiential frames are established and, ultimately, authorized.

Figure 14 Jesus praying in the Garden of Gethsemane at the Shrine of Christ's Passion (St. John, Indiana). Photo credit: James S. Bielo.

14

In Place, In Motion

In 1933, the Archdiocese of New York produced a devotional object designed to perform the Stations of the Cross anytime, anywhere. Intended especially for pray-ers housebound by age or illness, "The 'Way of the Cross' Dial" reimagined a historically mobile ritual.[1] In their modern form, the Stations consist of fourteen stops derived from biblical and extra-biblical Catholic sources, narrating Jesus's physical journey in Jerusalem from condemnation by Pilate to burial in a tomb.[2]

The Dial is handheld, made of lightweight cardboard and measuring 3 inches wide by 6 inches long. The border, stylized as an ancient architectural window, is colored purple and gold. The front provides prayers for the first seven stations, with "Around the Stations of the Cross" printed in purple at the top. The back provides the remaining seven, with brief instructions printed at the top asking the pray-er to both imagine and enact movement:

> Kneel down, make the Sign of the Cross and repeat a fervent Act of Contrition. Pass from Station to Station meditating on the suffering of JESUS for you and be sorry for your sins that made HIM suffer. At the end, kneeling, say one *OUR FAITH, HAIL MARY* and *GLORY BE TO THE FATHER*, for the intention of the Holy Father. (Emphasis in original)

On the right side of the object, there is a movable dial with a downward arrow. At the center, there is an oval window, which displays the name and image of the stations, appearing in turn as you rotate the dial. The texts provided to recite with each image are brief. For example, at the Second Station, "Jesus Carries the Cross," you are prompted to pray: "The pains of JESUS are caused by my sins."[3]

"The 'Way of the Cross' Dial" is part of a long-standing material tradition associated with the Stations. As early as 1520, devotional handbooks representing portions of the modern Stations were produced in western Europe for use in churches, home, and during travel (Thurston 1914: 72; cf. Shavel 2009: 141). In the latter half of the nineteenth century, religious images were produced en masse for use with handheld stereoscopes, creating a phenomenon of parlor devotionalism. Scenes from the life of Jesus, including series focused on the Stations, were among the most popular (Morgan 2007: 148; cf. Long 2003: 90). Handheld dials, books, stereoscope series, prayer cards, themed rosaries, and a host of other items—all form a lineage of objects designed to enhance personal prayer, provide a ritualized tie to tradition, and create a surrogate pilgrimage experience.

These objects highlight important material affordances, as they transform the physical kinesthesis of ritual performance yet maintain a symbolically potent form. They conjure a sense of movement while enabling stationary devotion. They accommodate immobility while at the same time facilitate a capacity to pray the Stations anywhere. As material forms they travel easily, drawing our attention back to circulation.

For some, devotional materiality like the Stations Dial salvages a ritual that is, or has become, inaccessible to them. For others, this mobile expression of the ritual fosters past memories and anticipates future performances. These objects do not, of course, replace more kinesthetic performances of the Stations, but they circulate in parallel with one another. Pilgrims to Jerusalem still walk the Old City streets, ostensibly following Jesus's journey from condemnation to burial. And, Christians the world over replicate the devotional journey in diverse configurations. This chapter traces the history of this ritual form and builds to a recent Stations replication in the US state of Indiana and the ways in which it integrates materiality, space, movement, and sensation to perform this authoritative ritual.

Stations: History, Genre, Performance

Contemporary pilgrims in Jerusalem can progress through fourteen commemorated spots: beginning just outside the *Ecce Homo* arch and concluding inside the Church of the Holy Sepulchre. Much of the path proceeds amid a congested marketplace, moving through narrow Old City streets crowded with vendors, travelers, and shrine custodians (Feldman 2016). Pilgrims visit and pray their way through the Stations year-round, though certainly the busiest and most celebrated time is during the Paschal season and especially Good Friday.

Like so much in the toured Jerusalem of today, the Stations are often presented to pilgrims as an ancient ritual, practiced unchanged through time. Their origin is, in fact, more recent. Herbert Thurston, a British Jesuit scholar, traced the long, fragmented history of the ritual in a 1914 book, *The Stations of the Cross*. It is from the thirteenth century that we have pilgrim accounts that document spots commemorated outside the Church of the Holy Sepulchre (21). In 1563, a Belgian Carmelite priest, Jan Pascha, first wrote out a set of Stations as an organized devotional ritual (83). Though, his devotional is not confined to the fourteen stations now recognized. In short, between 1300 and 1720, there was no widespread coherence in how many stations there were, which stations were included, or where they were commemorated in Jerusalem (58; 135). It is not until the 1730s that the modern ritual form still practiced is codified by Pope Clement XII (172).

Like any ritual form, the Stations are polysemic in nature, made meaningful in diverse ways by people with diverse ambitions. Its ritualized power owes more to its genre than any particular performance. Ritual practitioners morph the practice to meet their needs, making use of a traditional form but not confined to traditional interpretations.

Most commonly, the Stations are rendered rather literally, focused on the events of the Passion. Devotionally, pray-ers focus on Jesus's suffering and sacrifice and the confession of sin. Perhaps the most continuously used prayers for the Stations were written in 1761 by an Italian bishop, Alphonsus de Liguori. For example, at the Second Station when Jesus accepts his cross, the priest and people are called to recite:

PRIEST: Consider how Jesus, in making this journey with the Cross on His shoulders, thought of us and offered for us to His father the death He was about to undergo.

PEOPLE: My MOST beloved Jesus, I embrace all the tribulations Thou hast destined for me until death. I beseech Thee, by the merits of the pain Thou didst suffer in carrying Thy cross, to give me the necessary help, to carry mine with perfect patience and resignation. I love Thee, Jesus my Love; I repent of having offended Thee. Never permit me to separate myself from Thee again. Grant that I may love Thee always; and then do with me what Thou wilt.

Another traditional Catholic devotion reframes the ritual, focusing attention on the faith and sacrifice of Mother Mary. In some ways, this Marian devotion has a deeper history than the modern form. Pilgrim accounts from the fifteenth century included veneration of some stations in Jerusalem, but understood themselves to be following a ritual that had been performed by Mary in the wake of her son's death (Thurston 1914: 23). Consider the difference in presenting the Second Station from a 1984 Marian prayer book produced for the Our Lady of the Snows shrine in Belleville, Illinois. It begins:

> I look at my Son through my tears. He's bruised and beaten. The soldiers mock Him. But He stands so tall . . . so calm, as He lifts that horrible cross to His shoulder. Even in this dreadful moment I am so proud of His gentleness and His strength.[4]

The Stations have not only been mobilized for personal devotion, but they have also been used to express and engage intense sociopolitical conflict. For example, in her historical analysis of a seventeenth-century Stations' replication outside Vienna, Bodner (2013) observes how the site was part of a broader Counter-Reformation effort aimed at disempowering new Protestant movements. For Carlos Musart, one of the priests designing the devotional path, "the lifelike representation of Christ's suffering depicted in the Stations could move viewers to return to the Catholic faith and remain faithful to it" (24).

Contemporary Catholics and Protestants have also used the Stations to articulate political critiques of socioeconomic marginalization, oppression, and inequality. Inspired by mid- to late twentieth-century liberation theologies, these performances of the Stations connect Jesus's suffering to the ongoing suffering of peoples due to structural violence. Consider an example from the "Way of the Cross Toward Justice and Peace," a 1985 performance organized by the US Catholic Conference Campaign for Human Development. Their prayer for the Second Station begins with two Gospel readings and then presents the story of Franz Jagerstatter, "an uneducated farmer from a small village in Austria" conscripted by the Nazi military. It briefly tells the story of his refusal to serve:

> He was imprisoned in February 1943 and after a military trial, he was beheaded in August, 1943. The night before his execution the words he told his chaplain sealed his fate. "I cannot and may not take an oath in favor of a government that is fighting an unjust war."[5]

Recent examples have been documented in New York City (Ashley 1999), Chicago (Davalos 2004), Amsterdam (Wijnia 2020), and Cincinnati (Williams n.d.). In each case, fourteen stations are arranged in city streets and neighborhoods, seeking to transform public space and address public audiences. The objects of critique shift among the residential displacement of poor peoples through gentrification, military imperialism, mass incarceration, the human rights of immigrants, and corporate greed. As these reframings of the Stations illustrate, the genre of this ritual form is readily used as a space for creative theological and cultural action.

Replicating the Stations in "Life-Size"

As the modern ritual form cohered in the first half of the eighteenth century, it became commonplace for any Catholic Church or shrine environment to display some kind of artistic Stations representation (Leatherbarrow 1987: 107). Though less numerous, there is also an extensive tradition of creating "life-size" Stations spread throughout a spatial expanse. One of the earliest materializing the Bible sites is the *sacro monte* in Varallo, Italy. Founded in 1486 by Franciscan priests who had served as Holy Land custodians, the initial series of chapels depict Jesus's Passion and were designed as a Stations-like experience (Leatherbarrow 1987: 107; cf. Lasansky 2017). Some of the most visited Catholic pilgrimage sites in the world—such as Lourdes, Fatima, and Saint-Anne-de-Beaupré—include large, outdoor Stations arranged on manicured pathways.

Movement and measurement have been key elements for many life-size Stations replications. By placing pray-ers on extended devotional trails, these replications entail something of a kinesthetic iconicity. That is, they make the simulation of movement from one station to the next a constitutive feature of ritual practice. Historically, this iconicity has been intensified by site designers who claim that their stations are separated by the same distances as the original spots in Jerusalem.

This tradition of "pious measurement" (Shavel 2009: 134) stretches as far back as the Santo Stefano complex, a twelfth-century Holy Sepulchre replica in Bologna, Italy (Ousterhout 1981). Typically measured by the number of footsteps, the same performance of authenticity via spatial accuracy is found in Stations replicas from sixteenth-century France (Arad 2015), seventeenth-century Lithuania (Liutikas 2015), and seventeenth-century Austria (Bodner 2013). This tradition extends to the modern United States, illustrated by a southeastern Michigan Catholic parish founded in 1936. Still extant, the site entices visitors with this description: "The hill upon which [the Shrine of] St. Joseph stands very closely approximates in size and contour the Mount of Calvary. Historically, the distance from the crucifixion to the tomb is only 65 paces, the exact distance in the Irish Hills Way of the Cross."[6]

The Shrine of Christ's Passion

How do you conjure Jesus's Jerusalem journey in the flatlands of northern Indiana? As other materializing the Bible performances illustrate, topographies are adaptable and landscapes workable as stages for choreographing biblical scenes. Consider the Shrine of Christ's Passion in the rural town of St. John, 24 miles south of Chicago.

The shrine was envisioned by local real estate developers, Frank and Shirley Schilling.[7] In 2000, the couple was asked by their priest to help locate land for a new parish building. They chose a plot just west of a Marian statue that Frank's grandfather installed in 1954. Less than a mile separated the statue and the new building, and they wanted to create a path connecting the two. Frank is credited with imagining a series of biblically themed statues, though they initially had trouble locating an artist for the work.

In what the couple narrates as a "providential" event, they decided to drive, rather than fly, on a vacation trip to New Mexico. Traveling west on Interstate-40, they stopped to explore a 200-feet tall roadside cross in Groom, Texas. Encircling the base of the cross, they encountered life-size bronze sculptures depicting the fourteen stations. For Frank and Shirley, this crystallized their vision for the pathway, and they set about locating the artist who had crafted the bronze figures. Their search led them to a self-taught artisan named Mickey Wells, who operates a bronze sculpture studio in Amarillo. Wells accepted the contract and they began construction in 2001.

Seven years later, the Shrine of Christ's Passion opened to the public in spring 2008. What visitors find is a winding, 0.5 mile "prayer trail" set in a landscaped environment. Wanting to evoke a "Holy Land" setting, their site design includes 4,000 dump-truck loads of clay to elevate the flat farmland and 80 semi-truck loads of boulders from a Wisconsin quarry, the rocks from which mimic the white coloration of Jerusalem stone.

The trail features forty-four bronze figures, arranged into the traditional fourteen stations, but also preceded and followed by additional biblical scenes. Before encountering the first station of Jesus being condemned by Pilate, there is a Last Supper portrayal and a representation of Jesus praying in the Garden of Gethsemane while disciples sleep. Following the fourteenth station of Jesus being laid in the tomb, there are three scenes: an angel praying in an empty tomb, Jesus appearing to Mary Magdalene, and Jesus's ascension. Each station includes an audio narration, written by Shirley Schilling in collaboration with fellow parishioners and spoken by a Chicago-based journalist widely known for his radio work.

The shrine advertises itself as an "interdenominational" organization, though many of its elements index a theologically and culturally conservative Catholic identity. Their performance of the Stations treats the liturgy in traditional, personal devotional terms (not, for example, an engagement with liberation theology). Consider the shrine's narration of the Second Station:

The heavy cross was laid upon Jesus' bruised shoulders. He accepted His cross meekly, even joyously, because by that cross he intends to redeem the world. Christ stands silent and the anger of humanity rages around him. Can they endure His strength, His purity, His profound humility? They lash out, forcing the cross upon him. Lovingly, Christ seizes the opportunity to pull the cross to Himself. He covers Himself with our sin.

Just outside the main entrance, there is a marker, designed as a gravestone, with a bronze life-size kneeling Jesus. Directly invoking antiabortion discourses, the marker reads:

Dedicated to the Sanctity of Life
In Loving Memory
Of The
Innocent Victims of Abortion
"Before I Formed You in the Womb, I Knew You"

Jeremiah 1:5

The "sanctity of life" marker leads into the gift shop, through which you enter the outdoor prayer trail. Once on the trail, multiple senses of movement are integral to the ritual setting's embodied experience. To examine these senses, I distinguish three interrelated kinesthetic forms: *movement between*, *movement around*, and *movement of*.

The Shrine of Christ's Passion does not recreate the practice of claiming an exact measurement of steps in between stations. Still, the ritual is constituted by the practice of moving between stations in a particular, narrated sequence. An integral observation to make here is that the movement from one station to the next is not an empty ritual space, but a meaningful sensory and discursive space that connects one scene to the next (Plate 2016: 255). Most of the stations are separated by ~200 feet, and the creators wanted to mobilize that distance. Shirley Schilling, for example, reflected that "even if you know the story," which most any Christian visitor would, the separation affords a concentration on each scene individually.[8] The connecting pathways have only ambient stimuli, such as floral landscaping and instrumental music, but no other artwork or media for visitors to engage. The result is a space choreographed for reflecting on the previous scene and/or anticipating the next.

The stations are situated in alcoves extending off the central pathway with no barriers. Visitors can move around the bronze figures and be as near to them as they wish. During my time at the Shrine, it was common for visitors to stand directly next to the statues, leaning in to inspect them closely, and to touch the figures. A more detailed look at how visitors move around the scenes comes with an analysis of Instagram self-posing.[9] In various ways, visitors accept the choreographed cue to move around the figures and interact with them. Visitors held Jesus's hand at different stations, including posing themselves in positions of prayer. For example, some visitors imitated the sculpture of Jesus in the Garden of Gethsemane kneeling in prayer with elbows on a large rock. They posed on the other side of the rock, placing their palms on top of Jesus's cupped hands.

Visitors also joined scenes, role-playing in some instances. For example, a popular pose was to stand next to, behind, or beside Jesus and act as though they were helping carry the cross. A few added a strained grimace facial expression to enhance the play. The most popular self-posing scene was to sit with Jesus at the Last Supper display. When I interviewed Mickey Wells about his sculpture work for the shrine, he shared a story with me about this scene.[10] He said that he was originally contracted to complete a Da Vinci-esque scene that included the disciples as well. However, after the Jesus figure was installed, the Schillings observed that visitors liked to gather around Jesus, sit with him, take pictures, and even eat their lunches at the table. In turn, they asked Wells to stop production of the other figures and leave the Last Supper scene with only the solitary Jesus. Wells's sculpture has Jesus mid-blessing, holding a cup in his right hand and a loaf of bread in his left. Most visitors who self-posed here are touching Jesus in some way: an arm draped around him, holding his hand with head bowed in prayer, or hugging him. A few visitors joined the scene by placing one hand on the bread, as though present for the meal and accepting their turn to consume the sacrament.

A third sense of movement in the shrine's stations is *movement of*: that is, the biblical figures are depicted as being in motion. Perhaps the most dramatic illustration is station 11, "Jesus is Nailed to the Cross." The scene includes two figures: Jesus laying down on the cross with a nail halfway through his right wrist; and a Roman soldier, holding Jesus's arm down with his right hand (a second nail in his grasp) and his left arm mid-swing holding a hammer. Both faces are caught amid intense expression: Jesus in agonizing pain, the soldier with concentrated intent and seeming to be almost gleeful.

The in-motion quality of the statues was designed by Wells to intensify the affective impact on visitors. For the Schillings, it was exactly what they wanted. With the Ascension station, Shirley notes that the Jesus figure is best appreciated on a windy day because his hair is depicted as blowing and the interaction with weather conditions furthers a sense of realness.[11] In their Instagram posts, visitors took up a similar cue. For example, one Catholic tour group included this caption with their images:

Captured a few moments along the prayer trail today at the Shrine of Christ's Passion, but the photos don't do it justice. The life-sized statues bring new meaning to the Way of the Cross. It's a powerful and overwhelming spiritual experience to see the detail in the facial expressions and put yourself into the scene at each station #wayofthecross #shrineofchristspassion

For Mickey Wells, depicting movement was crucial. His foremost priority for the Stations statues was to convey emotional feeling, in particular as registered through Jesus's body in motion. He consulted other, primarily historical representations of the Stations and felt that too many treated Jesus as "too holy"—that is, not human enough. He wanted his sculptures to convey the physical difficulty, to show how Jesus suffered "just like you or I would."

This theological-artistic imperative guided his creative process. Consider, for example, a story from the making of Station Two, "Jesus Accepts His Cross." After consulting other representations, his next step was to photograph human models posing for each of the stations. A friend modeled for Station Two and attempted to appear strained as he was holding a cedar cross on his shoulder. Mickey thought the pose looked too contrived and wanted a more naturally exerted feel. He told his friend that his camera was having trouble and asked him to stay still until it was fixed. After about five minutes, Mickey noticed the friend starting to shift his weight and spread his feet apart. When the friend finally asked, "Can you hurry up, this thing's getting heavy," he started taking photos. For Mickey, the bodily expressions of physical movement needed to be captured with precision and with as much realism as possible.

Coda

From handheld devotional objects to life-size replications, the Stations of the Cross draw together multiple dynamics in materializing the Bible. Like all ritual, the Stations are performative (Bell 1992). Apart from local, context-specific felicity conditions, the efficacy of the Stations hinges on their capacity to move practitioners out of a here-and-now space-time. Again, like all ritual, this is fundamentally about play: about getting caught up in a legitimized experiential frame. The Stations seek to do this by drawing pray-ers into replicated biblical scenes as participants, not merely inhabiting the stance of being a detached onlooker. A key observation of this chapter is that this metaphorical sense of movement, of experiencing a space-time transformation, relies on multiple forms of actual kinesthetic movement.

As Coleman and Eade (2004) observe, movement is essential for understanding pilgrimage and religious tourism: traveling to, from, between, and within sites; the mobile dimensions and devotional labor of ritual action (walking, running, crawling, kneeling, dancing, lifting); and, the metaphors of movement that animate religious imaginations (cf. Pena 2011; Siekierski 2018). In this chapter, I have focused on what Coleman and Eade call "movement as embodied action" (2004: 16) and its varied expressions in a traditionally Catholic practice. From stationary mobility to crafting static figures in motion and the kinesthetic iconicity of constructing authenticity, movement is a constitutive element that authorizes the Stations of the Cross as ritual form and performance.

Figure 15 Inside the Hebrew Bible Experience at the Museum of the Bible (Washington, DC). Photo credit: James S. Bielo.

15

Interactivity

The Themed Entertainment Association based in Burbank, California, is a premier US organization for professionals in the design industry. Founded in 1991, its register of self-presentation integrates market diversity and the promise of affective experience:

> An international non-profit association representing the world's leading creators, developers, designers, and producers of *compelling places and experiences*. Our members bring the experience of *engaging storytelling* and entertainment to a vast number of *casinos, restaurants, retail stores, museums, zoos, theme parks and an ever-growing list of destinations* that aim to bring a higher level of visitor experiences worldwide.[1] (Emphasis added)

The experiential imperatives marked here ("compelling places," "engaging storytelling") and the range of destination genres illustrate what some term the Disneyization of society (Bryman 1999). Rather than stay confined to one leisure-economic space (the theme park), various forms of consumption and education have adopted the ambition to create "imaginary worlds that evoke a thematic coherence through architecture, landscaping, costuming, and other theatrical effects to establish a focused, integrated experience" (Chidester 2005: 146).

Every year, the Themed Entertainment Association hosts a series of professional conferences in the United States, Europe, and Asia, including one they call "SATE," an acronym that highlights some organizing commitments for the industry: story, architecture, technology, experience. For two days in September 2019, SATE members gathered in Seattle. One of the conference's twenty or so sessions was a two-hour panel, "The Greatest Story Ever Told."[2]

Nodding to the 1965 Jesus-themed epic film was no irony or sleight of hand. The panel's focus was on religiously oriented destinations as a largely untapped niche among themed entertainment producers. The panelists represented experiential design firms based in London, New York City, Salt Lake City, and

Savannah, Georgia; and each presenter reflected on the potential and challenges of "faith." The panel's conceit was that the themed entertainment industry was missing out on a sizable and enduring market segment.

The panel moderator was Geoff Thatcher, who founded a design firm in Savannah in 2017. To introduce the session, Thatcher began with a "confession" and a metapragmatic reflection. "We are all just a bit nervous to share this story with you today. We're a bit nervous to talk about faith because we know that talking about faith can make some people uncomfortable." This anxiety, he continued, "is based on personal experience." He then told a story about an unsuccessful bid he helped pitch to Cincinnati's National Underground Railroad Freedom Center.

Freedom Center opened in 2004, and while it has been praised by critics for its educational work on the history of racism in the United States, it has not attracted audiences in the numbers initially predicted. The firm Thatcher worked for at the time responded to the museum's Request for Proposals to rebrand and boost attendance. The question they were posing, Thatcher recalled, was this: How can Freedom Center attract the largely absent (and relatively lucrative) demographic of white suburban families?

After visiting the museum, Thatcher and his team noticed that abolitionist leaders profiled throughout the exhibits expressed their vision of freedom through the idiom of biblical language and salvific theology. Their pitch, "Faith to Freedom," centered on telling "the story of how faith inspired so many abolitionists" and "the story of how faith was used by others to justify slavery." "Faith," by which he seemed to exclusively mean Christianity, would be the narrative bridge between past and present to rebrand the museum and attract those missing "suburban soccer moms."

Freedom Center rejected their pitch. As Thatcher told it, the museum's chief marketing officer was actually incensed by the proposal, affronted for being mistaken as "a church." Thatcher told this story in the stance of a cautionary tale: of a missed opportunity because religion was treated as taboo and "faith" avoided. Ultimately, his appeal to the SATE audience was for everyone to "keep an open mind" and consider "faith" as a valuable register for the themed entertainment repertoire.

The fact of this panel's inclusion at a premier conference for experience design professionals marks a fascinating encounter between religious tourism and themed entertainment. While Thatcher's team was not able to materialize Faith to Freedom, other non-faith-based design firms have taken on faith-based projects. For example, Orlando-based ITEC Entertainment Corporation designed the Scriptorium exhibition for the Holy Land Experience in 2002 and the Billy Graham Library in Charlotte, North Carolina, which opened in 2007. In 2014, the main permanent exhibit at the St. John Paul II National Shrine in Washington, DC, opened, designed by Gallagher and Associates, a prestigious New York City-based firm. And, scheduled to open in 2021 is the Faith and Liberty Discovery Center, an American Bible Society project on Philadelphia's Independence Mall. This attraction is being designed by Local Projects, an acclaimed design firm based in Manhattan. Because these kinds of attractions materialize religion in the public sphere, often in the frame of an educational experience, they raise an important question: How is experience design helping to mold public engagements with religion?

Religious Publicity and Experience Design

Anthropologists have explored the pursuit, promotion, and management of religion in public life using concepts such as "religious publicity" (Engelke 2013) and "cultures of circulation" (Handman 2018). Emphasizing *publicity* as a process more than *public* as an achieved status, this work illuminates the social and material channels through which religion enters and occupies public spheres. By tracing the cultural production and circulation of religious representations, we are poised to better understand how social worlds are "infused" with the ideologies, ambitions, and material forms of religion (Handman 2018: 158).

Religion in public life is, fundamentally, a sensory matter. Soundscapes in urban contexts, for example, are key for establishing, negotiating, and debating religious presence (e.g., Bandak 2014). As a multisensory process, religious actors strategically mobilize the "aesthetic properties of movement, color, rhythm, [and] tone" as they enter public spaces (Elisha 2017: 78). In his analysis of religious publicity in England, Matthew Engelke (2013) observes that campaigns designed by the British Bible Society were oriented by a logic of "ambient faith": a sensory presence that oscillates between public and private, presence and absence, being sense-able and going un-sensed. From this finding, he poses a key question: "What, in any given place and time, are the legitimate and legitimating forms of proclamation" (xix)? That is, what media genres and attendant sensory practices are authorized in processes of religious publicity?

For contemporary museums and other "cultural attractions," questions of how best to engage audiences reflect an industry-wide shift toward "interactivity" (Whitcomb 2011). As an imperative, interactivity assumes that visitors learn more effectively and are engaged more thoroughly when they become active participants, when their sensoria are excited in diverse and often playful ways. Museums have employed interactive techniques since the 1880s (Whitcomb 2011: 353; cf. Griffiths 2008), but this paradigm was formalized with San Francisco's Exploratorium in 1969 (Barry 1998). Museums now favor exhibits that foster "a kind of sensory gymnasium" (Howes 2015: 265; cf. Classen 2017: 115). Led by science and children's museums, museums of all kinds lean into the pattern that "disinterested contemplation has been offset by affective participation" (Howes 2015: 264). Hein (2000) boldly (and, I think, accurately) describes this shift as a "conceptual revolution" (viii) in museology. Curated objects have become more a means than an end, with their "function being to generate a museum experience that is illuminating and satisfying" (6). What makes an experience satisfying is forged through the broader culture of modern entertainment: "Theatricality makes a story more compelling emotively, and so design and the art of spectacle compete with logic and evidence in the inducement of belief" (80).

A watershed example in the museological embrace of experiential design came with Washington, DC's US Holocaust Memorial Museum. Linenthal (1995) describes a ten-year period of "fits and starts," in which multiple exhibition firms were either fired or quit because their respective visions for the project did not gain traction with the advisory board and other stakeholders. This rotating door of designers stopped when Ralph Applebaum and Associates, a New York City-based firm, was hired to create "a 'storytelling' museum rather than a 'collection-based' museum" (142).

Interactivity and immersive storytelling in museums reflect a broader cultural change toward the "experience economy," in which a commodity is appraised "no longer by its actual use and exchange value, not solely by its representational value, but by its ability to transform the sensation of the subject" (Klingman 2007: 6). The contours of the experience economy were largely established by Disney principles of entertainment. The modern theme park, inaugurated by Disneyland in 1955, posed "a new kind of experiential product," in which "the carefully controlled sale of goods (souvenirs) and experiences (architecture, rides, and performances) [were] 'themed' to the corporate owner's proprietary image" (Davis 1997: 22).

Consumers in experience economies gravitate toward contexts defined by pleasure and play in branded worlds. Given the emphasis on sensation and the undergirding ideology that consumers should trust their sensory experiences, the experience economy is thoroughly an affective economy. Success—as product, event, brand, or destination—rests on consumers forming ideological attachments that are registered and practiced somatically. The experience economy capitalizes on the phenomenological dimension of human attention and our tendency to authorize "culturally elaborated ways of attending to and with one's body in surroundings that include the embodied presence of others" (to which designers would likely add the presence of new media technologies) (Csordas 1993: 138). Sensory immersion is a prime imperative in all this, and the ideal of becoming "caught up" in an experiential frame themed as distinct from everyday life has become among "the most influential ideological system[s] on the planet" (Stromberg 2009: 3).

DC's Museum of the Bible

One of the presenters on SATE's "The Greatest Story Ever Told" panel was Jonathan Alger, cofounder of C&G Partners, a Manhattan-based design firm. Jonathan was invited to participate because of C&G's involvement with DC's Museum of the Bible (MOTB). Opened in November 2017, MOTB received roughly two million visitors during its first two years. Located two blocks south of the Washington Mall, one-half mile from the US Capitol building, the museum is comprised of seven public floors and 430,000 square feet. From the building's purchase and renovation to exhibit installations, the project cost roughly one billion dollars. MOTB was envisioned and funded primarily by conservative evangelical Protestants and is a revealing case of religion in public life because most of the creative labor of design was conceived and executed by secular firms who do not typically work for faith-based clients.

C&G Partners was one of those firms. For over four years, a team of twelve to sixteen designers created "The Impact of the Bible," one of MOTB's 30,000-square-foot permanent installations. "Impact" is composed of a dizzying sequence of physical and digital interactive displays, materializing the claim that pivotal events in US history and a wide range of global achievements have formative links with biblical texts.

MOTB invited C&G Partners to design "Impact" because of the firm's extensive resume. To name a select few, the firm has contributed design work to the Library of Congress, Bronx Zoo, National 9/11 Memorial and Museum, National Museum of African American History and Culture, and the New York Yankees. By selecting prestigious experiential design firms, MOTB sought to challenge public perceptions of what a Museum of the Bible would be. In a March 2016 promotional interview, MOTB's director of community engagement described it as "not an old dusty museum."³ Boosting MOTB in this register anticipates and feeds a public suspicion that museums are beset by "lifelessness" (Berns 2016: 154).

Another firm, BRC Imagination Arts, completed two of MOTB's permanent installations: "The Hebrew Bible Experience," a 14,000-square-foot exhibit, and "The New Testament Theatre," a twelve-minute animated film projected onto a 270-degree panoramic screen. Based in Burbank, BRC boasts its own impressive resume: The Rock and Roll Hall of Fame, Abraham Lincoln Presidential Library and Museum, Kennedy Space Center, and Jameson Distillery Bow St. (again, just to name a few). In the museum's opening years, industry praise for the Hebrew Bible Experience has been especially notable: garnering multiple design awards, including the Themed Entertainment Association's 2020 "Award for Outstanding Achievement-Museum Exhibit."⁴ The exhibit's design was led by BRC's creative director, Matt Solari.⁵

Matt was born into a Roman Catholic family outside Atlantic City, New Jersey. He deconverted from Catholicism in high school when he came out as gay and now self-identifies as an atheist. After eighteen years working in dramatic theatre, he joined BRC in 2004. For four and a half years, he led a team of twenty-five designers to create the Hebrew Bible Experience.

For Matt, the key to experiential design is storytelling, and he describes designers in terms that are both mythic and romantic: members of a "sacred tribe" called to tell "stories that touch people at a core level" and "bring people together." With any project, he seeks to tell "universal" stories, addressing emotional themes that are "never old." Reflecting on the nature of this storytelling vocation, he affirms a commitment to "authentic" experience. "Audiences . . . want to be part of a narrative that connects with their own deep values and stories." The critical suspicion of "authenticity" that dominates scholarly discourse is absent from Matt's relationship with this commitment; authenticity is an achievable ambition in the best design work and an imperative that audiences rightfully crave. He places experiential design within the "hospitality industry," in which "the guest" is the first priority: "you want to create a sense of magic; you want to surprise and delight them."

These commitments structured his team's design of the Hebrew Bible Experience. "The biggest thing that kept me up [at night]," he said, was the fact that he was not Jewish, nor was most of his team. They continually asked themselves, "would we be able to tell a story that was authentic?" He did not want the exhibit to "foreshadow Jesus"; or, in theological terms, he wanted to avoid a supersessionist reading of Hebrew scriptures, in which Judaism is incomplete without a delivered messiah. What he did want was an experience that could affectively stir multiple audiences, interreligious and nonreligious alike. The narrative "through line" they chose was "a journey home," designed to evoke both a "physical" pilgrimage and the hope of "finding home." Wary of overdetermining visitor experiences, he wanted "home" to remain ambiguous so that audiences could assign their own, individualized interpretations to what and/or where home was and what finding it meant. Ultimately, the team's ambition was for visitors to leave "feeling joy [and] feeling connected to each other."

The Hebrew Bible Experience is a thirty-minute exhibit where visitors move through 14,000 square feet of themed space. There are no biblical antiquities on display, only BRC's imagineered biblical past. The fifteen galleries are filled with choreographed sounds, digital animations, immersive environments, fabricated objects, and various atmospheric changes. For Matt, the integration of spatial design, technologies, and narrative was oriented affectively: "each room has an emotional design," such as suffering and hope. His personal favorite, a gallery depicting the Passover (Exodus 11–12), is the most technologically austere. While some galleries feature panoramic digital screens, moving walls, and animations that mix realism and "shadow play," the Passover gallery is more minimal. There are no screens, just four sensory elements oriented by a single object in the middle of the room. A life-sized statue of a family huddled together is illuminated by changing lights, while overhead narration is mixed with crescendoing music and smoke streaming down at a varying pace. Matt loves the "simplicity" of it, but also the emotional ambiguity: Is that "anxiety or joy" etched on their faces? "It's up to [visitors] to decide."

BRC's work at MOTB reflects and recreates the sensory repertoire of experiential design. As Klingman (2007) observes, experiential design mobilizes sensory saturation to ignite affectively charged imaginations: "Through the look and feel of people, places, and things, experiential environments show rather than tell, delight rather than instruct. The effects are immediate, perceptual, and emotional" (42). For Matt and BRC, their desired imprint on MOTB's religious publicity was to satisfy diverse audiences, appealing to an affectively powerful, if ambiguous, value of belonging.

Exit

Transforming the "sensation of the subject" is the experience economy's prime imperative (Klingman 2007: 6). A wide range of consumer and educational institutions have embraced this social condition, from corporate brand environments to zoos, botanical gardens, airports, libraries, and a host of other attractions. Contemporary museums are also conforming, favoring "sensory gymnasium[s]" that excite "affective participation" over "disinterested contemplation" (Howes 2015: 264–5). For an increasing number of religious attractions, the sensory practices and ideologies of experiential design are mobilized in an effort to expand public presence.

As religious actors seek a presence in public life, their activity occurs through social and material processes of publicity (Engelke 2013). Our understanding of these processes is bolstered when we reckon with the fact that we live in an "age in which the conditions and qualities of being public matter as much as being public itself" (238). Analyzing these conditions and qualities means attending to how forms of representation and expression are deemed "legitimate and legitimating" (xix). What media genres and attendant sensory practices are authorized amid processes of religious publicity?

At MOTB, this question leads to the professional industry of experiential design, which integrates modern entertainment principles of theming and sensory immersion with multisensory interactivity and theatrical uses of multimodal technologies. As an expression of religious publicity, we can ask: to what end? The museum's wager is that the efficacy of experiential design is presumed in the experience economy, sensible and sense-able to diverse audiences. By parlaying the legitimacy of experiential design, MOTB seeks to generate and sustain a public excitement about all things Bible.

While MOTB is a conservative evangelical project in many ways, it is worth reflecting on the fact that most of the exhibit design work was produced by non-faith-based firms like BRC Imagination Arts. Despite their instrumental role in choreographing the sensory experience for visitors, design firms are often erased from analyses of museum exhibitions, including at MOTB (e.g., Moss and Baden 2017). Perhaps the rationale behind this erasure works on the assumption that designers are merely hired hands: certainly talented, but ultimately only materializing the preestablished vision of more relevant stakeholders. Based on my fieldwork, I am certain this was not the case for the experiential designers who worked on MOTB. They brought their own professional commitments for what visitors would and should experience.

Attending to the creative labor of designers reveals key insights for understanding museum spaces. This crystallized for me during an initial interview with Matt Solari. We were discussing the diverse audio strategies his team used to design the Hebrew Bible Experience: which sounds were chosen, how they were amplified, and the vital role of auditory experience for choreographing the "journey home" narrative. Matt noted that their sound needs ended up causing a major disruption to the museum's planned layout. For several years, the Hebrew Bible Experience and two related exhibits were slated to be on the fourth floor, while "The History of the Bible," another 30,000-square-foot permanent exhibit, was to be on the third floor. Eventually, BRC requested that this arrangement be swapped because the third floor had higher ceilings, and they needed the height to achieve their desired sound effects. The firm designing "History" had no objections, and the change was made.

Without talking to designers, this kind of spatial history goes unknown. In the case of MOTB, these are particularly important observations to unearth. Consider the fact that a number of scholars who have written critically (and insightfully) about the museum address the ordering of the permanent floors (e.g., Mitchell 2019). In their analysis of the space, the museum is organized in a way that presents a conservative evangelical narrative, a theological telos realized through sequential progression. In fact, the respective positions of the third and fourth floors emerged from a design request. These floors are ordered the way they are because of where Matt and his team needed to put the speakers.

Figure 16 Postcard of the Cyclorama of Jerusalem (Sainte-Anne-de-Beaupré, Quebec) (author's collection).

16

Engulfed I

Between 1884 and 1903, at least fourteen panoramic paintings were produced on the theme, "Jerusalem on the Day of the Crucifixion"[1]. They traveled through at least eleven countries and twenty-three cities: Belgium (Montaigu), Germany (Munich, Berlin, Altoetting), Austria (Vienna), England (London), Ireland (Belfast), Scotland (Glasgow), Switzerland (Einsiedeln), Australia (Adelaide, Melbourne, Sydney), New Zealand (Dunedin), Canada (Toronto, Montreal, Saint-Anne-de-Beaupré), and the United States (Chicago, Buffalo, New York City, Philadelphia, Cleveland, Boston, Minneapolis). Housed in specially designed buildings called cycloramas, the fourteen versions ranged in size from roughly 11,000 to 20,000 square feet. If the reviews of exhibition premiers are any indication, then Crucifixion cycloramas were a blockbuster in their day: as entertaining spectacle, impressive art, spiritual inspiration, and effective Christian pedagogy. In December 1890, the *South Australian Chronicle* reported on the opening of that country's first exhibition in the city of Adelaide. Thoroughly laudatory, it includes the following description, which cuts to the core of the cyclorama's experiential promise:

> Time, place, measurement, proportion—all are changed. One might almost believe the city and surroundings of Jerusalem truly there. Give but rein to the imagination and Fancy will speedily spread her magic pinions and fly the beholder back to "the sixth hour of the 14th day of Nisan, A.D. 29."[2]

To be transported, emplaced, immersed, to have your sense of space-time and your sensorial whereabouts disrupted: this was what cycloramas promised audiences as a choreographed attraction. In this era, before audiences' sensorial and entertainment repertoires were reconfigured by motion picture cinema, the cyclorama proclaimed an engulfing effect new to the public. In this chapter, I examine this phenomenon, from its popularity and profitability in the late nineteenth century to a twenty-first-century project to determine the heritage value of one of the world's three remaining Crucifixion cycloramas.

"As if Really on the Very Spot"

The technology of a 360-degree painting housed in a specially designed building was patented in Edinburgh in 1787 by an English painter named Robert Barker. The patent stipulates that the enclosure "must be a circular building or framing erected" and "must be lighted entirely from the top." Further, a viewing platform "shall prevent an observer going too near the drawing or painting, so as it may, from all parts it can be viewed, have its proper effect." That platform "may be elevated, at the will of an artist, so as to make observers, on whatever situation he may wish they should imagine themselves, feel as if really on the very spot."[3] The ambition of immersive displacement and design strategies that structured the viewer's experience were not later additions; they were integral to the technology's conception and early marketing.

Beginning in the early nineteenth century, the distinctive architecture of cyclorama buildings became common additions to cityscapes. A painting would remain on exhibition as long as it attracted paying crowds and then be replaced by another. Panoramas were generally one of two types: landscape scenes depicting natural wonders or major cities and events deemed historically significant (Uricchio 2011: 232). By the early twentieth century, battle scenes had emerged as the most common type. Representations of US Civil War battles, such as Gettysburg and Atlanta, were among the most popular (Uecker 2012).

Jerusalem appeared early in the panorama age: first in New York City in 1802 and subsequent versions in London (1816), Paris (1819), New York again (1837), Philadelphia (1840), Edinburgh and Glasgow (1837-38), at least three different paintings in London again (1851), Philadelphia again (1855), Boston (1875), and Paris again (1887).[4] Most were present-day representations of the city, though they tended to mix biblical and contemporary references. For example, one of the most popular was Frederick Catherwood's version that opened in New York in 1837. The panorama key for guiding visitors noted seventy-one spots, which ranged from scriptural references ("5. Where Christ wept over Jerusalem") to natural features ("17. Dead Sea"), sacred churches ("65. Church of St. Anna"), and imagined cultural scenarios ("46. Servants making coffee") (Davis 1996: 62).

When the Crucifixion theme first appeared in 1884, it marked an innovation for its play of space-time displacement. Its subject was not Jerusalem as it appears now to travelers, but Jerusalem as it was during the time of Jesus. Even more exacting, it represented a precise moment: Jesus hung on the cross having just breathed his last. This biblical representation sought to create a portal where audiences could connect to a defining moment of Christian temporality.

The first attempt in 1884 by a Belgian artist was installed near Scherpenheuvel, a Marian pilgrimage site, but received little attention. A second attempt in 1885 received widespread attention, and its style was copied by all subsequent versions. A German painter, Bruno Piglhein, was commissioned to paint the scene. He traveled to Jerusalem, along with two assistants he hired to help complete the project, where they spent several months observing, drawing, and photographing the city and landscape. They returned to Germany to complete the work, consulting with a Levantine historian throughout the process to inform their representational choices.

The finished product, nearly 20,000 square feet of painted circular canvas, exhibited in Munich from May 1886 through 1888, then moved to Berlin (1889–91) and finally Vienna, where it was destroyed by fire in April 1892 after being on display for two months. As with Catherwood's panorama, visitors were provided a numbered key to guide their experience. Fifty spots highlighted botanical features ("50. A large pine tree"), technology ("4. A watchtower (for watchers to protect the flocks)"), biblical sites in the immediate and distant landscape ("6. Emmaus, a village 11 km from Jerusalem"), and biblical characters in the scene ("16. Jesus of Nazareth, the Saviour of the world, expiring on the cross").[5] The work was a commercial and critical success. An 1887 review from a German periodical comments on the use of objects to complement the painted work and the immersive effect achieved:

> As soon as we stepped out on the platform we were taken in by an optical illusion so perfect that it had to be called to our attention: the painted ruins of an oriental mill are completed by actual blocks of stone that extend up to the platform in such a manner that the eye absolutely cannot distinguish the real pyramids of stone from the painted parts. There is no way to make out the borderline, and one feels immediately transported to the landscape. (quoted in Oetterman 1997: 277)

Piglhein's contract prohibited him from reproducing the work for ten years, but his assistants would produce several. One assistant, Karl Frosch, contracted with a US cyclorama company in 1886 and, with the help of a new team, produced at least six 20,000-square-foot copies. These exhibited in Chicago (first in 1887, then again for the 1893 Columbian Exposition), Buffalo (from 1888 to 1890, then again for the 1901 Pan-American Exposition), Minneapolis (1888–9), New York City (1888), Philadelphia (1888–90), Cleveland (1890), Boston (1891), Toronto (1893–7), and London (1890). The London exhibition created legal conflict, with the US company losing a copyright infringement lawsuit to the owners of Piglhein's contract.[6]

A group of American and French painters created a copy also modeled on Piglhein's 1886 version (Caron 2016). Produced in New York City in 1887–8, this 16,200-square-foot version exhibited in Montreal from 1889 to 1894 and was then moved adjacent to the shrine at Saint-Anne-de-Beaupré, a Catholic pilgrimage center north of Quebec City. This cyclorama, "Jerusalem on the Day of the Crucifixion," is one of three still extant versions and was open for 123 years before closing in October 2018.

Two versions emerged in 1890, one authorized by the owners of the 1886 copyright and one not. The authorized version exhibited in Glasgow (1890–1) and then Belfast (1892). An advertising flyer for the Glasgow exhibition concludes by drawing together the promises of immersive realism, the connection to Christian temporality, and some leisure and commercial options:

> The visitor, passing from the busy world without, beholds around him the almost lifelike portrayal of the most interesting city in the world, and of that "chief event of time" around which the tenderest memories of all Christians must ever gather. In connection with the Cyclorama is a pleasant Lounge; a Reading Room, furnished with Papers and Periodicals; a collection of choice and valuable Engravings; and Maps, Plans, and Books descriptive of Palestine, Jerusalem, &c.[7]

The unauthorized version toured Australia, beginning in Adelaide (1890–3), then Melbourne (1893–5), Sydney (1895–1902), and back to Melbourne (1902–4) (Colligan 2002). As with the London installation, the Adelaide cyclorama company was successfully sued by the German copyright holders in 1892 (though, unlike the previous suit, a settlement was reached that enabled subsequent exhibitions through 1904).[8]

At least three other versions, all closely influenced by Piglhein's 1886 original, appeared between 1892 and 1903. A smaller version, roughly 11,000 square feet, was produced for a Catholic pilgrimage center in Einsiedeln, Switzerland. The original was destroyed by fire in 1960, and a replica version has exhibited there since 1962. Another fire destroyed a short-lived copy in Dunedin, New Zealand, in 1893 (the fire engulfing the art after just one month of display). And, a roughly 12,000-square-foot version has been on display since 1903 near a Catholic pilgrimage center in Altoetting, Germany.

The Crucifixion cycloramas produced between 1886 and 1903 were immensely popular. Directors of the Adelaide cyclorama company reported more than 130,000 visitors in its three years of operation (Colligan 2002: 203). A writer for

New York's *The Critic* magazine reflected in 1888 that "the illusion of actuality is perfect."⁹ In 1887, a *Chicago Tribune* writer emphasized the attraction's value in both artistic and religious terms:

> Like every cyclorama, it is more than a painting; but as a painting the work was admitted by acknowledged judges to be of a very superior order. Aside from its religious interest, which is absorbing beyond description, the picture cannot fail to attract any one, whatever his country or creed.¹⁰

And, in 1888 a writer for *The Buffalo Evening News* lauded the attraction for its capacity to re-enliven the reading of scripture:

> The Bible is to many as a twice-told tale that has lost its first awful significance, but such scenes as this and the remembrance of the patient, suffering, noble face of the man who, in all His majesty, was portrayed in the great picture at the fair standing before Pilate, make it all seem terribly real.¹¹

The juxtaposition of the Chicago and Buffalo reviews is instructive, as it appeals to different authorizing frames: one artistic, one religious. Irrespective of the frame, the widespread embrace of the Crucifixion cycloramas owed to a legitimation that they were not merely artful imaginings but provided an accurate portrayal of the scriptural past. This tracks with Uricchio's (2011) observation that the genre of the panorama was invested with representational authority by the viewing public: "[cycloramas] were often inscribed within the period's tendency to record, catalogue, and teach" (232). For Jerusalem on the Day of the Crucifixion, this traced to the fact that Piglhein and his team spent months in Palestine and collaborated with a historian for the 1886 version. The authority generated by these appeals to authenticity carried over to subsequent versions, as did some repeated misinformation about who painted which version.¹² Ideologies of authenticity circulated in tandem with Orientalist ideologies. For example, an 1887 review of the Chicago exhibition treats modern Palestinians as walking scriptural referents: "Ideal heads were sought to be used in portraying prominent Bible characters."¹³

Immersion and Illusion

The cyclorama's experiential ambition was to immerse visitors, to disrupt their sense of spatio-temporal orientation. As popular entertainment and as religious pedagogy, this ambition was oriented by an affective choreography. Immersion was achieved through an engineering of sensory response, the coordinating of technologies to send "shivers down your spine," to excite gooseflesh on the skin, to raise up those tiny hairs all over your body (Griffiths 2008). How did it seek to achieve this visceral response? What was its repertoire of illusory techniques?

Recalling Barker's patent, the architecture of the cyclorama building was an integral part of the design. In my ethnographic work with religious imagineers and secular experiential designers, they voiced an imperative to "surprise" visitors and to orchestrate "big reveal" moments when visitors' sensoria could be caught off guard (Bielo 2018, 2020). The architecture of the cyclorama anticipated these modern techniques of exhibit design. The pathway of entry to the painting is a prime example. After an initial waiting area, visitors walk through a dark, narrow corridor and ascend a spiraling flight of enclosed stairs. Following this path where the surroundings are drawn close to the body, visitors stepped out onto the viewing platform where they are engulfed by the painting and its layers of depth (recall Piglhein's inclusion of "Emmaus, a village 11 km from Jerusalem").

The play with light was also an architectural technique. Interior lights were dimmed to mimic "the solar eclipse" that some Christian traditions record for the Crucifixion day (Oetterman 1997: 276). The building's structure interacted with this. Portions of the ceiling were often made of glass, allowing natural light and weather conditions to enter, replicating the shifting tones of being out-of-doors (Griffiths 2008: 41). This reinforced the space-time disorientation. The indoor visitors were invited to get caught up in imagining themselves positioned atop a hill adjacent to Calvary, suddenly becoming eyewitnesses to Jesus's death.

Objects of various kinds were mobilized as stagecraft. Dark cloths of vellum were hung above the platform like a canopy and draped along the painting's sides. This created an embedded effect, as though visitors were gazing upon a scene that kept going beyond their field of vision as opposed to viewing a work of art set in a bounded frame. Material props were arranged at the base of paintings, adding a three-dimensional element. Recall the 1887 German review quoted earlier, the "optical illusion" it praised was about the interaction between objects ("actual blocks of stone that extend up to the platform") and the composition of the painting. In addition to the guiding key, visitors were offered (or sold) a pair of binoculars for observing small details that were not otherwise visible. For some this may have indexed a theatre experience, while for others it may have fostered the play of being outdoors. In either case, the design was to draw visitors closer to the painting, further engulfing them into the scriptural drama.

Sonic effects were also used to complement visuality, amplifying the fact that "seeing is not disembodied or immaterial and vision should not be isolated from other forms of sensation" (Morgan 2012: xvii). Composed music was the primary strategy and often mentioned by advertising and reviews. The 1890 Glasgow flyer quoted earlier includes in bold print at the bottom, "Music at Intervals on the Grand Organ." An 1895 *Sydney Morning Herald* review noted that music was used to help frame visitors' transition from the street into the building: "while they were waiting their turn [to enter] excellent vocal and instrumental music was rendered."[14]

In 2009, the Altoetting cyclorama invested in the potential of sound to enhance the visitor experience. They hired a German sound engineer, Moritz Fehr, to design a soundscape specifically for the Crucifixion panorama. The result is a thirty-minute composition, playing on a loop, projected through speakers onto the painting and "redirected back to the visitor platform." The speakers are obscured from view, mounted above the platform, and "hidden in the faux terrain" in front of the painting. In his description of the composition, Fehr cites his use of techniques to represent sounds "in distance and subtle movement." And, he contrasts a potential approach with his own, which carries forward the ambition to engulf: "[the soundscape] is not intended to illustrate the given visual impression of the Panorama, but to broaden the perception of the illusionistic Medium through spatial sound and therefore enhance the immersive experience."[15]

Architecture, objects, and sound represent non-textual aspects of the cyclorama's choreography, but discursive components have always also been present. Early reviews noted the presence of a lecturer who would speak about the painting and the historical context of first-century Jerusalem. When the *New Zealand Evening Star* reported on the impending opening, it mentioned a lecturer: "The Rev. G. Chapman accompanies the exhibition, and in his lecture will thoroughly explain the different points of interest, besides exhaustively treating the customs and habits of the Jews, the sieges of the city, and many other historical facts in and about the time of the life of our Saviour."

While lecturers like Rev. Chapman were common for late nineteenth-century audiences, printed guidebooks are a more enduring material artifact. As we might expect, these texts are not shy about celebrating the cyclorama's immersive promise. For example, a 1900 booklet for the Saint-Anne-de-Beaupré installation walks visitors through each of the painting's sections in sixteen detailed pages. It begins with a space-time location that very precisely orients the visitor away from their present here and now: "The spectator stands upon a rocky plateau surrounded by deep ravines. The time is the sixth hour on the day corresponding to the modern 7th day of April, in the year 29, A.D." And, it closes with an invitation to follow a specific experiential choreography:

Having examined the picture in detail, and from the place where you stand, glance once more to the scene of the Crucifixion, to the tents, to the magnificent buildings of Herod. Try to take in as much as possible of this striking painting at a single glance. We feel sure that you will agree with the innumerable others, who have been here before that this PAINTING, is without doubt a masterpiece almost beyond conception.[16]

Heritagizing a Cyclorama

Visitors to the Altoetting and Einsiedeln panoramas continue to be engulfed, but the world's third (and oldest) remaining Crucifixion cyclorama at Saint-Anne-de-Beaupré closed to the public in 2018. Though existing side-by-side with a Catholic pilgrimage shrine, it has always been a separate entity. The cyclorama was purchased by two brothers in 1957, and sixty years later, the family who inherited the property is ready to release ownership. The family listed the cyclorama for sale in 2017 for US$5 million, a move that alarmed scholars, artists, and government officials.

In August 2017, the Quebec Ministry of Culture intervened, placing both the building and the painting under consideration for heritage classification. Two years later, the inquiry concluded and both were approved. The respective declarations of "heritage object" and "heritage building" do not prohibit the family from selling. But, they do mean that a buyer cannot move the building or the painting, and that any owner is obliged to actively upkeep both to mitigate deterioration.

Jean-Pierre Sirois-Trahan, a professor of cinema history at Laval University in Quebec City, is a leading proponent of the heritage declaration. In 2017, he published an appeal for the provincial government to approve the classification and to purchase the site.[17] He identifies a number of qualities that make the cyclorama "an international treasure": the size of the painting with respect to other panoramas from the same era; its status as the only nineteenth-century panorama in Canada; the artistic detail ("the rendering is so precise that we can see characters in the streets of Jerusalem with telescopes and not with the naked eye!"); and the broader fact that only fifteen large-scale panoramas from the nineteenth century remain worldwide. At no point does he invoke the status of the painting as a once-popular devotional attraction or its original purpose as a medium of Christian pedagogy. In fact, he invokes the opposite: "many people have never entered it, thinking that it is *only* a religious spectacle" (emphasis in original). A similar rationale appeared in a story about the heritage decision published in *Le Soleil*, a daily newspaper in Quebec City: "if we put aside the religious aspect, it is an immersive experience that can please everyone."[18]

Since 2017, the Quebec cyclorama has been enmeshed in a process of "heritagization" (Meyer 2019). This concept helps us recognize that formal declarations of "heritage," and their attendant material and symbolic consequences, occur as a sociopolitical process. Heritage does not simply exist; it is worked for, argued for, negotiated, contested, proclaimed, publicized, and managed. A striking feature of the cyclorama's heritagizing is the way in which it is reframed from a religious attraction to a work of artistic and national significance. Its value is redefined, away from devotion and religious instruction and toward its aesthetic qualities, the lack of comparable works in Canada, and its artefactual status as uniquely representing a bygone era.

The heritagization at work here resembles examples from Western Europe. In nations like France and the Netherlands, church buildings and other forms of Christian material culture are also being reframed in secular terms. What were once active elements for religious communities are being transformed into "cultural" objects deemed historically important for their artistic and national influence (e.g., Oliphant 2015; Meyer 2019; Wijnia 2021). The example of the Quebec cyclorama does present a revealing contrast to other French Canadian examples, such as the wayside crosses detailed by Hillary Kaell (2017). Based on her ethnographic work with wayside cross caretakers, she argues that scholarly and governmental discourses of heritage can erase the vitality of ongoing devotional labor. Unlike the crosses, which are volunteer community efforts, the cyclorama was a for-profit tourist site. Its closure means that visitors, some of who continued to engage the attraction in a religious register, will have little voice in how the cyclorama will be formally remembered. The work of memory, of heritagization, seems to be the domain of scholars and provincial officials who are poised to assign value in nonreligious frames.

Coda

In the modern history of biblical tourism, the Crucifixion cyclorama is a rich touchstone. For a brief period, it was a widely celebrated attraction, critically and commercially successful. In an age when global travel was not completely commonplace and composed images did not totally saturate everyday life, they offered audiences something novel and exciting. In the context of other visual technologies that promised immersion (e.g. the handheld stereoscope and moving panoramas), the cyclorama was praised as especially effective. It choreographed a sensory experience with the ambition to transport visitors away from their present to a biblical past, to disorient and reorient their space-time, to engulf them in a scriptural drama.

Scholars writing about the cyclorama's history draw comparisons between this technological media and the digital virtual reality (VR) that appeared a century later (e.g., Colligan 2002; Markantes 2005; Meier 2018). While there is no direct link between the two, it is true that as technologies they share similar ambitions. If there is something in the modern sensorium that craves to be engulfed, they scratch the same itch using their respective material repertoires. In "Engulfed II," we linger on these interests and explore some VR performances of materializing the Bible.

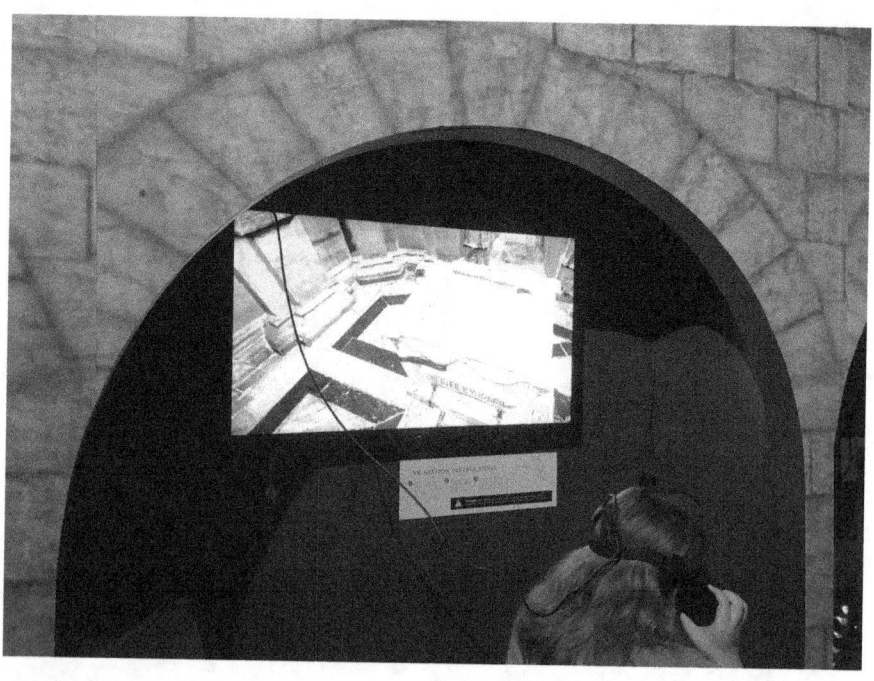

Figure 17 Virtual Reality at the National Geographic Tomb of Christ Experience (Washington, DC). Photo credit: James S. Bielo.

Engulfed II

On successive days in August 2018, I experienced two uses of virtual reality (VR) as biblical tourism. Both occurred in Washington, DC museums and both materialized an experience of being in the Christian Holy Land. However, their respective choreographies and my sensory evaluation of their relative success diverged widely.

Explore!

"Soar across the Sea of Galilee, climb the stairs to the Temple Mount, explore the path of the good Samaritan and visit the Church of the Holy Sepulchre during midnight services." This is how DC's Museum of the Bible publicized their VR experience. *Explore! A Virtual Reality Tour of the Lands of the Bible* is an eight-minute jaunt across twenty-four traditional pilgrimage sites; their sequence roughly traces the life, ministry, and death of Jesus of Nazareth.

Explore! is exhibited at the Museum of the Bible, but it was produced by SonTerra Labs, a VR company founded by Gary Crossland, an evangelical writer and teacher.[1] Crossland began filming in the Holy Land in 2005 and, in 2013, began filming exclusively on 360-degree rigs equipped with up to ten cameras. When the museum was ready to create an exhibit space dedicated to VR, it came together quickly because Crossland built the eight-minute tour from already collected footage. In other words, the content of this VR experience was not designed for this particular exhibition, but rather the experience was designed around an already extant body of visual work.

The museum as a whole includes seven public floors and more than 430,000 square feet of exhibit space. There are several permanent installations and there are four rooms reserved for temporary exhibitions, two on the basement lower level and two on the fifth floor. The sizable first-floor lobby area is primarily dedicated to visitor orientation and gathering space, but also includes the gift shop, children's game area, and two exhibit rooms. Given this layout, the location of *Explore!* is significant. It is in the lobby area, directly across from the ticket desk; the first exhibit space visitors encounter when arriving and the last one they pass when exiting. It costs extra (US$9.99), and certainly not all visitors opt to go in, but for many it helps set the experiential frame for their encounter with the museum as a whole.

When first entering the space, my attention was drawn to the room's pillars, covered with colorful vintage-themed travel posters. "Egypt This Winter," "Old City Jerusalem," "Patmos Greece, pick your own olives!" VR headset stations were arranged around the room, accompanying ten seating areas with four swiveling stools each. The museum docent coached me briefly on how to engage. Adjust the headset volume and tighten the straps to my liking; stay seated, as the experience can induce a disorienting sense of vertigo; be sure to look all around in every direction; and "have fun."

For eight minutes, I viewed a fast-paced progression from one pilgrimage site to another: from the Sea of Galilee to the Church of the Holy Sepulchre. The footage was filmed at a high resolution and, apart from a few blurry spots, the image was crystal clear. Most of the still scenes were filmed as a time lapse, creating a speedy affect from images of waves crashing and people moving rapidly. Other scenes were filmed with slight movement. They were mostly filmed with an elevated camera rig, which meant you looked down to the ground at a higher-than-average vantage point and looked down on the tops of heads in peopled spaces. If you dislike heights, a few shots would be difficult to tolerate. Filmed on extension rigs, you move out from mountain top ledges to look down into canyons. Roughly every twenty seconds the scene shifts. Each new scene is introduced with a brief text in the bottom corner of the screen: a place name and a New Testament chapter and verse citation associated with that place. All the while an upbeat instrumental score plays, evoking adventure travel more than devotional contemplation.

Tomb of Christ

"Discover the fascinating history of the Church of the Holy Sepulchre and be transported to Jerusalem for an immersive 3-D experience unlike anything you've seen in a museum before." This is how the National Geographic Museum publicized a temporary exhibition with multiple VR components. *Tomb of*

Christ: The Church of the Holy Sepulchre Experience is a multiroom walk through exhibit that explores the history and renovation of global Christendom's most revered pilgrimage site.

Built in the fourth century, located in Jerusalem's Old City, the central features of the Church of the Holy Sepulchre are shrines marking the claimed locations of Jesus's crucifixion, burial, and resurrection. During 2016–17, a team of scientists and artisans from the National Technical University of Athens completed conservation and restoration projects on the main shrine (the Edicule) that had been rebuilt in the sixteenth century. National Geographic was invited to document the project with multiple technologies, including high-resolution scanning, photography, and video.

From November 2017 through December 2018, DC's National Geographic Museum hosted the *Tomb of Christ* exhibition. The exhibit design and production was led by Falcon Creative, an experiential design firm based in Orlando. Falcon's team used National Geographic's documentation materials to create several immersive experiences, all of which were guided by the design imperative of storytelling. The creative lead noted in a print interview with an industry periodical: "We approach all of our projects from the storytelling experience standpoint first: *What do we want to tell the guests? What do we want them to experience and feel?*" (emphasis in original).[2] The team's primary strategy was to replicate the sensation of being inside the church, the embodied presence of being face-to-face with the shrine.

As a visitor, you enter *Tomb of Christ* in a group of roughly twenty people, pulsed in by twelve-minute intervals. You move through four rooms: the first three are timed, while the final room allows you to linger as long as you like before exiting. Room One is an orientation, using two layered digital projections (one larger on the wall and one smaller on a slanted table in front of the wall) to introduce the church and its storied history. Room Two is the first fully immersive space, replicating the sensation of being inside the church. Every surface except the ceiling was used: there were two wall-sized digital projections, while the other two walls and floor were papered to resemble the church's stonework. A narrator guide explained different features inside the church, as the projection mapping on two of the walls shifted to showcase the church's various rooms and shrines. Room Three attempts to intensify the immersive effect, as visitors pick up 3-D eyewear before entering. Once inside, projection mapping on every surface moves you through digital replications of the church in various periods over time, culminating in video footage from the Holy Fire ceremony, which takes places annually the day before Orthodox Easter.

Room Four is the largest and most diverse. After a visual timeline of Jerusalem on a wall, a series of interactive kiosks are arranged for nonlinear flow. Accompanied by signage and video monitors, these tactile installations enable visitors to enact the technologies used in the process of documentation, conservation, and restoration: ground-penetrating radar, thermography, LIDAR (remote sensing method), 3-D printing, and photogrammetry. The room's final element is the headset VR experience. Three booths were arranged side-by-side, each with a swivel chair, headset with earphones, and a screen which projects for other visitors what the VR participant is seeing. Inside the headset, the image is a 3-D digital reconstruction of the church based on National Geographic's photogrammetry work. You begin outside in the courtyard and are free to look around for as long as you like. To move ahead, you stare at highlighted spots for about thirty seconds, which then advances you forward through the space. The voice of the same narrator from Room Two appears sporadically to explain different shrines inside the church. Throughout, background music played in a devotional or contemplative register, subtle but always present.

Choreographies

After experiencing these two VR performances, I reflected on how my sensory response to each overlapped and diverged. Overall, I found *Tomb of Christ* to be far more engaging and memorable. I wanted to go through the whole thing again immediately, an impulse I did not have for *Explore!*. On the one hand, it puzzled me that a digitized reconstruction felt more immersive, more real, more bodily exciting than a 360-degree film. In my field notes, I wrote that *Explore!* reminded me more of an extended commercial for booking a Holy Land trip than it did a simulated experience of being there.

The question I have asked myself since is, why? Why did a digital simulation engulf me more than footage of an actual environment? I posed this question to a group of students and faculty at Wesleyan University in October 2019. For the students, the answer was obvious: it was a matter of agency. *Tomb of Christ* felt more real because I could control when and where I moved, rather than being whisked along on a linear, predecided course. I suspect they are right, that this capacity of decision making and self-determination has much to do with the disparate senses of immersion. But, perhaps there is also more to the story that is worth fleshing out, more to say about what facilitates this form of mediated immersion. Consider five other possibilities. Two of which are also about the affordances of the technology itself, the other three are about the broader exhibit choreography, and all of them say something about me as a culturally specific visitor.

First, the two exhibits afforded different perspectival stances. Because of its filming vantage points and use of time lapse, *Explore!* placed me in spatial and temporal positions divergent from my everyday experience of reality. I'm not typically elevated in a crowd, floating above a canyon, or watching locations at intensified speeds. In contrast, *Tomb of Christ* kept me at ground level and also allowed me to be in closer proximity with physical objects and built environments. In *Explore!*, I was mostly situated at a remove from the world around me, not drawn near as though I could reach out and touch what lay in my field of vision.

Second, I responded quite differently to the respective sound choices. The devotional-contemplative register of *Tomb of Christ* was, at least, not distracting and perhaps resonated with an expectation I had for a ritualized frame. The adventure register of *Explore!* was distracting and even off-putting, perhaps because it keyed the commodified experience of being sold a packaged tour. When I interviewed the exhibit coordinator, I asked about the selection of music, which he figured differently. He said that it "just felt right," that the Holy Land "is an adventure." While the music did mirror the fast-paced dynamic of scenes changing every twenty seconds, for me it conjured alienation rather than intimacy.

Third, *Tomb of Christ*'s inclusion of a monitor where other visitors can visually participate in what the headset wearer is experiencing was effective. Perhaps the rationale had a practical dimension. For some visitors, it might maintain interest, enticing them to linger for a turn even if all three booths were occupied. For others, it might satisfy their curiosity for what happens inside the headset, mitigating longer wait queues. For me, the monitors worked against something that scholars and critics have noted as a limitation of VR: donning a headset is an isolating act that lacks sociality (e.g., Griffiths 2008). This technique transformed the experience from private to public, making one's path through the church a part of the exhibit that can be shared among visitors.

Fourth, the two exhibits are structurally different from one another, which shaped my differential appreciation of them. *Explore!* is contained within one room and the VR experience is the sum total of the exhibit. *Tomb of Christ* is spatially larger, with a series of exhibits that conclude (culminate?) with the VR experience. In the industry periodical interview, Falcon's creative lead for the project reflected on how the team approached the integration and placement of VR:

> There's a lot of debate about VR, and we always caution our clients that VR is a very personal and isolating experience. When you put on a VR headset, you are, for the most part, alone in an environment. There's pros and cons to that, but we think some of the more successful attractions are the ones you can enjoy with family. We lean more toward creating a larger space where we surround guests with media. In this case, we have 3D media that stretches around the perimeter of the room and continues onto the floor. It is a group experience. *As a secondary opportunity*, there also are VR stations. After you've experienced the main scene in 3D, you can then put on a VR headset to explore the church in more detail—to choose your own path and spend a little more time looking at specific elements (emphasis added).³

He begins by noting the apprehension around VR's lack of sociality and concludes with a nod to what the Wesleyan students anticipated, that VR is at its best when it enables a sense of agency for the user. What resonates most closely between my experience and the designer's rationale is the relationship among the multiple rooms. The VR experience did not need to stand alone as an immersive technology, but it worked in tandem with and as a complement to other strategies.

Finally, the two exhibits operate in divergent interpretive frames, which reflect their host institutions. *Explore!* operates as a version of surrogate pilgrimage, celebrating the transformative potential of encountering the sites where Jesus walked (e.g., Kaell 2014; Feldman 2016). *Tomb of Christ* aims for something more nuanced and more inclusive. The exhibit is pitched in a religion-science frame, operating in a double-voiced way more so than proposing any particular relational configuration between the two. In my initial field notes, I noted that the exhibit spoke in two registers: celebrating scientific achievement and avoiding any explicit promotion of Christianity, while also wanting to be edifying for Christian visitors. This double-voiced character was present throughout, beginning in the queue line outside Room One where a short video played on a loop and cited the project as being of equal interest for both "scientific" and "faith" audiences. Wall signage repeated this message at various points. Toward the beginning of Room Four one sign read:

> While we can track the age of quarries and buildings, we can't prove what events occurred at this place in Jerusalem long ago. The religious significance of what lies hidden beneath the polished limestone and marble slabs of the church's

Edicule remains a matter of personal faith. But, people of all faiths can appreciate the beauty and long history of this storied building.

The exhibit's glossy souvenir booklet does the same. At one point, the text lists off a range of identities that visitors might identify with:

> Whether you consider yourself a devout believer, a curious agnostic, or simply a lover of culture and travel, the dramatic history, cultural significance, and stunning art and architecture of such places can captivate us all.

In short, *Tomb of Christ* operates in a frame that attempts to resonate with multiple identities. As someone who identifies as both a committed Christian and a social scientist, this double-voiced frame worked for me. For some it might feel wishy-washy (trying to satisfy too many audiences), for others as veiled evangelizing (given National Geographic's shift to 73 percent ownership by the Murdoch media empire in 2015). The broader interpretive frame for the VR experience enabled me to shift between religious and scientific registers without having to unite them in any specific way.

Conclusion

Digital virtual reality systems began circulating in the late 1960s, but "VR" catapulted into our present in 2016 with the commercial release of personalized headsets that compete for consumer attention and dollars. Existing and purported applications range widely: from computer gaming to athletic and military training, medical and therapeutic rehabilitation, and many others. Museums of all varieties have also been attracted to VR applications. Arguably, it is among the liveliest questions for curatorial and exhibition staffs. For example, the international for-profit company MuseumNext dedicated a January 2017 conference to VR and museums in Australia and regularly publishes online articles about the subject, such as a January 2020 feature that asks, "Virtual Reality is a big trend in museums, but what are the best examples of museums using VR?"[4]

Museums that materialize the Bible—as temporary exhibits, like National Geographic, or as core to their mission, like MOTB—are no exception. Given the phenomena explored throughout this book, this is totally unsurprising. VR's promise of sensory immersion reflects and recreates the long-standing tradition of seeking to conjure experiential access to biblical lifeworlds: from architectural replications to use of scriptural flora in gardens and cooking and, of course, the cyclorama as a technology of sensory immersion equally hyped in its own era.

VR exhibits like *Explore!* and *Tomb of Christ* help us refine our understanding of how the promises, performances, and sensory engagements of biblical tourism continue to develop. Certainly, there are many fascinating questions to ask about how relationships between the physical and the virtual will be used to materialize the Bible, and how producers and consumers will seek to authorize "virtual pilgrimage" (e.g., MacWilliams 2002). And, as sure as the cyclorama and VR headsets were mobilized for biblical experiences, so too will the next technological innovation.

But, not all that seems new under the sun is altogether new. As emerging technologies like VR are mobilized, there remains the capacity to recreate long-standing ideologies. An enduring observation about modern, especially Protestant, representations of the Holy Land is that they incline toward obscuring or erasing non-Christian peoples, cultures, and histories (e.g., Long 2003; Coleman 2007; Kaell 2014; Feldman 2016). Despite all their differences, we see this in both *Explore!* and *Tomb of Christ*. Landscapes and built environments are mostly emptied of people, conjuring the very unreal scenario of an isolated, fully personalized encounter with Holy Land pilgrimage spots. As anyone who has visited the Church of the Holy Sepulchre knows, the possibility of being in the space all alone is either unheard of or the privileged outcome of special arrangements. While technologies may afford new experiential opportunities, how tethered will they stay to the encultured ways of experiencing they inherit?

Classification

The third set of chapters in Section III approach the theme of choreographing experience by way of classification—that is, the process of categorizing, naming, and otherwise ordering materiality. Here, I am inspired by Morgan's (2017) proposal for tracing the social life of religious material culture (cf. Rakow 2020b). While his framework was oriented by handheld objects, it is equally generative for understanding places that materialize the Bible. Classification choreographs because it specifies and situates materiality within broader systems of practice and valuation.

Classification fuses issues of meaning and power, as it draws together efforts to render materiality sensible (and, sense-able) and efforts to authorize what something is, where it belongs, and what it is good for. Such efforts are present throughout this book. We might highlight the forms of self-identification that are claimed by biblical tourism sites. A place might call itself a "garden," "shrine," "exhibition," "museum," or "theme park," and in selecting one they conjure certain expectations and mobilize particular registers of authority.

All classifications are a social process, which means they are subject to change, objection, dialogic accumulation, erasure, and are historically and culturally contingent. Creationist "museums" identify as such in order to advance their claim of cultural legitimacy and scientific viability. Critics reject this appeal with their own fervor, arguing that creationist sites are, by definition of a body like the International Council of Museums, something else. Authorizing definitions have their own social histories and to grant or refuse belonging within definitional boundaries is always an act of granting or refusing legitimacy.

The three chapters in this set each focus on a particular materializing the Bible site to examine dynamics of classification: (18) a Kentucky tour guide who asserts a place to be sacred through storytelling, and who is categorized by himself, visitors, and myself as ethnographer; (19) a nonextant expression of

African American yard work in Georgia, and the risk of erasing its particular theological identity when it is remembered in strictly artistic terms; and, (20) the social life of a Holy Land replica in Connecticut, and the ways in which dominant classifications of "kitsch" and "outsider art" obscure richly affective local attachments to place.

Figure 18 Tour group at Garden of Hope (Covington, Kentucky). Photo credit: James S. Bielo.

18

In the Garden

Biblical tourism is a densely mediated phenomenon. Infrastructures of travel, communication, and commerce; national and transnational economics and politics; the social contexts of touring; the consumption, production, and circulation of media content—all conspire to shape practice and memory. One of the most formative, and sometimes most memorable, mediators of tourism and pilgrimage is the living, breathing, moving, and talking guide. Guides can play a central role in constituting the travelers' experience, structuring the where and how of movement, and constructing meaning all along the way (Mesaritou, Coleman, and Eade 2016; cf. Cohen 1985).

Tour guides range from highly scripted, dime-a-dozen types who are indistinguishably deployed at sites to virtuosos who can uniquely transform how a place is experienced. In any case, it is a wonderfully complex kind of social performance, as guides "constantly negotiate changing perceptions of self and other, guiding work and daily life, intimacy and economic exchange, past and present" (Feldman and Skinner 2018: 10).

The complexity and virtuosity of guiding is illuminated by Jackie Feldman's auto-ethnography of being a Jewish guide for Christian pilgrims in Israel-Palestine (2016). Reflecting on more than thirty years of guiding, Feldman demonstrates how guides are integral for shaping the pilgrimage experience. Guides do not determine what visitors experience or remember, but they do structure the field of possibilities in impressionable ways. Feldman exerted an active presence as a pilgrim guide, making itinerary decisions about where to go, which route to take, how places and histories are narrated, and managing the attention orbit of travelers (what to notice, minimize, celebrate, obscure, or erase). "Seduction" is the description he settles on to characterize the guide-pilgrim encounter, meaning that the aim of the guide is to "win their confidence, engage their emotions, satisfy their expectations" (116).

In this chapter, I follow a key piece of Feldman's approach by highlighting storytelling as a vital element of the guiding performance. He describes pilgrimage as a coproduction between guide and traveler, and it is narrative most of all that makes this dialogical encounter successful or not: "the use of appropriate feeling tones, the selective creation of empathy with key figures of the past, and imaginative and personalizing descriptions of historical events are often more important than virtuoso displays of knowledge of fact and figures" (26; cf. Fine and Speer 1985: 77). This resonates with Lauren Kerby's ethnography of Christian heritage tours to Washington, DC (2020). Akin to Feldman, Kerby argues that the engine for this form of religious tourism is the circulation of fundamentalist stories that claim to reveal the true history of the nation. In shifting among religio-political identities—from founders of the nation to exiles from power, victims of "secularism," and saviors of national greatness—"all [Christian heritage tourists] require to recreate themselves is a good story" (19). By keeping select stories in circulation, guides help choreograph tours, reproduce organizing ideologies, and assert experiential frames for travelers.

"Street Rat" Choreography

Covington is a small city in northern Kentucky, across the Ohio River from Cincinnati.[1] At the end of a No Outlet road, amid a working-class neighborhood, atop a steep rise that affords an unobstructed view of the Cincinnati skyline, is a 2.5-acre place called the Garden of Hope. Envisioned by a Southern Baptist pastor who visited Jerusalem in 1938, the centerpiece is a 1:1 scale replica of the Garden Tomb. Opened to the public on Palm Sunday 1958, the Garden of Hope hosted 150,000 annual visitors in its first two years (Hicks 2009). After its founder died unexpectedly in 1960, the Garden passed through numerous custodians and owners and has seen periods of extended neglect, sporadic restoration, and recurrent vandalism. In 2018, it recorded less than a thousand visitors. Covington's Garden of Hope is a "largely forgotten" site of religious tourism, representing a kind of sacred space often neglected (by scholars and visitors) in favor of more conspicuously popular destinations (Irvine 2018: 376).

The Garden is largely forgotten, but not entirely. The work of a few custodians keeps the place open year-round, including its primary tour guide: Steve. Born in 1947 and born again on "December the 23rd, 1978, 7:45 p.m.," Steve is, in local terms, "a character." To welcome each group of visitors, he describes himself as a "die-hard Covington street rat," born and raised within a mile of the Garden. After serving a three-year tour in Vietnam, Steve worked lower management jobs until retiring due to a stroke that rendered him "55 percent blind." Since his forced retirement, he has devoted himself to the Garden: guiding "over eight thousand people" since becoming the primary guide in 2003.

During my fieldwork with Steve, he met every tour group in roughly the same outfit: white crew socks and sneakers, blue denim shorts, a Garden of Hope T-shirt, and US Navy Veteran hat. In many ways, he presents as an unpolished ambassador to visitors. We were talking before one tour when he nonchalantly took out his dentures and stuffed them in the front pocket of his shorts. A callous on his gum was bothering him, and I expected he might leave the dentures out until the group arrived for a brief respite from the pain. Wrong. He left them out for the entire tour. From one tour to the next, Steve is prone to shift dates about the site's history and provide incorrect information about other details (e.g., the founding date of the Garden Tomb in Jerusalem). There are certain key facts about the Garden's history that he always shares, but his guiding performance is largely a tangle of non sequiturs: humorous and devotional stories from his and others' experiences onsite, joking with visitors, and always a bit of singing.

In a foundational article about the role of the guide, Eric Cohen (1985) observes that keeping travelers happy is a key aspect of guiding labor, and a reliance on humor is "a particularly important element in the role performance of not fully qualified guides... who may compensate for their inferior competence as guides by playing the 'good fellow' or clown" (13). While some visitors may interpret Steve this way, I think it misunderstands him. Sites of pilgrimage and religious tourism are not all straight-laced piety all the time (Coleman and Elsner 2004). Steve's humor, variously teasing and self-deprecating, seems always to be part of his reverence for the Garden, never a departure from it. His guiding performance evokes the southern US evangelical preaching tradition, which moves nimbly between levity and gravity (Blanton 2015).

All guides must reckon with the question of legitimacy. Who are they, and why should anyone pay attention, let alone trust them? Mesaritou, Coleman, and Eade (2016) articulate a key question: "From where do guides draw their legitimation and how and for whom does the knowledge they produce become authoritative" (5)? For Holy Land guides licensed by the state of Israel, extensive training is required. Feldman (2016) describes a two-year course with twelve hours of instruction every week and seventy-five full-day tours apprenticing with a seasoned guide (11, 25). This training is centered on an interdisciplinary knowledge of history, geography, geology, and botany, and a physical intimacy with the "land of the Bible."

Steve is different. He has no advanced education in theology or history; he is not an ordained minister in any tradition; and, he has no previous guiding experience. But, his guiding prowess has nothing to do with scholarly expertise or formalized training. His legitimacy is drawn from his born-again identity and his localized, passionate attachment to the Garden. Steve's guiding authority resembles what Skinner (2016) details in his analysis of a Northern Irish guide. A former Republican Army member, the guide's presence had no pretension to impartiality or objectivity; he embodied a definitive point of view. "Here was a martyr. Here was an ally. Here was an enemy. Here was a tour guide with a difference: an intimacy, a passion, a personal connection, a living history with the subject of his work" (26). As a "die-hard Covington street rat," Steve loves the Garden of Hope and loves to share it with people. He loves to show off a piece of his home, and he loves to tell stories that perform his unwavering commitment that this is a special place.

Lucy in a Vat, an Angel in Overalls

Years of guiding can yield a well-honed repertoire of stories designed to transform "undifferentiated space into significant place" (Feldman 2016: 53). The same is certainly true with Steve. His stories are a patchwork of historical claims, personal anecdotes, jokes, and tales of miracles onsite.

At the Garden Tomb in Jerusalem, there is a replica of a first-century wine press near the tomb. In an effort to heighten the Garden of Hope's immersive quality, a replica of this wine press replica was added in the early 1960s. In his tour, Steve rarely makes mention of the Jerusalem wine press and has nothing to say about the archaeology of first-century Palestine. His narrative route goes a different direction, and he always begins by asking for a willing participant from the tour group:

> STEVE: Do we have any teachers here? Retired teachers? {a woman raises her hand and he walks over, extending his arm to accompany her} Da-da-da-dum. Lock onto me. {they link arms and walk over to the wine press replica} Those of you who have looked at my sign, you are disqualified. Do not say a word. I know who you are. Teachers are very smart people, agreed? What's that in the ground over here, right there? {pointing to replica}
>
> VISITOR: A well?
>
> STEVE: A well, thank you. {he shakes her hand} I've proved my point. Wrong answer. {group laughs} Let's go back to TV land and the *I Love*

Lucy show. Lucy was in Naples, Italy, in a big wooden vat and she's stomping grapes. That's a wine press, ladies and gentleman. That's the way they made wine back in the days of Jesus. Women would stomp it up. They didn't have any Sweet-n-Low or Splenda, so what they would do is put vinegar in there. A few years ago, I tried that. My wife comes home and I got a big bowl of grapes and I'm there with a mallet and I'm making sure I'm mashing it up. And she says, "What are you doing?" And I says, "I'm making wine." And I put the vinegar there, and I mixed it up really good, I took a big solid drink of it. I ran to the sink and I puked for about 10 minutes. Take your time, look in the tomb, get a picture of it, then we're going to the Chapel {another replica onsite}, where we're not getting married. {group laughs}

Much about Steve's guiding style is on display here. He engages people one-on-one, creating a miniature drama within the broader story he is telling. He shifts registers fluidly, from quiz show host to a sing-song lilt ("da-da-da-dum"), explanation, and narrative. He is direct with visitors, jokingly blunt and assertive. ("Do not say a word. I know who you are.") Baby boomer pop culture lingers alongside a cursory biblical sketch. A silly, self-deprecating story ends abruptly, which leads without segue to tour directions. If it all sounds messy, that's because it is. Steve is. But, that does not mean he is ineffective; groups typically smiled throughout the routine and responded to every cue.

Steve's repertoire also includes stories central to the Garden's sacrality. One, which he tells to groups when they first gather in front of the tomb replica, is a miraculous story of divine intervention about how the very space where they stood had been made. He begins the story by setting the scene: it was spring 1957 and the Garden's in-progress construction was emerging from its first winter. The Garden's founder, Morris Coers, discovered that the land beneath the tomb was sliding, destabilizing the hillside. Coers and his team of workers tried every construction technique they knew, but nothing worked.

Engineers evaluated the problem, but they all said the same thing, the Garden of Hope was no longer safe. Then, a stranger appeared one day outta nowhere: six foot six, 360 pounds, bib overalls, a straw hat, and no shoes. The shoes were on his shoulder. He went to [Coers] and said, "I hear you got a problem." The minister's only five foot seven. He looks up and says, "Well, yeah, we do." "Don't tell me about it, put it on paper." The man sketched a design for a retaining wall, like the railroads use. They started building right away, but the man was gone.

> Nobody got his name or where he was from. When you're standing on the patio in front of the tomb today, you're standing on an 18-foot high wall made of concrete and steel. We haven't lost an inch of dirt since.

Steve's performance of this miracle story uses several hallmark narrative features to establish its truth: precise setting of time and place; exacting details of physical appearance; constructed dialogue between Coers and the stranger (Bauman 1986). Of course, Steve was ten years old in the temporal context of the story. While he grew up near the Garden and visited as a child, he never knew the Coers family and held no special reverence for the Garden until after his born-again conversion in the late 1970s. He knows this story not from firsthand knowledge but as the rest of us do: as folklore.

This story circulated in print for more than a decade before Steve started guiding in 2003. The first version appeared in a popular devotional book, *Where Angels Walk* (1992). Set amid "true stories of heavenly visitors" around the world, in a section entitled "Master Builders," is an account of "the man in the bib overalls" (129). The story is also referenced in several *Kentucky Post* profiles of the Garden (1995–2007). The first *Post* story, "Maybe angel wore overalls in Kentucky," was published to help advertise a book tour for *Where Angels Walk*. The author was coming to a bookstore in Covington, and the news story promoted both the book and the Garden. The columnist writes a version of the story he heard from a man named Bob Palmer, a guide at the Garden who preceded Steve. It describes "a large man in bib overalls" who appeared out of nowhere, offered to help Pastor Coers, and disappeared as suddenly without a trace.

During my fieldwork at the Garden, Steve asked me to apprentice with him as a guide, which I happily agreed to do. To help me prepare, he lent me a tour script he had received when he began guiding. There is no name on the script, and Steve did not know who authored it; perhaps it was Bob Palmer. The script includes a version of the Angels in Overalls story, much of it taken verbatim from *Where Angels Walk*. The script adheres to the same broad outline as Steve's telling, though it lacks Steve's attention to detail: no exact height or weight, and no mention of a hat or shoes. This version also concludes more indecisively: "Was he an angel (as many said)??? Could have been, or merely a man like you and I who was sent by God and became the man of the hour." In Steve's guiding performance, there is no question: the man was an angel sent to rescue the Garden from collapse. "I believe in angels, they've visited me in my house, what about you," he pointedly asked groups, before shifting without pause to details about the tomb replica construction.

"The Hidden Jewel"

During a life history interview with Steve, he described the Garden as "the hidden jewel of northern Kentucky because 99 percent of greater Cincinnati and northern Kentucky and surrounding area still do not know that we are here." Steve is immensely proud of his role in sharing the good news of the Garden, of helping people discover a sacred place in their own (and his) backyard. At times, the Garden's hiddenness also frustrates him. On occasion, one-on-one with me and with some tour groups, he described how he approached numerous churches in the area to sponsor the Garden, never with success. This lack of support puzzles and bothers Steve, which came through at the start of a tour in July 2017.

In the summers of 2016 and 2017, the Garden experienced a swell of visitors, much more than Steve was accustomed to guiding. In July 2016, the creationist theme park Ark Encounter opened 40 miles south of the Garden. Local tour agencies started selling packaged tours, with stops at the Ark, Creation Museum (20 miles west of the Garden), the Garden of Hope, and several other sites of Christian interest in the area. Steve was mostly enthused about this opportunity to show off the hidden jewel, though it also stoked his frustrations.

It was a steamy afternoon, high humidity and temperature in the mid-90s. We sat in the shade, awaiting the group's arrival. Steve usually carried something to drink when touring, sometimes water, sometimes a Mountain Dew. That day he had brought a Tang-type orange powder to mix in water, which he was preparing in a McDonalds Styrofoam cup. Accidentally, his stirring straw poked a hole in the side, and the orange drink started leaking on his pants. He fumbled briefly and laughed, taking the ill-timed spill in good humor as the bus arrived promptly at 3:30 p.m.

The group had over fifty people, making it one of the largest tours I observed Steve guide. They had come from central Pennsylvania and included members from several Protestant churches. Steve welcomed them and asked how they had enjoyed their day touring Ark Encounter. He often contrasted the Garden with the two creationist sites by saying the focus "here" is on the New Testament and "there" it is the Old Testament, but today he took a different tact. He began by saying that he wants to "get a hold of" Ken Ham (CEO of the ministry responsible for Ark Encounter and the Creation Museum) and ask about "investing" in the Garden. Steve quipped, "They got millions, ours is a buck ninety-five," and the group laughed with appreciation. "But we got somethin' they ain't got. Jesus! All's they got is dinosaurs." Steve's gibe at the creationist past garnered a few nervous laughs, and several people looked around at each other uneasily. He continued, "Let me ask you a question. Where in the Bible does it say Noah brought dinosaurs on the ark?" One visitor picked up Steve's cue, "Nowhere." "Thank you! That's exactly right." With this, Steve shifted sharply into the story of Morris Coers and the Garden's founding.

The rest of the tour continued as usual. Steve delivered his repertoire of stories and concluded with a prayer, blessing the group and thanking God for the opportunity to once again show off "your hidden jewel." As the group left, I saw several people placing cash into the donation slot, and Steve sold seven souvenir T-shirts, more than average for a group this size. Despite the awkward opening, something about Steve and/or the Garden itself won people over.

Steve is not universally liked by tour groups. He will freely recall negative Trip Adviser reviews and other critical feedback he's received over the years. On several occasions during tours, visitors found quiet ways to ask me if Steve was "for real" or to double check information they were hearing from him. But, for many visitors, Steve's guiding illuminates and transforms the Garden into a sacred place. In June 2018, I accompanied a group of six Catholic men from Dayton, Ohio. Bob, a man in his sixties, organized the visit; he had only recently learned of the Garden despite visiting family in Covington for decades. As the tour concluded, several men asked Steve for his autograph on their souvenir brochures and were visibly pleased when he agreed to join them for a group photo. While saying good-bye, Bob excitedly proclaimed Steve to be "our Baptist brother!" In a follow-up email exchange, Bob wrote to me that Coers' story was "inspiring," but it was Steve who defined their experience: "[He] gave it a glow that, without him, would have been missing. He made the resurrection of Jesus come alive and that was a very good thing—for those of us who may never visit Israel."

Perhaps it seems a strange leap, from stories of vomiting up homemade wine to the resurrection of Jesus. How does a somewhat coarse, somewhat unreliable narrator amount to a glow? Where does Steve "draw [his] legitimation" and how do his representations become authoritative (Mesaritou, Coleman, and Eade 2016: 5)? Steve helps us remember that pilgrimage can be playful and that humor is not necessarily at odds with or apart from devotional reverence (cf. Coleman and Elsner 2004). Though he is not a minister and does not perform in a preaching register, Steve's guiding performance does resonate with an evangelical sermonic tradition, in which an "anointed" speaker integrates the light-hearted and the eternal (Blanton 2015). Most of all, Steve mobilizes the power of storytelling to construct an authoritative guiding self: a local "die-hard Covington street rat" who knows the Garden intimately and wants you to love it as much as he does.

Figure 19 Rev. Ruth in his Bible Park, charcoal drawing. Photo credit: Art Rosenbaum.

19

Rev. Ruth's Yard Poetics

John Ruth lived eighty-three years in rural Woodville, Georgia. For much of that time, he lived off a two-lane road in a one-story home set amid tall, thin longleaf pine trees.[1] On April 19, 1954, the forty-year-old Mr. Ruth began a project in his yard, beneath the pines. It consumed his attention and labor for the next four decades.

Sometimes called the "Drive-Thru Bible Garden," John Ruth's project did not involve planting scriptural flora. It was a mixed-media environment focused on re-presenting biblical stories and designed as a personalized testimonial display to all who drove by (Promey 2018). A pathway, for cars or feet, wound through 23 acres and connected six numbered areas. Each area, and the spaces between, featured sculptures (e.g., Noah's ark), paintings (e.g., six days of creation), everyday objects that had been re-signified (e.g., a cistern hand-pump for Jacob's well), and hand-lettered signs hung on pine trees—some detailing instructions for visitors while others were prayers, poems, and scripture-in-script (as full verse or citation).

Based on interviews with Mr. Ruth between 1988 and 1992, folklorist Susannah Koerber (2004: 92) notes that he created his Garden as an alternative to the more formally institutionalized experience of local Protestant churches (cf. Wojcik 2008: 181). The local Baptist congregation he attended refused to recognize his divine calling to preach. So, he became "Reverend Ruth" in tandem with making a place that materialized biblical history and evangelized for and about Jesus. When Rev. Ruth died in 1997, his Garden died with him. The paintings, sculptures, objects, and signs were dismantled. The whereabouts of the materials are unknown, likely they do not remain at all, and the pine trees used as shelter, stage, and canvas were all felled.

I feature Rev. Ruth's project in this chapter because his Garden is an almost entirely "forgotten" site (Irvine 2018) and a distinctly African American expression of materializing the Bible. It is preserved only piecemeal by a few artists who spent time with the reverend. Unlike other "visionary art environments" featured in this book (see Chapter 20 and Holy Land, USA, in Waterbury, Connecticut), the Drive-Thru Bible Garden did not survive the passing of its founder and never experienced a restoration. By assembling a scattered archive of Rev. Ruth's Garden, by remembering this place through analysis, I ask how it adds to our comparative understanding of scriptural materiality and place-making. Ultimately, my goal is to demonstrate that a strictly artistic classification obscures or erases the theological material poetics that animated John Ruth's life's work (Wojcik 2008).

Yard Work

Rev. Ruth's Garden emerged from the tradition of "yard work": a practice of expressive place-making that is common throughout the southeastern United States, particularly among African Americans (Gundaker 1993; Gundaker 2000; Gundaker and McWillie 2004; Gundaker 2014). Yard work recontextualizes everyday objects and fashions new forms from mundane materials, all in service of making public the identity, cosmology, and spiritual ambitions of creators. This tradition is not defined by a singular style but includes a repertoire of shared techniques, such as using multiple forms of script writing, color coding, separating wild and cultivated nature, setting up buffers and filters at entry points, and honoring ancestors (to name a few) (Gundaker and McWillie 2004: 11).

African American yard work is often classified, sought after, collected, and exhibited as an expression of vernacular (aka, outsider, visionary, and/or self-taught) art. While this has brought deserved recognition to some individual artists, it also bears the tension of subsuming a diverse cultural tradition into the categories and structures of international art markets. Classifying yard work as vernacular art risks extracting it from distinctive cultural histories and racialized experiences (Gundaker 1993: 63, 71; cf. Wojcik 2008). Without denying the spark of individual creativity, we must recognize yard work as a dialogical production, as individuals are engaged with a shared set of expressive practices and local social experiences. Further, designations such as "outsider art" can run contrary to the identity and ambition of makers, namely the dissonance of treating an inherently religious project in secular terms (Gundaker and McWillie 2004: 23–240). The theological signatures that animate yard work can be dulled or erased; specific claims about, say, the Bible or Jesus can be transformed into more vague, universalizing notions about "spirituality" and "human creativity" (cf. Patterson 2016; Promey 2018).

Yard work is best conceptualized as a creolized cultural production, drawing together west African, European, American Indian, and Black Atlantic signs, styles, and materialities (Gundaker 2014). Individual yards reflect the "reiteration and improvisation" of signifying practices, re-creating while adding to the expressive tradition (Gundaker 1993: 67). Yards exist in liminal spaces, betwixt and between roadways and houses, and in turn have both public and private qualities. Given its outward-facing quality, yard work is also self-work and the presentation of the decorated yard is a presentation of self. Working within the creole tradition, individuals use yard work to say something about themselves, the state of the world and their place in it, and relations among past, present, and future realities (material, social, and theological). For African Americans, yard work reflects a racialized social experience and is one means of "coming to terms with oppression and seeking a positive outlook in even the most soul-daunting circumstances" (Gundaker and McWillie 2004: 154).

Rev. Ruth's Bible Garden emerged from this well of expressive culture. Like other yard makers, John Ruth practiced a material poetics that drew together "artefacts, the environment and bodies [with] metaphor, creativity, imagination, dreams, and mystery" (Lundberg 2008: 2). Such material poetics are grounded in a relational state of being, in which makers forge durable bonds among their identities, sensations, and cosmologies, the materialities they work with and through, and other actors they live among (human and nonhuman, animate and inanimate). Further, such poetics are always performative; they are ways of doing things in the world. Yard work is "more than adornment," and it is "a metalanguage not reducible to speech or writing with which to comment on the human condition and take responsibility for directing its course" (Gundaker and McWillie 2004: 10, 12). As a presentation of self, yard work is ultimately about materializing a transformation: of objects, land, and lives (Gundaker and McWillie 2004: 153). This was true for John Ruth, who became "Rev." and not only "Mr." through the yard he made.

April 26, 1988

The material archive for Rev. Ruth's Garden is more minimal than for any other site in this book. It was never widely known (Koerber 2004: 40), and the only known video footage is a fifty-six-minute tour recorded on April 26, 1988.

Housed with the University of Georgia Libraries' Folklore Collection, it was filmed by a local artist named Art Rosenbaum. Art visited the Garden several times during the 1980s and developed a warm acquaintanceship with John Ruth. For this filmed tour, Art brought a group of first-time visitors, including an art professor from the University of Georgia and about ten students. Rev. Ruth led this group, presumably interested in his Garden as a form of vernacular art, on a tour and explained each installation in turn. The atmosphere is convivial with several shared moments of robust laughter, but this should not obscure the multiple moments when the reverend witnesses to the group, informing them that "the end of time is coming" and "there is only one true God."

Rev. Ruth orients the group in front of an opening sign near the two-lane road. Resonant with other African American yards, this sign honors the ancestors, naming the relatives by whom the Garden was "made possible" and to whom it was dedicated "in memory of." Before the Rev. shifts to "Number One" (i.e., the first main area), Art asks him the kind of ethnographically minded question I might have asked on such a tour. Ruth's answer makes clear his ambition for this place:

> ROSENBAUM: Reverend Ruth, can you tell these folks what the idea of the Bible park was and how long you been working on it?
>
> RUTH: The Bible Garden is 33 years old now. Thirty-three years old, exactly, last year. Thirty-three years old. Now, the purpose of Bible Garden is to bring out history and religion. Christian religion, mainly. And, to bring out that one man, a Jew man. One Jew man is the ruler of the universe. Now, we all may not believe that. He's gonna rule anyway. The Jew man is the son of Abraham. He's also son of David, flesh and blood. Later, he became Son of God by Virgin Mary. Four thousand-four. Creation started, the beginning, four thousand-four. And, at the end of four thousand-four, he was born. Now, we have two thousand years since that time. Bout to come to the end of that now. So, the water is poisoned, the air is poisoned, everything's been poisoned. So, now the earth's gonna have to be cleaned up from man. And he's gonna clean it up. The earth cannot continue as it is. We cannot have peace with man. Man cannot bring peace. Peace treaty will be signed one after another, but there will be no peace. No matter how many leaders may come to sign peace, there will be no peace. But, when the other king comes, which is called Jesus Christ, there will be peace. Only then and only then will there be peace. We're gonna have it. I'm looking for peace.

"Number One" is composed of two signs, which frame the Garden with a kind of Alpha and Omega representation of the New Testament. The first sign, hand-lettering on a rectangular piece of plywood, cites Matt. 1:1. An abbreviated genealogy for Jesus is spelled out along with Ruth's foundational theological claim that Jesus is the "one true God." Next to this is a sculpted horse painted white to represent the apocalyptic vision of Rev. 6:2. The horse is lettered with verses to proclaim scriptural inerrancy and messianic return; one side has 2 Tim. 3:16 written out, and the other a shortened version of Rev. 22:18-19 (the closing text of the Protestant Bible).

Walking on the path to "Number Two" there are more installations. A retired cistern hand-pump sits alone in a clearing to represent Jacob's well. Across from this, there is Holy Land imagery: three large sculpted camels next to an even larger plywood sign. Painted on the sign are a date palm and stones next to a body of water (Sea of Galilee? Jordan River?). Two scriptural citations—1 Cor. 2:2 and Matt. 2:2—are set above song lyrics written by Rev. Ruth:

> Long long ago, far across the sea, just for you and me, a little baby born in Bethlehem, He is the son of David, Son of Abraham, a little baby born in Bethlehem.

This is one of several spaces within the Garden where Ruth's words existed alongside scriptural words. These instances mark Ruth's divine ordination as "Reverend," and they reflect a distinctive feature of African American yard making. Yards are a place-based expression of a broader expressive culture and they often integrate multiple performance genres. For example, Gundaker (1993: 68) notes the parallels between the use of fashioned seats in yards and song references to seats in the Black Spiritual tradition (cf. Gundaker 2014: 242). Here, Ruth integrates his short song into the storytelling of biblical history.

"Number Two" returns to Matt. 2:2, which Ruth uses on this tour to explain the significance of the virgin birth, "Jesus Christ was the only man born without a man. . . . So, he's the Son of God. What God? The one true God of Abraham, Isaac, and Jacob." This section includes several other hand-lettered signs: a dedication for the Garden's opening ("April 19, 1954"), an acknowledgment of six individuals who helped support the Garden's founding, and a sign that mixes instruction for visitors with a bit of social-theological critique. The latter instructs visitors that the Garden is "free to see" and that "He [God] will accept only free will offerings." It then presents an articulation of racial equality in the presence of God, listing off "Jew, white, yellow, red, brown, black"; one of several spaces where Rev. Ruth used the Garden to speak back to his experience growing up as a Black man in the Jim Crow South (cf. Koerber 2004: 106).

Before arriving at "Number Three" Rev. Ruth stops the group in front of a large pine tree that has grown with three trunks. In a scientific register, multi-trunk growth is hazardous for tree health and typically a sign that the tree will have a shorter-than-average life. Bible Garden transforms a hazard to a hallelujah. "This tree grew special here for me," Rev. Ruth explains to the group. Each trunk is labeled with a circular, hand-lettered sign, and reads right to left: "Symbol of one true God of Abraham"; "His Son Jesus Christ"; "Holy Ghost agree three into one." For Rev. Ruth, this tree was a divine signature in nature telling him where the Garden should be. By mobilizing the local landscape in this way, he re-created a common yard work pattern of associating trees with "the dead and higher powers" (Gundaker and McWillie 2004: 123; cf. Gundaker 1993: 61).

"Number Three" returns to Matt. 1:1, shifting from genealogy to "Jesus' earthly parents," and features sculpted representations of Mary, Joseph, and a donkey. Rev. Ruth uses this installation to reiterate his theology of Christian exceptionalism, as the only tradition bearing witness to "the one true God." Next to the sculptures is the longest of the Garden's hand-lettered signs, another poem written by the reverend. Here, the historical verse shifts from biblical history to Christianized militarism in the eighth century. It read:

> Mohamm's influence began to spread
> Many Christians had lost their heads
> He tried to overthrow Christian religion
> And gave Europe a new decision
> But Charles Martel was very strong
> He felt that Mohamm was surely wrong
> The Battle of Tours defeated Mohamm
> And turned his army clean around
> Charles Martel was not a king
> But a mayor in the King's ring
> He saved Christianity for Christian work
> And left Mohamm's army in a twirl
> The King was a weak child at that time
> So Charles Martel had to make up his mind
> He led the people from year to year
> With Christian love and tender care
> Charles' death brought Pepin on the sea
> And a plot to fill his little dream
> He went to the pope of ancient Rome
> And used his words to own the throne
> It is better for he with power to be king
> Than he who has name, and no power in the ring
> These words coming from the Roman Pope
> Gave Pepin the King a new hope

Later Pepin left the kingdom to his sons
Carloman died and Charles continued on
Of all kings he won the greatest fame
...
...
...²

"Number Four" and "Number Five" shift to Hebrew Bible/Old Testament chronology. Here, multiple expressive forms are integrated, for example, six painted concrete squares depicting the days of creation; a hole dug in the ground as "a symbol of hell"; and a Noah's ark sculpture with painted rainbow sign above it. Rev. Ruth narrates this section in the frame of biblical inerrancy and literalism: "Some people say this is just a fairy tale, didn't really happen. But, Noah's ark really happened." Throughout the tour, he is always keener to discuss theology than artistry. While touring this section, the art professor invites Ruth to elaborate on his process for drawing into the wet concrete. The reverend simply confirms that, "yes," this was his method and moves on.

"Number Six," the culminating installation, surrounds a white cinderblock sculpture in the shape of a cross with several different media. There are two European-styled paintings: depictions of the Last Supper and the Agony in the Garden that immediately recall Leonardo da Vinci and Heinrich Hofmann, respectively. Encircling the cross are twelve trees, each bearing a plywood circle with the name of an apostle hand-lettered on them. Like the multi-trunk pine, Rev. Ruth sensed the landscape in labeling this set of twelve trees. God used nature to communicate where the Garden should be, and Rev. Ruth listened. He extends this mobilization of land in a newer growth section of trees just outside the ring of twelve. A tree with a crooked trunk had grown and as he walked the group over to it he explained that there stood Judas Iscariot: "There's the ole' crook. That ole' crook, he's the one who sold Jesus. There's ole' crook, see him?"

John Ruth was seventy-four years old when he led this tour; he moved nimbly and would live for another nine years. The Garden was a forty-year devotion, a material poetics of prayer and testimony that he continually added to and tinkered with. This open-ended quality of never being finished is consistent with the broader expressive tradition of yard work (Gundaker and McWillie 2004). When presenting the Judas tree to the group, he noted that he had yet to attach a circular name sign to match the other twelve, but that he would soon do so. He then invited them to return again in the future, promising an undefined, but heightened experience:

Y'all gonna come back here? Make a promise you come back. You be shocked when you come back. I'm gonna have something wonderful out here. Not gonna believe it. Not gonna believe what I'm gonna have for you when you come back.

Coda

The Drive-Thru Bible Garden was a life's work for John Ruth. In it and through it he materialized for himself and for visitors his vision of Christian commitment. Ruth mobilized numerous expressive forms and genres to choreograph his Garden: sculpture, paintings, re-signified objects, altered and categorized landscape features, and hand-lettered signs with scriptural texts, poems, songs, and memorials. Akin to other individual creators of biblically themed attractions, Ruth's Garden was a theological, biographical, and aesthetic imprint on a local place (Beal 2005). While deeply personal and personalized, Ruth's Garden should not be reduced to an idiosyncratic spiritual expression. The place he made was shaped by definable social forces: a literalist Protestant theological tradition, his racialized experience as a Black man, and the creolized tradition of African American yard work.

In this chapter, I have rendered Rev. Ruth's Garden as a kind of material poetics, forged through expressive traditions and social conditions. Following Lundberg (2008), conceiving yard work as material poetics means recognizing the relational dynamic among objects, landscape, bodily experience, theology, and Ruth's guiding performance. Like all poetic forms, made places are not strictly referential, they are performative. It is not just about expressing something; it is about making something happen. In the case of John Ruth, his Drive-Through Bible Garden marked a personal transformation (from "Mr." to "Rev.") and acted as a materialized prayer and evangelical witness. Ruth's Garden is now absent from the physical landscape, and it lives on almost exclusively in the scattered archive of artistic documentation. We should be grateful that this archive exists, but also careful to not let the discursive construction of the Garden as "outsider art" dull or erase what Rev. Ruth made it to be: a dogmatically Protestant material poetics.

Figure 20 Holy Land, USA (Waterbury, Connecticut). Photo credit: Dave Williams.

20

Four Crosses Over Waterbury

I first visited Holy Land, USA, in Waterbury, Connecticut, on December 22, 2015[1]. I was there with my fiancée and her parents; we were spending Christmas with her grandmother, June Williams, who had lived her whole life in the neighboring city of Naugatuck. They had heard of the site for most of their lives but had never been to experience the hundreds of miniaturized replicas of biblical scenes and stories spread across 17 acres.

Local residents purchased Waterbury's Holy Land in 2013 with the aim of restoration, but it had been closed to visitors since 1984. We stepped around the "No Trespassing" sign and encountered the accumulated ravage of thirty years' worth of weather, vandals, and neglect. Some replicas were totally indiscernible, others missing pieces and halves, and nearly all cracked and leaning. The colors of some painted signs and carvings were faded beyond recognition, others faintly visible. The sense of abandonment was heightened by the day's weather. The sky was densely overcast, clouds thick enough that you could look directly at the sun's outline. The air temperature was below freezing, intensified by a steady wind that whipped and howled around and through the crumbling replicas.

Standing atop Pine Hill, the panoramic view is unobstructed. You look out onto diverging rivers, crisscrossing freeways, residential neighborhoods, church steeples, treetop hills in the distance, and the imprint of a deindustrialized economy—sprawling, aging factories that conjure up other "Rust Belt" scenes. We walked, careful of our footing and tensed up by the cold, snapping pictures and trying to imagine the site prior to ruination. But, it was not all bleak.

Amid the gray sky, dead winter brush, and deteriorating replicas stood a newly built pillar. Standing 4 feet high, composed of stone and mortar, it takes the shape of a large tree stump because it is built around one. Written in red letters on a white background, three words on one side read "Tower of Babel." The fresh paint stood out starkly against the surroundings, suggesting the stirring of new life. Above the Tower, the source was revealed by a small plaque screwed into exposed tree rings:

Eagle Project
by
Jacob Dinklocker
Troop 41 BSA
June 1, 2015

A Local Place

Sites like Holy Land, USA, are an often-written about, often-photographed presence on the US landscape. Public discourse is dominated by two interpretive frames: *kitsch* and *folk art*. In the *kitsch* frame these sites are gawked at, objects of bemusement and/or ridicule. They are spectacles, oddities, fascinating for their utter strangeness. They appear regularly in books like *Weird New England* (2005: 237). *Roadside America*, a popular travel guide first published in 1986, describes Holy Land, USA, as a "post-nuclear, *Road Warrior* vision of the Holy Land. Most of the rambling spread consists of impenetrable assemblages of junk" (154). In November 2002, the site was spoofed by Stephen Colbert on *The Daily Show*. In his characteristic style, Colbert dons a tan cargo vest to explore "a religious Epcot." In the *kitsch* frame, such sites are fun to engage with, but worthy of lampooning not aspiration.

A second way to classify such sites is to attribute the status of *folk art*. This frame circulates less widely and resonates in a more specialized register. In this frame, sites like Holy Land, USA, have value because they represent the creative work of a "folk," visionary," or "outsider" artist. The preferred term varies, but the spirit remains: someone who expresses a personalized artistic vision through unpredictable media and without formal training. The subject matter is far less important than the location, the style, and the relation between the artist's work and their biography (cf. Promey 2018). *The Clarion*, published by the American Folk Art Museum, featured a profile of Holy Land, USA, soon after its peak popularity. While critical of the theology, the author praised the artistry: "I felt that I was sharing an inner-vision made real, a manifestation of a man's lifelong dream come true and it was this feeling that made me exclaim that surely this was the real thing" (Ludwig 1979: 31).

These interpretive frames work for audiences because they render sites sensible in particular ways: valued for parodic or artistic worth. These frames also perform some erasure; that is, they obscure or make invisible other forms of value. Each in their own way, *kitsch* and *folk art* extract sites from their local resonances. I concluded the opening vignette with a Boy Scout's contribution as an example of how sites are locally valued, invested in by community members and emerging from collective labor (devotional and otherwise). The following sketch of Holy Land, USA, follows this course, demonstrating the necessity of an alternative interpretive frame, one attentive to local feelings of attachment and importance for Waterbury's Holy Land.

Waterbury's Holy Land

The site eventually named Holy Land, USA, was envisioned by a man named John Greco. Born in Waterbury in 1895 to Italian immigrants, he was part of the working class, the son of a shoemaker. His family moved back to Italy for part of his youth, returning to Waterbury when he was thirteen. Born into a devout Roman Catholic family, John initially sought the priesthood before health concerns forced a change. He graduated from Yale Law School and started a practice in Waterbury. Part of the lore around Greco is his lifelong loyalty to Waterbury's poor, providing discounted or free legal help as needed. He remained a committed Catholic his entire life, and prior to starting Holy Land, he founded two Catholic evangelist organizations: one focused on street preaching and one (anticipating a culture war to come) focused on "putting Christ back into Christmas."[2] These organizations traveled outside the region and his efforts with them earned him broader recognition (in 1957, for example, he was named a Knight of Saint Gregory by Pope Pius XII). But, the local memory of Greco is centered on his enduring bond with Waterbury: born there, returned there, lived there, served there, created there, died and buried there.

1956–84

Greco was sixty-one years old when he began working on Waterbury's Holy Land. It was October 1956, and with the help of volunteers from his evangelist group they installed the first of four crosses that would stand onsite. Archival sources report varying heights, from 20 to 35 feet, though all emphasize the use of light to make the cross visible at night from the city below. A local sign maker, Ralph Giuliano, designed the cross, which included a series of neon tubes. They emitted a bright glow and were removable so that the cross' color could change with the liturgical calendar. It was a community effort, Giuliano remembers: "There was no money involved, it was all, you know, everybody chipped in."[3]

Greco's reported inspiration for creating the site also varies. In one version, he was moved by a friend's description of seeing the Mount Royal Cross on a trip through Montreal.[4] In another, Greco drew from his experience as a traveling evangelist teaching youth in the Civilian Conservation Corps, and the success of visual aids to sustain attention.[5] A third story recalls the popularity of nativity scenes that his evangelist organization created for Waterbury and other cities at Christmas time, and the idea of a permanent, more elaborate biblical representation.[6] A final version centers on landscape affinities between Pine Hill and biblical stories. Greco described it this way in one news interview: "Everything in the Bible took place on the heights and all the cities were built on the heights. The laws of Moses came on the heights, Christ preached his first sermon on a mount, and he died on a mountain. All these things took place on a hill like we have here."[7]

A lone cross on a hilltop was never the plan, and in December 1958 the first series of Greco's miniature replicas opened for public touring. Initially called Bethlehem Village, later changed to Bible Land, and finally Holy Land, USA, the replicas grew to over 200 structures. Arranged in no particular narrative sequence, and interspersed with hand-painted signs of biblical quotes, people in biblical dress, and animals mentioned in the Bible were scenes from the Hebrew Bible/Old Testament (e.g., Garden of Eden), Catholic tradition (e.g., Scala Sancta), and the New Testament (e.g., the Bethlehem Inn where Mary and Joseph were refused). One of the last additions was an exhibit donated from the Vatican Pavilion at the 1964–5 New York World's Fair.

With the exception of the Vatican Pavilion donation, Waterbury's Holy Land is a mélange of discarded materials. No single archival source lists every material used, but the following inventory emerged from reading across sources: plaster, concrete, statues of saints, pews and stained glass from churches, lumber, tin, plastic sheeting, plastic plants, marble, chicken wire, stone, brick, scrap metal, aluminum, copper, cement, radio and television cases, hand rails, soup pots, stovepipes, mannequins, tires, oil drums, window frames, bathtubs, freezers, water heaters, ashcans, and a mobile home trailer.

Kitsch and *folk art* classifications celebrate the transformation of this "motley detritus."[8] In the former it is part of the gawking, in the latter it is an integral element of a visionary art environment. Alternatively, we can understand this materiality as part of the bond between site and city. Waterbury's Holy Land was, quite literally, built from the stuff of Waterbury. Frank Davino—a friend of Greco, urban planner for the city, and longtime advocate for the site's preservation—described it this way: "A good 35 percent, maybe 40 percent or more, of all the material up there came from the houses and buildings, factories, that we tore down during the course of the urban renewal process."[9]

A taller cross was installed in 1969 and subsequent years saw the site at its tourist zenith. An August 1971 story reported 2,000 visitors a week during the summer months and a May 1974 story reported a peak of 44,000 annual visitors.[10] The site was always open eight months a year (April through December), and news reports emphasized the excited busyness of tour buses queuing to navigate the hill's ascent. These stories also emphasize the diversity of visitors: Catholic and non-Catholic, from multiple states, youth and older adults, African Americans, whites, and immigrants from various places. Remembering her first visit in 1976, historian Mary Baine Campbell (2003) recalled "Salvadoran, Filipino, and Haitian immigrants, on actual pilgrimages from New York City, Newark, and Hartford."

The first account of troubles comes in 1977. In the course of a year brush fire destroyed the Garden of Eden display, a road closure due to highway expansion confused and turned away would-be visitors, and the first of what would be many vandalism cases was reported. The number of annual visitors declined to 20,000 and Greco, then eighty-two, was increasingly unable to maintain his levels of physical care for the site.[11] By the time *The Clarion* profile was published, its author described the site as being "in virtual ruin" (Ludwig 1979: 39).

Holy Land, USA,'s decline closely parallels the economic decline of Waterbury. From the Civil War through the Second World War, Waterbury rose to industrial prominence, leading the nation in brass manufacturing (cf. Maher 2015). This attracted an ethnically diverse workforce, and the city developed a working-class culture known for immigrant enclaves. When the Second World War ended, factories attempted to maintain production levels, but commercial interests could not maintain the wartime pace. By 1950, factory jobs were being eliminated that would not come back. This coincided with automation, domestic and global relocations of labor, industry diversification (away from brass and toward metals like aluminum), and an aging infrastructure that was costly to sustain. By 1980, fewer than 5,000 factory jobs remained of the 50,000 that were available during the Second World War.

1984–2013

In April 1984, the original Holy Land, USA, was closed for the first time in its history. Greco hoped to reopen the site after making repairs, but volunteer labor was scarce and fundraising efforts yielded little. Greco died in March 1986, leaving the site without a visionary leader. In 1980, he had willed the site to a Catholic order of nuns, the Religious Teachers Filippini, who began staffing two sisters onsite in 1972. The Filippini Sisters are treated ambivalently in news stories. In some reporting, they are dedicated custodians who cared for Greco in his later years and did everything they could to help the site survive. In other cases, they are neglectful of the site and resistant to any revival plans.

After Greco's death, the replicas decayed, vandalism and theft increased, and the site developed a local reputation as being seedy. An attempt in 1988 to demolish portions of the site was halted only by a group of protesters who placed their bodies in front of bulldozers.[12] The Committee to Preserve Holy Land was formed at this time and received support from artists committed to the site's *folk art* value.[13] The Committee reported nearly 3,000 signatures in an August 1988 letter to the Museum of American Folk Art.

The rallying support of local residents and folk art advocates impeded any large-scale destruction, but did not generate the support needed for restoration. The site continued to decay and its reputation worsened, fueled by the sad event of a murdered body being stashed onsite in 1988.[14] The next renewal effort came in 2000, led by a local retired priest and backed by the Hartford Archbishop. Despite an initially optimistic tone, the effort was characterized as "failed" by 2005.[15] This was not the first time Holy Land, USA, had received support from the Archdiocese, previous Archbishops had blessed new additions created by Greco.[16] The relationship between the site and the Archdiocese is yet another case of ambivalence. While moments of legitimation occur, no financial help was provided during post-1984 fundraising campaigns and diocesan representatives would sometimes distance "the Church" from the site, saying once that it did "not reflect contemporary Christian thought."[17]

By 2008, the 1969 cross had become unstable and the Sisters organized to replace it with a third iteration. Again blessed by the archbishop, it was shorter, thinner, and lit by exterior spotlights rather than illuminated from within. The 2008 cross was widely panned by local residents. A *Republican-American* story derided the cross as "wimpy," failing "to have a presence" or make a "real statement in the environment it touches."[18] A local resident wrote a letter to the editor offering "kudos" to the story's writer "for having the guts to report what almost everyone in the Greater Waterbury [area] has been thinking."[19] Four years later the sentiment lingered. A city resident bemoaned the new cross and remembered growing up in an immigrant household near Pine Hill. Her father, a Muslim from Kosovo, loved the cross because it symbolized "religious freedom." For her, the "two toothpicks on a hill" did not have the same landmark affect: "Paris has the Eiffel Tower; London has Big Ben; New York has the Statue of Liberty; and Waterbury had the cross."[20]

The site's reputation worsened horrifically in July 2010 when a sixteen-year-old girl was raped and murdered onsite. This prompted some to call for a total razing, to transform the abandoned site into a public park.[21] This tragedy also prompted the Sisters to list the land for sale. They set the initial price at $775,000, over a million dollars less than the city's assessed value, and for two years multiple bidders came forward only to be rejected, including a $200,000 cash offer from a group organized by Frank Davino.

2013–present

In June 2013, the Sisters agreed to a sale of $350,000, with the proviso that the site be guaranteed to remain as Holy Land, USA, in perpetuity. The buyer was a private nonprofit, led by the city mayor and a local business owner. The story the mayor tells most often is that the idea traces to his 2011 election campaign. He repeatedly encountered requests from older adults to restore the cross, perhaps akin to the 2012 editorial quoted earlier.[22]

The city response was overwhelmingly positive, but did not always speak in one accord. A July 2013 editorial recommended adding symbols to represent Jewish and Muslim citizens, a multicultural suggestion that was not explored. The newly formed nonprofit did not have cash in hand but raised the funds swiftly and closed the sale in October. By all accounts it was a broadly supported effort; over 900 contributors, from 46 towns in Connecticut and five states, giving between one dollar and $100,000. By 2016, they had reported 4,500 contributors.[23]

Their first priority was to replace the 2008 cross. This fourth iteration would approximate the height of the 1969 cross and again be illuminated from within (though, with a technological upgrade, exchanging neon tubing for 5,000 LED bulbs). Like the 1956 cross, the 2013 cross designer was a Waterbury native with family ties to John Greco. Joe Pisani owns a steel fabrication company in Naugatuck and built the cross free of charge (an estimated gift of US$375,000). Pisani described it as a kind of generalized reciprocity, as it was Greco who helped his father secure citizenship free of charge. The site was dear to his family growing up, especially his mother, who he honored by placing her rosary beads in the concrete pedestal that supports the new cross.[24]

The cross was lit on December 22, 2013, a ceremony attended by 1,000 city residents. For many, the site's revival was an emotionally charged process. A priest speaking at a dedication mass for the new cross choked back tears when describing its significance: "I came back from a few tours in Vietnam. I flew into Bradley airport. My father picked me up and we came into Waterbury. I saw the cross; I was home again. The fact that it's up again in the glory that it was, is so important to the people of this city."[25] Many of the stories leading up to, and reporting on, the December lighting ceremony quoted residents who fondly recalled memories of experiencing the original Holy Land, USA, during its peak years: picking blueberries on the hillside, helping Greco care for the replicas, taking pictures onsite after First Communions and Confirmations, having Sunday picnics onsite after church, and walking the pathways in prayerful meditation.

As of December 2020, the nonprofit has not yet fully reopened the park, but in the years after the crosslighting, they have organized several events to attract people and attention. Three public masses have been held (September 2014, August 2018, and April 2019). The Hartford Archdiocese again lent its approval, with the archbishop presiding over the August 2018 mass. Two of the masses were held in honor of another Waterbury native, Father Michael McGivney, who founded the Knights of Columbus. McGivney was canonized by Pope Francis in 2020, making him the first US-born male saint. Like the revival of Holy Land, McGivney's cause is a city cause. The other major event works in a more popular register. Beginning in July 2015, the city relocated its fireworks display from its traditional site at a public park to Holy Land, USA. The same editorial writer who called for a multicultural display on Pine Hill seized this moment to remind *Republican-American* readers that this ritual is an opportunity for inclusion: "for Waterburians to get together in recognizing the site as public property, welcoming people of all religious and ethnic backgrounds."

In the *kitsch* and *folk art* frames, Holy Land, USA, is remembered primarily as the work of a lone individual (respectively, Greco as eccentric zealot or Greco as dedicated artist). This erases the fact that for both Greco and the new owners the labor of building and caretaking has always been a collective endeavor. Pisani donated the cross and numerous other hands have been at work. Land clearing and paving companies donated equipment and labor to building new roads onsite. The "Tower of Babel" is one of at least four Boy Scout contributions onsite. Another Eagle project rebuilt the base of an original statue made by Greco. "I wanted to do something that would last and contribute to Waterbury," the Scout said of his work.[26] In April 2019, a Catholic school teacher tweeted a photo of her students working together: "My 6th grade teamed up with their 1st grade buddies to paint rocks for our beautify

Holy Land Waterbury project. Middle school students will go to Holy Land tomorrow to clean." Numerous obituaries printed in the *Republican-American* after 2013 request that donations be made to "Holy Land USA Waterbury" in lieu of gifts to families.

The relationship between site and city has been reciprocal. In April 2014, the cross was illumined blue to support National Autism Awareness Month, and in October 2018 it glowed pink for National Breast Cancer Awareness Month.[27] Along with acts of publicity and solidarity, some of the site has continued to circulate. Most notably, the much maligned 2008 cross found a new home in November 2019. A local Assemblies of God church transported, cleaned, and reinstalled the cross in their parking lot.[28] While it was roundly deemed the lesser of the four crosses, it was still a piece of Waterbury's Holy Land.

June's Clippings

When John Greco was designing his initial series of miniature replicas, he traveled to Palestine for the first time. He wanted to see the sites he sought to re-create at home. Like thousands of other pilgrims before and after him, he collected landscape items (rocks and soil) and incorporated them into Bethlehem Village.[29] Creating a bond with scripture was always Greco's stated mission: "to open the Bible to the public," he would often say.[30] Like so many other sites discussed in this book, this is one framework for understanding the original Holy Land, USA—the affective intimacy produced through materializing the Bible. This chapter, though, is concerned with more than just the original Holy Land, USA. It has taken up the site's broader life course. My primary aim has been to work against the erasure of local resonance, to draw out the significance not of Holy Land, USA, as a tourist attraction, but of Waterbury's Holy Land as a localized place.

To fully apprehend Greco, we might also remember his identity as an Italian Catholic and the way his work fits within a cultural tradition of shrine creation (Sciorra 1989).

And certainly, this story of four crosses resonates with scholarship on the symbolic power of crosses to shape landscapes (Kaell 2017). As Promey (2018) observes, the cross is effective as a form of display because it draws together a general yet unambiguous proclamation of religious identity with a ubiquitous cultural penchant for publicity. In her discussion of the cross at California's

Salvation Mountain, Promey also notes that a *folk art* classification draws attention away from the site's localized history and context, secularizing it for broader appreciation and use.

Whichever frame we prefer, we must keep visible the social dynamics by which Holy Land, USA, came to symbolize local belonging. While plenty of heartfelt nostalgia is evident in the archival sources, my clearest sense of this attachment has come from my wife's grandmother, June. This chapter owes a tremendous debt to her diligence in mailing me newspaper stories about the site's restoration efforts. She would often include a short note with the clippings, expressing her hopes for the site's (and, by extension, Waterbury's) success. Attached to a February 2017 story about the new cross being vandalized with spray paint, she lamented: "one step forward, two steps back." To accompany a May 2018 story about a new road being constructed onsite, she wrote: "I wish the message was Holy Land totally restored. By bits and pieces perhaps one day that will be the message." And, she cheered in a note included with an April 2019 story about the installation of a new welcome gate: "from all indications of the frequency of articles in the Rep-Am progress is being made on the reconstruction of the park. Good news!" Voices like June's, Joe Pisani's, the many letters to the editor, and even aspects of John Greco are too easily erased by *kitsch* and *folk art* classifications. Sites like Holy Land, USA, are always also home places, bound in manifold ways to local lives.

Conclusion

This book has charted a journey through the phenomenon of materializing the Bible: how the written words of scripture are transformed into experiential, choreographed environments. Section I, "Variations on Replication," juxtaposes performances that recontextualize in some particular present elements from the (actual or imagined) biblical past. From 1:1 replicas of Moses's Tabernacle to a theatrical reenactment of the book of Job, these examples illustrate how replication accomplishes the affective work of promising experiential access to the sacred stories of scripture. Section II, "The Power of Nature," turns to the natural world associated with Christian scripture and how it is mobilized as a privileged media. Examples like biblical gardens, zoos, and cookbooks reveal an ideology of sensory indexicality, which claims a direct connection between the present and the scriptural past through experiential encounters with nature. Section III, "Choreographing Experience," examines some of the lived interactions with the affordances of materializing the Bible performances. Through processes of circulation, design, and classification, these chapters demonstrate how these performances are oriented and engineered.

Ultimately, this book demonstrates that materializing the Bible works as an authorizing practice to intensify intimacies with scripture and circulate potent ideologies. To close, I want us to revisit the leading dimension of this argument: processes of authorization. While there are many threads of connective tissue crisscrossing these twenty chapters, I consider the dynamics of materiality and authority to be the most pronounced. As a forward-looking coda, I end by identifying a direction this project seeds as an opportunity for comparative inquiry.

Materializing Authority

A key finding of this project is that people assert, challenge, and negotiate authority through their performances of materializing the Bible. Looking across these chapters and examples, I want to highlight three processes by which the authorizing work of materializing plays out. These are illustrative, not exhaustive, and I invite readers to discover other mechanisms or even to reconfigure this analysis in other terms.

Authenticity. Claims of verisimilitude are one circuit of authorizing. While the experiential promise is consistent, to access the scriptural past, the media shifts. Architectural forms, smells, tastes, landscapes, ritual, and everyday objects: all are put forward as realistic material representations. The promise of authentic biblical replication is always a thoroughly sensorial promise. The aroma of biblical flora and the spatial sense of being next to or inside a "full-scale" Noah's ark function by the same logic: realism registered through bodily encounters with technology and place.

Mobilizing authenticity in this way is often pitched as a corrective to some widespread misunderstanding, as a challenge to other authorizing agents. We see this in moments such as biblical archaeology being used to critique Western artistic representations of scriptural scenes (Chapter 6), or when a biblical garden tour is used to critique common practices of scriptural translation (Chapter 7). Materializing the Bible performances integrate these claims and challenges into their experiential frames, asking people to trust their rendering of what is real, accurate, and truthful.

The register of authenticity also shifts. In many examples, the realness at stake is about historical verisimilitude: the size and shape of a re-created Tabernacle in the Wilderness, the distance between stations on a Way of the Cross. In others, the realness is more about conjuring a particular affective experience. Some sites, like DC's Museum of the Bible, ask visitors to shift registers as they move among choreographed spaces. "The World of Jesus of Nazareth" (Chapter 6) is an imagineered rendering of the biblical past. It operates historically, drawing together live actors, mural art, sounds of nature (e.g., birdsong) and technology (e.g., house construction), and fabrications of nature (e.g. olive trees) and technology (e.g., olive press); all choreographed to conjure an experience of first-century Nazareth. Located directly adjacent on the same exhibit floor, "The Hebrew Bible Experience" (Chapter 15) is also an imagineered rendering of the biblical past, blending dozens of multimedia sensory effects. It is not, however, oriented around any kind of veracity to historical detail. The register of authenticity is more affective, organized by the design team's narrative of "a journey home."

To claim authenticity is to claim an authoritative stance. The experiential promise is about scriptural realism—historical, affective, and otherwise—but this is not really the end game. The ultimate goal is trust: not only a trust in how a particular institution, tradition, or charismatic figure renders the biblical past, but how those actors exist in the present.

Authorizing Actors. If claiming authenticity is about authority, acts of assessing and classifying authenticity are equally expressions of power. In a seminal article in the anthropology of tourism, Bruner (1994) writes: "The more fundamental question ... is not if an object or site is authentic, but rather who has the authority to authenticate" (400). This dynamic animates many materializing the Bible performances and we see diverse agents playing differing roles in this process.

Some sites exist on land owned by a denomination and are formally recognized. From the many Catholic shrine environments to the Pentecostal Fields of the Wood, these sites are authenticated by a governing Christian body. Their legitimacy is institutionalized, bound up with the social and theological history of a tradition. Other sites seek this kind of recognition, but struggle to fully obtain it. A prime example is Holy Land, USA, in Waterbury, Connecticut (Chapter 20). Since its founding in 1956, the site has been variously embraced, ignored, and overtly distanced by the regional Archdiocese. The hope of unwavering support highlights the spiritual and social capital that is at stake for local places. The reality of contingent support reflects the ambivalence that can adhere to places when they are created outside a tradition's authorizing structures.

Religious institutions are not the only ones that grant or withhold endorsement and material investment. Materializing the Bible performances can also enter the authorizing orbit of secular institutions. Several chapters (e.g., 3, 19, 20) illustrate how this can happen in the frame of assigning artistic genre and value. In other cases, national and international actors assign artistic or historical value in the frame of heritage. The example of Quebec's cyclorama of Jerusalem on the Day of the Crucifixion illustrates this work of heritagizing most clearly (Chapter 16). In being declared a place and object of national heritage by the provincial government, the cyclorama is protected from demolition, relocation, and is ensured to receive regular maintenance to minimize deterioration. As materializing the Bible performances are authorized by secular institutions, an important dynamic emerges. Artistic and heritage value can be pitched as distinct from theological and devotional value, potentially displacing public recognition of religious significance.

If religious and secular institutions play a role in authenticating materializing the Bible performances, so too do local actors. Examples like the Garden of Hope's tour guide Steve (Chapter 18) and Rev. Ruth's Drive-Thru Bible Garden (Chapter 19) draw this into sharp relief. Steve and John Ruth had different orientations to their respective sites: one a custodian, the other a maker. But, they both developed a love for their site that imbued their acts of sharing it with others. The authority to tell the stories of their places did not derive from official designation, encyclopedic knowledge, or charismatic revelation. It derived from the affective intensity of their attachments to place.

Local or international, bureaucratic or grassroots, the work of authorizing is vital for the continuation of a site. The phenomenon of materializing the Bible encompasses places of widely varying longevity. Some are centuries old (e.g., the Sacred Mount of Varallo discussed in the Introduction) while others lasted only a few years (e.g., Orlando's Bible Land discussed in Chapter 11). In Chapter 6, "Ways of Remaining," we took up the question of how the social life of materiality can extend beyond an original context. Authorizing processes further illuminate this dynamic, and they have much to say about how places are remembered and forgotten.

Interdiscursivity. Section I introduced the theme that materializing the Bible performances are interdiscursive; that is, they "fold within them" multiple genres, frames, and histories (Bartesaghi and Noy 2015: 1). This is much more than a mere fact of composition; it is a process by which performances are produced, altered, and experienced over time. In turn, interdiscursivity is another process for asserting, challenging, and negotiating authority. These chapters demonstrate how various discourses intermix, constellating together in particular contexts.

Take, for example, Fields of the Wood in Murphy, North Carolina (Chapter 12). The site originated amid a Pentecostal revival, and a spot onsite commemorates divine revelation: the very place where God spoke to A. J. Tomlinson in 1903. This charismatic discourse combines with others onsite, such as the uniquely Protestant tradition of replicating the Garden Tomb. Added to Fields in 1944, this replica ties the site to the Holy Land. Speculated to be the authentic burial site of Jesus, the Garden Tomb has served as an alternative to the Church of the Holy Sepulchre in Jerusalem since 1867. Despite all archaeological evidence against its historical veracity, the Garden Tomb has proven to be a more satisfying experience for many Protestant Holy Land travelers who favor the open-air atmosphere over the Old City church, which is densely adorned with Catholic and Eastern Orthodox sensory elements. Other sites also integrate surrogate Holy Land experiences, Protestant replica traditions, and the memorializing of divine presence, such as northern Kentucky's Garden of Hope (Chapters 10 and 18). In doing so, Fields of the Wood, Garden of Hope, and other sites demonstrate that authority is not reducible to any single founding moment, person, or institution but, rather, is an interdiscursive product that accumulates over time.

The integration of scientific and entertainment discourses in materializing the Bible is a configuration that finds diverse expression across these chapters. Chautauqua's landscape model of "biblical Palestine" (Introduction, Chapter 10), miniature models of Jerusalem (Chapter 2), biblical gardens (Chapter 7), National Geographic's "Tomb of Christ" exhibition (Chapter 17): each use science to claim authenticity, from Holy Land geography and botany to digital technologies of 3-D measurement and infrared photography. At the same time, these sites use entertainment to intensify affective attachments: from theatrical reenactment to dramatic narration, role play, sensory immersion, and VR gaming. These interdiscursive configurations of science-entertainment work in tandem to authorize, always mobilizing sensory experience to connect people to place and performance.

* * *

This book has roamed across cultural, theological, and temporal contexts. The range and richness of examples might be drawn together in multiple ways; for me, the interplay of materiality and authority is the brightest thread. Here, I have highlighted a few organizing processes by which materializing the Bible works as an authorizing practice: claiming authenticity; assessing and classifying authenticity; the interdiscursive nature of performances. Whatever other insights readers might generate about materializing the Bible from these chapters, I hope that the constant presence of asserting, challenging, and negotiating authority is foremost. Authorizing processes are always about power relations and that, ultimately, is the ambition of this book: to explore how materializing the Bible is a phenomenon defined by expressions of power.

A Future Direction

Any book worth reading generates more than it resolves. In this spirit, I want to close by seeding an area of inquiry this book's framework might be extended to. Certainly, there are still more materializing the Bible stories to tell. I think about temporary, seasonal performances that are mobilized for social engagement. Consider, for example, churches in the US southwest who lace nativity scenes at Christmas time with political commentary, placing Jesus, Mary, and Joseph in chain-link cages to critique the federal policy of family separation at the US-Mexico border.[1] I think, too, about how biblical texts and other sacred scriptures are materialized outside of Christian traditions. There are many examples to think with, such as religious replication at a Hasidic-run Jewish children's museum in Brooklyn (Fader et al. 2007); Buddhist and Hindu theme parks (Paine 2019); or, a Qur'anic botanical garden in Qatar founded in 2008.[2]

These directions are certainly worth exploring, but I want to face a different direction. I want us to think about how the conceptual repertoire of this book is useful beyond the study of particular theological traditions. Ties between materiality and authority, affective history-making, replication, sensory indexicality, choreography, circulation, design, classification, heritagizing: this constellation of interests and approaches can also be used to explore other sacred performances. The area of inquiry I highlight is not an emergent phenomenon, though it is the subject of ongoing cultural production: sacred spaces that materialize stories of African American identity, history, inequality, and flourishing amid suffering.

There are more than 300 sites in the United States focused on exhibiting or curating historical and contemporary resources in order to materialize African American lives, events, communities, and institutions.[3] Some are focused on single places or individuals, while others have a more encompassing sweep. They tell stories of enslavement, struggles for freedom, Jim Crow violence, Civil Rights victories, mass incarceration, police brutality, and the collective organizing and healing that unfolds against the backdrop of enduring structural racism and white supremacy.

Since 2000, a number of widely publicized sites have been added to prominent locations in US cities. To cite just a few examples, there is the National Underground Railroad Freedom Center, situated squarely between professional football and baseball stadiums in Cincinnati (2004); the National Center for Civil and Human Rights in downtown Atlanta, part of a tourist complex that includes the Georgia Aquarium, World of Coca-Cola, and Children's Museum (2014); the National Museum of African American History and Culture located just south of the White House on DC's Washington Mall (2016); and, planned to open in 2021 in downtown Tulsa is Greenwood Rising, centered on the 1921 massacre of several hundred Black people and razing of the Black Wall Street district.

In a comparative analysis of two African American museums, religious studies scholar Richard Newton (2020) argues that these sites "operate as sacred spaces within the complex of signifying practices [associated] with Black religion" (2). Their sacrality emerges from the histories and experiences they memorialize, but also their promised capacity to reorient visitors' consciousness. As Newton observes, they are a "social technology from which one can signify an alternative orientation to the world" (2). These sites also circulate as sacred spaces in tourist economies. I encountered an example in winter 2020, before the grinding halt of Covid-19. The Episcopal Cathedral I belonged to in Cincinnati was advertising a May trip co-led by the Cathedral dean and the president of the Union of Black Episcopalians. The itinerary for the week-long trip included ten African American museums throughout southern states, and was billed as an "American Civil Rights Pilgrimage."

Like examples of religious publicity explored here (e.g., Chapters 4, 6, 15, and 17), the newest wave of African American museums has embraced the sensory and affective techniques of the experience economy. In Newton's analysis, he observes that the relationship among body, technology, and place is vital for the design of these sites: "[they] craft sensorial experiences with the potential to haunt visitors into reckoning with the realities of Black pasts, presents, and futures" (2). Indeed, some of the same design firms whose creative labor is creating biblically themed attractions like DC's Museum of the Bible are also crafting materialities for African American museums.

This first registered for me during an interview with Alin, C&G's lead designer for the Museum of the Bible's "Impact of the Bible" exhibition (Chapter 15). We were discussing his team's strategy for mixing different "interactive" and "reactive" techniques, and I asked how the Museum of the Bible compared with other projects they had worked on. Their approach was consistent: focused on "storytelling" and "authenticity"; using digital technologies to enhance physical experience; and, creating "enough room for people to take what they want [from the exhibit]." As an analogue example, he referenced their work on Atlanta's National Center for Civil and Human Rights. Alin was pleased to hear that I had been to the Center in summer 2015, and I shared that the most memorable display for me was a re-created 1950s diner.

As a visitor, you sit on a swiveling stool in front of a lunch counter, facing a wall mural of a restaurant. You put on a pair of headphones, place your hands on a pair of sensors, and close your eyes. The headphone audio track plays a barrage of increasingly violent yells and insults that demand that you leave the diner immediately. The challenge is to keep your hands in place, and the sensors alert you when you flinch. While I managed to keep my hands in place for the duration of the recording, I opened my eyes feeling viscerally unsettled. Alin led the design of this display and cited it as a prime example of how to use a "snapshot of a moment, but not any exact moment" to materialize the broader story of "discrimination."

C&G Partners is not the only design firm whose portfolio includes different kinds of sacred space. Local Projects, another New York City-based firm, contributed to DC's National Museum of African American History and Culture and led the design of the Legacy Museum, which opened in downtown Montgomery, Alabama in 2018. This firm has also led the design for two projects planning to open in 2021: the American Bible Society's Faith and Liberty Discovery Center on Philadelphia's Independence Mall, and Tulsa's Greenwood Rising.

Observing that the same firms are choreographing biblical and race-consciousness tourism is less about the firms themselves, and more about the broader signature of the experience economy. Both forms of materializing are structured by a shared repertoire of affective ambitions and sensory techniques. Consider two examples.

Just as museums and design firms are creating headset VR experiences to re-create travel to Holy Land sites of biblical commemoration (Chapter 17), there are VR renderings of Civil Rights experiences. In early 2020, Local Projects collaborated with several media companies to debut a traveling exhibition that uses VR technology to place visitors in the crowd on August 28, 1963, to witness Martin Luther King's "I have a Dream" speech. The promised immersion integrates multiple sensory dimensions: an audio recording of the speech layered with ambient sounds, such as crowd murmurs and summer cicadas; a wireless headset to allow freedom of movement, affording visitors the ability to approach and encircle Dr. King; composite images based on photographs from the March; and, a digital replication of Dr. King based on archival video.[4]

Sites materializing African American histories also rely on sensory encounters with unique material culture items. Some are human crafted, archaeological artifacts from the slave and Jim Crow eras. Cincinnati's National Underground Railroad Freedom Center displays "The Slave Pen," an early 1800s cabin once used to detain slaves, reassembled from its original location on a Kentucky farm. DC's National Museum displays the casket of Emmett Till, whose violent lynching in 1955 followed by the acquittal of his murderers proved a powerful mobilizing force for Civil Rights activists. From his visit to Montgomery's Legacy Museum, Newton (2020) makes special mention of "a wall lined with hundreds of jars of soil, each collected from the ground where a Black person was lynched in the United States of America" (13). The latter is especially striking in light of this book's discussion of the power of nature (Chapters 7, 8, 9, and 10). Akin to interactions with Jerusalem soil, Galilee water, and Jordan rocks, there is a sensory indexicality at work where the stuff of nature generates privileged access to an affective past.

This book has explored the phenomenon of materializing the Bible. My hope is that the methodology and conceptual repertoire developed here does not end with the critical study of Christianity or scriptural religion, but inspires comparative inquiry. In the US context, I can think of no more meaningful or necessary direction to extend the analysis than to the cultural production of a different sacred: materializing the struggle for racial justice and equality. This direction, like materializing the Bible, centers on authority and is revealed through the intersection of physical forms, sensory choreographies, and curated places engineered to intensify intimacies.

Notes

Introduction

1 "Sabu Visits the Twin Cities Alone," *John Prine Live* (1988).

Chapter 1

1 The following sketch of the Jerusalem exhibit at the St. Louis World's Fair is based on primary and secondary sources. For the latter, I relied on Vogel (1993), Rubin (2000), Long (2003), Parezo and Fowler (2009), Shamir (2012), Feldman (2016), and Lindsey (2017). Primary texts included *Prospectus of The Jerusalem Exhibit Co.* (1904), "Jerusalem Reproduced at the World's Fair" (*The San Francisco Sunday Call*, 1904), "The Walled City of Jerusalem – in St. Louis" (*The Cosmopolitan Magazine*, 1904), and several articles from *The World's Fair Bulletin* (1903–4).
2 "Jerusalem Reproduced at the World's Fair" (*The San Francisco Sunday Call*, 1904).
3 *Prospectus of The Jerusalem Exhibit Co.* (1904: 10).
4 *Prospectus of The Jerusalem Exhibit Co.* (1904: 14).
5 "City of Jerusalem," *World's Fair Bulletin* (1904, August 4 (10): 35–9).
6 In addition to the twelve extant replications, the project catalogue has identified at least seven nonextant Tabernacles (six in the United States and one in Israel).
7 "Advantageous Use of Modern Tabernacle," *The Ministry* 8 (1): 7, 1935.
8 "Man's 1948 creation followed divine plan," *St. Petersburg Times* (May 9, 2001).
9 The following analysis of Tabernacle tours is based on seven group tour video-recordings from three sites: The New Holy Land Tabernacle at the Great Passion Play (Eureka Springs, Arkansas), Messiah's Mansion (based in Harrah, Oklahoma), and the Wilderness Tabernacle (Timna Park, Israel). Recording dates and sources are as follows: New Holy Land (1994, DVD originally sold at Great Passion Play gift shop and acquired by author through eBay), Messiah's Mansion (2011, 2012, 2014; YouTube), Wilderness Tabernacle (2015, 2017, 2019; YouTube).
10 "Old Testament tabernacle rises in Fountain Valley," *Orange County Register* (November 11, 2016).

11 "The Jewish Jesus in the California Desert: A Report from the Tabernacle Experience," *Interfaith Observer* (October 15, 2016). www.theinterfaithobserver.org/journal-articles/2016/9/23/a-report-from-the-tabernacle-experience (accessed: June 12, 2020).

Chapter 2

1. Not all Jerusalem miniatures have been created by Christians or for Christian devotional, evangelistic, and pedagogical purposes. For example, a well-known model premiered at Jerusalem's Holy Land hotel in 1966, fostering both mass tourism and Israeli nation-building. This 1:50 scale model depicts the city in 66 CE, a time when Jerusalem was at its "greatest geographic extent" and is remembered to be of "central importance in the Zionist ethos" (Paden 2019: 3). The model was commissioned by the hotel's owner to attract tourist-pilgrims and was designed by an archaeologist at Hebrew University. Its relocation to the Israel Museum in 2006 "greatly enhanced its status as both a national exhibit and a scientifically accurate representation" (4). This model was used as the basis for designing the floor model at Orlando's Holy Land Experience.
2. The proliferation of Jerusalem miniatures also developed alongside Victorian-era World's Fairs, beginning in 1851, which made prolific use of miniature dioramas and models (Krasniewicz 2015).
3. The following is based on a visit to the Holy Land Experience in March 2014, where I observed two Jerusalem model presentations. This analysis was supplemented by a souvenir DVD (2004), which features a fifty-six-minute explanation of the model, and two YouTube recordings of model presentations (a thirty-minute presentation from December 2018 and a twenty-minute presentation from September 2017).
4. The following is based on a field visit to the model and interview with a College staff member in March 2019, as well as audio-recordings of the model's narration made available by the College and brief discussion of the model in a written history of the College (Beckham 2009).

Chapter 3

1. This chapter is based on a series of archival materials. Books by Orlin and Irene Corey were invaluable as artistic statements and recollections from *Job*'s production and touring: *The Book of Job Drama* (1960) by Orlin, *The Mask of Reality: An Approach to Design for Theatre* (1968) by Irene, and *An Odyssey of Masquers: The Everyman Players* (1988) by Orlin. Fifteen published reviews from US newspapers

were analyzed, dating from 1959 to 1972. And, playbills and brochures from 1957, 1959, 1962, and 1971 were analyzed. I am grateful to the Western Kentucky University Libraries for providing a digitized brochure and Sandra Baird at the Georgetown Library's Special Collections for arranging access to their wonderful collection of *Job* materials.
2. *The Book of Job* tourist brochure (Pineville, Kentucky), 1962.
3. *The Book of Job*, preface to script, 1960.
4. Ibid.
5. Playbill for *the Book of Job*, 1962.
6. Ibid.
7. *The Book of Job*, preface to script, 1960.
8. "Theatre: 'Book of Job': Choric Version Seen at Christ Church," *New York Times* (February 10, 1962).
9. *An Odyssey of Masquers*, 150.
10. Ibid, 153.
11. "What Is Man? 'Book of Job' Seeks Answers," *The Tennessean* (July 31, 1960).
12. *An Odyssey of Masquers*, 152.
13. Ibid, 155.
14. *The Mask of Reality*, 14.
15. "Pilgrimage of a Play," by R.D. Judd (Dean of Graduate Education, Georgetown College), published as a preface to *the Book of Job* play script (Anchorage Press, 1960).
16. Ibid, 17.
17. Ibid, 4.
18. Ibid, 16–17.
19. "Awe-Inspiring Outdoor Drama," *Dayton Daily News* (August 17, 1969).
20. *The Book of Job*, preface to script, 1960.
21. "Theatre: 'Book of Job': Choric Version Seen at Christ Church," *New York Times* (February 10, 1962).
22. "Awe-Inspiring Outdoor Drama," *Dayton Daily News* (August 17, 1969).
23. *An Odyssey of Masquers*, 155.
24. "Awe-Inspiring Outdoor Drama," *Dayton Daily News* (August 17, 1969).
25. "The Coreys Interpret 'The Book of Job,'" *The Cincinnati Enquirer* (July 13, 1970).
26. *An Odyssey of Masquers*, 101.
27. This tension continues to figure in related forms of religious drama, such as Pentecostal praise dancers who are determined to not have their "ministry" mistaken for mere "performance" (Elisha 2017).
28. "Religious Subjects as Matter for Dramatic Treatment," *New York Times* (December 16, 1906).
29. Flyer, "The Speech Department and 'The Maskrafters' of Georgetown College Present 'Job,' a religious drama of the Holy Bible" (1952).

30 *The Book of Job,* preface to script, 1960.
31 *An Odyssey of Masquers,* 3.
32 Ibid, 235.
33 Ibid, 2.
34 Ibid, 55.
35 Ibid, 158.
36 "'Outdoor Drama' Is Different," *The Cincinnati Enquirer* (August 1, 1971).
37 "'Job' Well Received by British Baptists," source unknown. Documented dated 1958, Georgetown College Library archives.

Chapter 4

1 This chapter is based on forty-three months of fieldwork with the creative team who led the design of Ark Encounter (October 2011–June 2014). The primary forms of data collection were observing and interviewing team members while they worked at their cubicles and recording team meetings. When possible, I would audio-record informal interviews with the artists. Each artist's cubicle was filled with concept art and other forms of material culture tied to their creative labor, which served as ideal elicitation devices. I relied heavily on fieldwork photography (with a cache of more than 750 jpeg images) and audio-recorded semi-structured interviews with each team member. All quotations come from field notes and interviews with team members, unless otherwise noted.
2 Source: arkencounter.com/blog/2017/11/02/interviewing-noah-then-and-now/ (accessed: August 4, 2020)
3 Source: dev.johngrooters.com/projects/noah-interview (accessed: August 4, 2020)
4 Source: ncse.ngo/kentucky-gets-ark-shaped-second-creation-museum (accessed: August 4, 2020)

Chapter 5

1 The following is based on a *c.* 1975 guidebook for the Grotto of the Redemption and a 1946 radio interview with P. M. Dobberstein (source: www.westbendgrotto.com/history/; accessed February 18, 2019).
2 This portrait is based on the following data sources: author interview with Randy Hofman (November 7, 2017); a ninety-seven-minute DVD, *Biblical Sand Sculptures*; and three periodical profiles sent to the author by the artist (*Clubhouse* by Focus on the Family, July 2004; *Shore Living Magazine,* December 2006; *Charisma,* December 2008).

3 The following is based on a thirty-six-minute tour of the attraction posted on YouTube in April 2015, as well as analysis of denominational promotional materials about the temple. The tour is conducted by a trained docent, Miguel, who is dressed as a Tabernacle "High Priest." Narrated in Portuguese, complemented by English subtitles, Miguel leads an interviewer on a guided tour of the grounds, intermixed with dramatic action filming and documentary footage.

4 The UCKG was founded in 1977. Its origins trace to an outdoor worship gathering in Rio de Janeiro led by Edir Macedo, a local man who had converted to Pentecostalism through a Canadian missionary working in Brazil, and who continues to serve as the denomination's head "Bishop." Today, the UCKG claims 5,000 churches throughout Brazil and a presence in 96 countries. As neo-Pentecostals, the UCKG fosters ritual and theological structures common among prosperity churches, such as divine healing and positive confession (Coleman 2000).

Chapter 6

1 Source: https://www.colliertownship.net/188/Neville-Woods---Bible-Walk (accessed: May 25, 2020).

2 This sketch of Bible Walk is based on a semi-structured interview with Bill Warren conducted by the author in November 2017, written communication with Bill, and several texts: "Woodland Retreat Advances on Collier" (*The Pittsburgh Press*, August 23, 1979); "Bible Park Pits Couple Against Collier" (*The Pittsburgh Press*, December 24, 1980); "Dispute on Bible path is raising holy furor" (*Pittsburgh Post-Gazette*, August 28, 1980); and a filed legal brief, "Warren et Ux v. Collier Twp. Bd. Of Comrs" (1981).

3 Source: https://www.biblewalk.us/contact/ (accessed: May 25, 2020).

4 Personal communication with Pastor Tom Klusmeyer (January 2020).

5 Source: https://collections.mcq.org/mosaiques/sosies-de-cire (accessed: May 25, 2020).

6 1970 brochure, "Christus Gardens" (author's collection).

7 Author's visit to Holy Land Experience (March 2014).

8 "Man's 1948 creation followed divine plan," *St. Petersburg Times* (May 9, 2001).

9 This analysis is grounded in several data sources. (1) Four visits to MOTB between November 2017 and January 2020, each of which included observing and photographing *Nazareth*. (2) Semi-structured interviews with two members of the *Nazareth* design team, the art director and a sculptor. (3) Detailed guidebooks for MOTB and *Nazareth Village*. (4) YouTube videos of footage inside *Nazareth*, including promotional items produced professionally by or in conjunction with the museum and amateur footage recorded by visitors.

10 For example, https://blooloop.com/link/worlds-technologically-advanced-museum-42m-high-tech-experience-bible-museum/ (accessed: May 22, 2020).
11 For example, the song "Jesus Was a Carpenter," written by Christopher Wren and released by Johnny Cash on his 1970 album, *Hello, I'm Johnny Cash*.
12 Source: www.youtube.com/watch?v=yB7dqyCxeco&t=980s (accessed: May 22, 2020).

Chapter 7

1 "The Months in Palestine," *Sunday School Journal for Teachers and Young People* (February 1871, Vol. III, No. 2, 37) (author's collection).
2 This chapter's analysis is grounded in four data sources collected between May 2015 and April 2017. (1) I toured and photographed eighteen biblical gardens (primarily in the United States, but also in Israel and Croatia). Four visits were guided by garden caretakers and most included detailed guiding pamphlets. (2) I corresponded via email with garden founders and caretakers in the United States, England, Ireland, Germany, and Australia; several of whom sent me detailed garden guides and histories. (3) I maintain a comprehensive database of gardens worldwide and have assembled a rich corpus of materials from online sources: garden mission statements, event calendars, photo galleries, guidebooks, maps, blogs, promotional videos, virtual tours, histories, annual reports, and strategic plans. (4) The project's material archive includes diverse items related to the theme of biblical flora. This chapter focuses only on Christian biblical gardens ($N = 148$ extant globally) and does not include Jewish biblical gardens ($N = 34$ extant globally).
3 Source: *The San Bernardino County Sun*, July 19, 1937.
4 Source: "Carmel Biblical Garden: A Planting Historically Forty Centuries Old," *Sunset Magazine* (January 1941) (author's collection).
5 There are more than fifty gardens in both the United States and Germany. The remaining gardens are in Australia, Austria, Canada, Croatia, Denmark, England, France, Hungary, Ireland, Israel, Italy, Japan, Kenya, Malta, the Netherlands, New Zealand, Poland, Portugal, Russia, Scotland, Switzerland, Ukraine, and Wales.
6 Source: "Biblical Garden in Myczkowce," published by the Caritas Centre of Recreation and Rehabilitation (2014). (author's collection, contributed by Zofia Wlodarczyk).
7 Source: Canberra Bible Garden guidebook. (author's collection, contributed by Yeng Cheng-Chang).
8 Source: email communication between founder and author (July 2016).
9 Source: http://noankbaptistchurch.org/meeting-house-history/ (accessed: May 21, 2020).

10 The Section II introductory essay defines "sensory indexicality" as a process in which the sensorium is used to claim a direct, unmediated connection between humans and nature, undisturbed by time, history, or culture.
11 Source: https://www.youtube.com/watch?v=1bV-UGdOu0I (accessed: May 21, 2020).

Chapter 8

1 Quotations are from Creation Museum signage as it appeared in June 2013.
2 For example: biblicalisraeltours.com/2016/01/migrating-birds-in-israel/ (accessed: June 27, 2020). See also: Christian Broadcasting Network's 2013 report on an annual Holy Land birdwatching festival in northern Israel: www.youtube.com/watch?v=zT16axhScM0 (accessed: June 27, 2020).
3 Source: gfm.intervarsity.org/resources/birdwatching-prayer (accessed: June 27, 2020).
4 The Creation Kingdom Zoo (Gate City, Virginia) was founded in 2010. Noah's Ark Zoo Farm (Bristol, England) was founded in 1998. The Living Torah Museum (Brooklyn, New York) was founded in 2002. And, the Biblical Museum of Natural History (Beit Shemesh, Israel) was founded in 2014.
5 The following analysis of the Jerusalem Biblical Zoo-turned-Tisch Family Zoological Gardens is based on several sources: newspaper and periodical stories and reviews of the zoo published between 1953 and 2011; an illustrated children's book, *The Biblical Zoo: The Story of a Very Special Zoo in the Land of the Bible* (1960); "Noah's Journey," a virtual tour on CD-ROM (*c.* 2000) produced by the zoo; and, Braverman (2013).
6 "The Biblical Zoo in Jerusalem," *New Scientist* (November 16, 1961), 431.
7 Susan R. Nevil, *The Biblical Zoo: The Story of a Very Special Zoo in the Land of the Bible* (1960), 2.
8 "The Biblical Zoo," *Negro History Bulletin* 25(6): 135.
9 "Visit animals of Noah's Ark," *Chicago Tribune* (February 18, 1973).
10 "Jerusalem's Modern Ark," *New York Times* (March 6, 1983).
11 "Isaiah's biblical zoo," *The Sunday Times* (December 4, 1977).
12 "Jerusalem's Modern Ark," *New York Times* (March 6, 1983).
13 "Jerusalem's Modern Ark," *New York Times* (March 6, 1983).
14 "Israel to get squirrels," *New York Times* (July 25, 1958).
15 See, for example, the zoo's discussion of the deer in their conservation program: www.jerusalemzoo.org/persian-fallow-deer (accessed: June 28, 2020). See also, "How Bambi Met James Bond to Save Israel's 'Extinct' Deer," *The Wall Street Journal* (February 1, 2010), and a scientific article about the project published in the journal *Conservation Biology* (Zidon et al. 2009).

16 Two long time Israeli tour guides, who have also written prolifically about Christian Holy Land pilgrimage, confirmed that tour itineraries rarely include the zoo (personal communication with Jackie Feldman and Amos Ron, June 24, 2020).

Chapter 9

1 This mission statement is printed on the site's circulating materials and stenciled on a wall inside the building's main entrance. The description here is based on the author's site visit and informal interview with a docent in May 2015. In addition, the project archive includes a review of the site in the periodical *Biblical Archaeology Review* (November/December 2008) and a recorded tour of the meal room performed by the site's founder in 2012 with a fundamentalist television program *Christ in Prophecy* (source: www.youtube.com/watch?v=BFC-00cjUgs—accessed: May 4, 2020).
2 The Section II introductory essay defines "sensory indexicality" as a process in which the sensorium is used to claim a direct, unmediated connection between humans and nature, undisturbed by time, history, or culture.
3 This database of biblical cookbooks was completed in May 2020. The list results from searching Amazon and eBay for a series of related terms (e.g., "biblical foods," "biblical meal"). The project archive includes copies of the five books analyzed here, first published respectively in 1958, 1971, 1976, 1981, and 1998.
4 Source: www.npr.org/sections/thesalt/2020/02/06/803186316/dates-like-jesus-ate-scientists-revive-ancient-trees-from-2-000-year-old-seeds (accessed: May 9, 2020).
5 Source: www.youtube.com/watch?v=WfwkAQsAKeU (accessed: May 9, 2020).
6 Source: gazette.com/life/is-a-biblical-food-the-next-foodie-fad-this-chef/article_a6a97bb6-9b16-11e8-8d53-672e5cb2c90f.html (accessed: May 9, 2020). See also, "Manna from a museum" (Foodie and the Beast podcast interview with Chef Todd Gray, March 25, 2018).

Chapter 10

1 'Come Ye, Who "Are Heavily Laden."' *The Cincinnati Post*, May 10, 1956.
2 "Chapel of Dreams" (Television-Radio reviews). *The Billboard*, May 5, 1951.
3 Oral history interview with Samuel Mattar; Cincinnati, Ohio (April 2018).
4 This practice of extracting nature is not unique to Christians or the Holy Land. Jewish travelers have done much the same (Kirshenblatt-Gimblett 1998: 5), and pilgrims to other sacred sites regularly ritualize landscape fragments (e.g., Hendricksen 2017).

5 As Hazard (2013) and Bialecki (2014) observe, this framework intersects with the work of many scholars across disciplines. Their bibliographies are excellent places to begin exploring new materialism, as is Coole and Frost (2010).

Chapter 11

1 The fifty brochures analyzed here represent twenty-seven different sites, six of which are nonextant. Per decade, the dates of production in the sample are composed as follows: 1920s (1); 1950s (3); 1960s (9); 1970s (9); 1980s (5); 1990s: (2); 2000s (3); 2010s (18).

Chapter 12

1 This inscribed postcard is part of the project archive. I acquired it through eBay in May 2018.
2 This chapter is grounded in an analysis of physical cards collected as part of the project's print archive. The analysis included 302 postcard views (including 12 souvenir postcard folders with multiple views), produced between 1910 and 2019, and representing forty-eight different sites of religious tourism-pilgrimage. Nine of the cards were inscribed with messages. Cards were purchased from eBay, antique malls, tourist gift shops, and donated by research interviewees. Following Jaworski (2012) and Gillen (2013), the analysis was multimodal, focusing on image-text interactions.
3 This brief history of the postcard is drawn primarily from Woody (1998), Smith (2001), Gillen (2013), and Meikle (2015).
4 This portrait of Fields of the Wood is based on the author's visit in May 2015.

Chapter 13

1 This chapter is grounded in an analysis of 500 self-poses at MOTB posted to Instagram between July and September 2019. The images came from 263 different accounts. Rather than work toward a fixed N, I followed the saturation principle: I stopped when distinct patterns emerged and further data only confirmed those patterns, ceasing to produce new insights. The results at 350 images continued at 400 and still at 500. I located images using the MOTB geotag (cf. Porter 2019). MOTB's Instagram account was minimally useful because it primarily posts promotional images and only periodically reposts self-poses. Hashtag searching

seemed promising, but an unwieldy range of hashtags are used for MOTB onsite posts and several common tags (e.g., #museumofthebible) are also used for offsite images. Using the Instagram geotag reflects a distinctive media practice: Instagram posts are thirty-one times more likely than Tweets to include geotag data (Laestadius 2017).

2   These superlatives are drawn from sixty news and opinion articles reviewing MOTB, dating to one month before, and two months after, its opening. Articles were published by diverse venues, from major commercial and public media organizations (e.g., *PBS*) to leading newspapers and periodicals (e.g., *The Atlantic*), and niche outlets (e.g., Catholic, Jewish, LDS, and evangelical forums).

3   A 2019 Themed Entertainment Association award for "outstanding achievement—museum exhibit." And, a 2018 Gold Award from the Experience Design and Technology awards for "Best Museum Environment."

Chapter 14

1   One 1933 Way of the Cross Dial is part of the project archive. I acquired the item on eBay in August 2017.

2   The traditional stations are as follows: (1) Jesus is condemned by Pilate; (2) Jesus accepts His cross; (3) Jesus falls the first time; (4) Jesus meets his mother Mary; (5) Simon of Cyrene helps Jesus carry the cross; (6) Veronica offers a veil to Jesus; (7) Jesus falls a second time; (8) Jesus meets "the daughters of Jerusalem"; (9) Jesus falls a final time; (10) Jesus is stripped of his garments; (11) Jesus is nailed to the cross; (12) Jesus dies on the cross; (13) Jesus is taken from the cross and held by his mother; (14) Jesus is laid in the Sepulchre. In 1991, Pope John Paul II introduced an alternative "scriptural" way of the cross, which re-narrates the journey focusing only on biblical references. It begins with Jesus's prayer in the Garden of Gethsemane the night before his crucifixion.

3   Author's collection.

4   Author's collection.

5   Author's collection.

6   Source: sites.google.com/site/stjosephbrooklynmi/stations-of-the-cross (accessed: April 18, 2020).

7   The shrine history presented here is drawn primarily from two sources. First, a nearly one hour interview with Frank and Shirley Schilling on an Alabama Catholic TV program in October 2010: shrineofchristspassion.org/gallery/ (accessed: April 19, 2020). Second, a DVD sold in the shrine gift shop, *The Making of The Shrine of Christ's Passion* (16 minutes, 2012; author's collection).

8   *The Making of The Shrine of Christ's Passion* (DVD, 16 minutes, 2012).

9 I analyzed over 600 posts from over 500 different Instagram accounts dating between April 2020 and April 2011. For more on this methodology, see Chapter 13.
10 Semi-structured interview conducted by the author with the artist; April 24, 2020.
11 *The Making of The Shrine of Christ's Passion* (DVD, 16 minutes, 2012).

Chapter 15

1 Source: www.teaconnect.org/index.cfm (accessed: July 26, 2020).
2 Source: www.youtube.com/watch?v=4BKeBOw84CQ (accessed: July 26, 2020).
3 Source: Interview with Lauren McAfee Green and Michael McAfee (Christian Thinkers Society, March 28, 2016).
4 Source: www.teaconnect.org/Thea-Awards/Past-Awards/index.cfm?id=8335&redirect=y (accessed: July 28, 2020).
5 This portrait is a composite based on three data sources: a seventy-five-minute interview with the author in October 2018; a seventeen-minute podcast interview, "Telling an Authentic Story" (Confessions of a Marketer, October 2018); and, a seventeen-minute presentation, "Creating the Inclusive Museum through Storytelling" at the MuseumNext conference (Indianapolis, Indiana, September 2016).

Chapter 16

1 This chapter is based primarily on archival and textual data from the project's collection and accessed through public domain sources online.
2 "The Cyclorama, Jerusalem at the Time of the Crucifixion," *South Australian Chronicle* (December 6, 1890).
3 *The Repertory of Arts and Manufactures: consisting of original communications, specifications of patent inventions, and selections of useful practical papers from the transactions of the philosophical societies of all nations, &c. &c.*, Vol. IV., 1794.
4 See Altick (1978), Hyde (1988), Colligan (2002), Comment (1999), Davis (1996), Oetterman (1997), Wharton (2006), and Griffiths (2008).
5 "Survey of the chief persons and other important objects in the Panorama representing the Lord Jesus Christ's crucifixion on Golgotha" (1886).
6 "Fishburn v. Hollingshead," in *The Law Times Reports of Cases Decided* (1891). Digitized copy of original accessed courtesy of Ohio State University libraries (March 19, 2020).
7 Digitized copy of original accessed from National Library of Scotland online (March 19, 2020).

8. "Fishburn Brothers v. Adelaide Cyclorama Company Limited," in *The South Australian Law Reports* (1892). Digitized copy of original accessed courtesy of Stanford University libraries. (March 19, 2020).
9. "Art Notes," *The Critic: A Weekly Review of Literature and the Arts* (June 23, 1888).
10. "Jerusalem the Day of the Crucifixion," *Chicago Daily Tribune* (September 7, 1887).
11. Quoted in "A Buffalo Survivor: The Cyclorama Building," *The Buffalo News* (May 25, 2018).
12. For example, a *c.* 1900 guidebook, *c.* 1940 picture book, *c.* 1950 postcard folder, *c.* 1970 brochure, and *c.* 1975 souvenir book from the Quebec cyclorama all mistakenly attribute this version to Piglhein (materials in author's collection).
13. "Chicago's Great Painting!" *The Current: Politics, Literature, Science and Art* (December 10, 1887).
14. "Cyclorama-Jerusalem," *Sydney Morning Herald* (1895).
15. Fehr includes a description for each of his projects on his professional website: www.moritzfehr.de/jerusalem_panorama.html (accessed: March 20, 2020).
16. "Cyclorama of Jerusalem on the Day of the Crucifixion: The Grandest Permanent Exhibition of the Nineteenth Century," 1900 (author's collection).
17. The Cyclorama of Sainte-Anne-de-Beaupré: an international treasure in danger. *1895: Review of the French Research Association on the History of Cinema* 83: 259–61.
18. "The Cyclorama of Jerusalem will be a heritage asset," *Le Soleil* (August 7, 2019).

Chapter 17

1. Author interview with Gary Crossland, October 2018.
2. Source: amusementtoday.com/falcons-creative-group-realizes-high-tech-nat-geo-d-c-exhibit/ (accessed: April 8, 2020).
3. Ibid.
4. Source: www.museumnext.com/article/how-museums-are-using-virtual-reality/ (accessed: April 9, 2020).

Chapter 18

1. This chapter is based on ethnographic, archival, and oral history data collected over sixteen months in 2017–18. I conducted informal and semi-structured interviews with site custodians and guides, and participant observation work with eleven tour groups. This included apprenticing as a guide and assisting with guiding four groups. Archival materials were analyzed from the Cincinnati Public Library, the Kenton

County Public Library, Northern Kentucky University, and the Garden of Hope. Claire Vaughn, an undergraduate research assistant, contributed to the ethnographic data collection, and our conversations about the Garden have been formative for this analysis. This chapter centers on the site's primary guide, Steve, and all quoting comes from a life history interview with Steve, field notes, and video recordings of tour performances.

Chapter 19

1. This chapter is grounded in four sources. (1) A fifty-six-minute video tour of the Drive-Thru Bible Garden, led by John Ruth. "Video of Reverend John Ruth at Bible Park, Woodville, Georgia, 1988 April 26." Georgia Folklore Collection, Walter J. Brown Media Archives and Peabody Awards Collection, University of Georgia Libraries, Athens, Georgia. (2) An oral history interview with Art Rosenbaum, who filmed the 1988 footage (June 19, 2020). (3) A short chapter on John Ruth and his Garden in *Light of the Spirit: Portraits of Southern Outsider Artists* (Goekjian and Peacock 1998). (4) Photographs of the Bible Garden by: Jim Linderman (personal blog); Robert Foster (SPACES website); and Karekin Goekjian (High Museum of Art website).
2. This text represents a transcription from the 1988 tour footage. Unfortunately, three lines at the end of the poem are not visible and are represented here by ". . . ."

Chapter 20

1. This chapter is informed by our visit in December 2015, though the analysis focuses largely on archival materials. I examined forty-five news stories and twelve letters to the editor from the *Republican-American* (2008–19), thirty-seven news stories and one letter to the editor from regional (e.g., *Hartford Courant*) and national (e.g., *New York Times*) outlets, 1960–2018. The project archive for Holy Land, USA, includes additional materials (e.g., visitor guidebooks). I am especially grateful to June Williams for her diligence in sending me Holy Land-related *Republican-American* stories.
2. Silas Bronson Library (Waterbury, Connecticut) "Hall of Fame" biography.
3. Interview with Ralph Giuliano for "HolyLand," a twenty-minute promotional video produced for the nonprofit Holy Land USA – Waterbury founded in 2013. Source: vimeo.com/user3158424/review/92159554/359198587b (accessed January 4, 2020).
4. "Lawyer Builds 12-acre Holy Land replica in Connecticut," *The Boston Globe*, October 13, 1975.

5. "'Holy Land' Draws 44,000 to Waterbury," *The Hartford Courant*, May 18, 1974.
6. "A Pilgrimage to Waterbury: where a lighted cross stood sentinel over a miniature Holy Land," *Connecticut Explored*, Summer 2008.
7. "17-acre 'Holy Land' in Waterbury Nearly Finished," *The New York Times*, March 4, 1974.
8. "Connecticut Holy Land Seeks Help," *The Boston Globe*, October 14, 1986.
9. Oral history interview with Frank Davino, August 5, 2013. Source: frankdavino.com/tag/holy-land-usa/ (accessed January 4, 2020).
10. "Waterbury 'Holy Land' Draws Crowds," *The Catholic Transcript*, August 13, 1971; "'Holy Land' Draws 44,000 to Waterbury," *The Hartford Courant*, May 18, 1974.
11. "Miniature Holy Land Undergoes Ordeal," *The New York Times*, August 20, 1977.
12. "7 protest demolition of 'Holy Land' park," *The Journal News*, July 10, 1988.
13. "Kitsch Crusade: Artists Rally for Holy Land," *The New York Times*, August 5, 1988.
14. "At Waterbury's Holy Land, a dream falls into decay," *The Hartford Courant*, September 28, 1988.
15. "A Hilltop Landmark Undergoes a Revival," *The New York Times*, November 4, 2001; "Some Still Hope to Revive Holy Land USA," *The Hartford Courant*, August 26, 2005.
16. "New Holy Land Exhibits are Dedicated," *The Catholic Transcript*, December 16, 1976.
17. "Work at Holy Land a concern to defenders of complex," *The Hartford Courant*, February 21, 1990.
18. "New Holy Land cross fails to live up to site's potential," *Republican-American*, September 1, 2008.
19. "Holy Land's new cross completely underwhelming," *Republican-American*, September 5, 2008.
20. "Some in Waterbury still miss seeing the lighted cross," *Republican-American*, August 13, 2012.
21. "Bulldoze Holy Land to make way for park," *Republican-American*, August 9, 2010.
22. "Resurrecting Holy Land," *The New Journal: The Magazine about Yale and New Haven*, November 18, 2016.
23. Ibid.
24. "2014 Newsmaker: Joe Pisani, Naugatuck businessman," *Republican-American*, January 2, 2015.
25. Source: Holy Land USA—Waterbury promotional video: vimeo.com/user3158424/review/92159554/359198587b (accessed January 4, 2020).
26. "Resurrecting Holy Land," *Republican-American*, August 23, 2015.
27. "'Light It Blue' for Autism Awareness," *The Waterbury Observer*, March 26, 2014; "Holy Land cross to glow pink," *Republican-American*, October 19, 2018.
28. "Rising Up," *Republican-American*, November 14, 2019.

29 "A Pilgrimage to Waterbury: where a lighted cross stood sentinel over a miniature Holy Land," *Connecticut Explored,* Summer 2008.
30 "Waterbury 'Holy Land' Draws Crowds," *The Catholic Transcript,* August 13, 1971.

Conclusion

1 Source: hyperallergic.com/532228/a-church-nativity-scene-makes-a-statement-about-border-detentions/ (accessed: December 29, 2020).
2 Source: qbg.org.qa/ (accessed: December 29, 2020).
3 Source: blackmuseums.org/directory/ (accessed: December 29, 2020).
4 "This Virtual Reality Exhibit Brings Martin Luther King Jr.'s 'I Have a Dream' Speech to Life." *Smithsonian Magazine* (February 20, 2020). Source: https://www.smithsonianmag.com/smart-news/virtual-reality-exhibit-brings-martin-luther-king-jrs-iconic-i-have-dream-speech-life-180974232/ (accessed: December 30, 2020).

Bibliography

Selected Primary References

Anderson, Joan Wester (1992) *Where Angels Walk: True Stories of Heavenly Visitors*. Sea Cliff, NY: Barton and Brett.

Beard, Frank (1908) *Bible Symbols, or The Bible in Pictures*. Oakland: The Smithsonian Co. Publishers.

Beckham, Christopher (2009) *Born in the Heart of God: A History of Clear Creek Baptist Bible College, 1926-2008*. Nashville: Fields Publishing, Inc.

Blue, Debbie (2013) *Consider the Birds: A Provocative Guide to Birds of the Bible*. Nashville: Abingdon.

Campbell, Mary Baine (2003) "Holy Land USA: Thirteen Photographs, a Poem, and Two Excurses." *Religion & Literature* 35 (2/3): 143–71.

Citro, Joseph A. (2005) *Weird New England: Your Travel Guide to New England's Local Legends and Best Kept Secrets*. New York: Sterling.

Corey, Irene (1968) *The Mask of Reality: An Approach to Design for Theatre*. Woodstock, IL: Anchorage Press.

Corey, Irene, Orlin Corey, Ken Holamo (1988) *An Odyssey of Masquers: The Everyman Players*. New Orleans: Rivendell House.

Corey, Orlin (1960) *The Book of Job*. Anchorage, KY: The Children's Theatre Press.

Du Bois, Patterson (1896) *The Point of Contact in Teaching*. London: Sunday School Union.

Ewing, Francis (1835) *Bible Natural History: Or, a Description of the Animals, Plants, and Minerals Mentioned in the Sacred Scriptures, with Copious References and Explanation of Texts*. Philadelphia: American Sunday School Union.

Gaden, Eileen (1976) *Biblical Garden Cookery*. Chappaqua, NY: Christian Herald Books.

Goekjian, Karekin and Robert Peacock (1998) *Light of the Spirit: Portraits of Southern Outsider Artists*. Jackson: University Press of Mississippi.

Harbaugh, Henry (1854) *The Birds of the Bible*. Philadelphia: Lindsay & Blakiston.

Harris, Thaddeus Mason (1820) *Natural History of the Bible; Or, a Description of All the Quadrupeds, Birds, Fishes, Reptiles, and Insects, Trees, Plants, Flowers, Gums, and Precious Stones, Mentioned in the Sacred Scriptures*. Boston: Wells and Lilly.

Hasselquist, Fredrik (1766 [1757]) *Voyages and Travels in the Levant; in the Years 1749, 50, 51, 52. Containing Observations in Natural History, Physic, Agriculture, and Commerce: Particularly on the Holy Land, and the Natural History of the Scriptures*. London: The Royal Society.

Kauffmann, Joel 2005. *The Nazareth Jesus Knew*. Nazareth: Nazareth Village.

Kimball, Kate F. (1913) "Leaves from the Life of Bishop John H. Vincent: I. The Palestine Class – A Unique Experiment in Pedagogy in the Fifties." *The Chautauquan: A Weekly Newsmagazine* 72 (1): 273-76.

King, Eleanor Anthony (1941) *Bible Plants for American Gardens*. New York: Dover.

Larsen, Earnest (1968) *Good Old Plastic Jesus*. Liguori, MO: Liguorian Books.

Longsworth, Polly, ed. (2009) "'And Do Not Forget Emily': Confidante Abby Wood on Dickinson's Lonely Religious Rebellion." *The New England Quarterly* LXXXII (2): 335-46.

Ludwig, Allan I. (1979) "Holy Land U.S.A.: A Consideration of Naïve and Visionary Art." *The Clarion* 28-39.

McKibben, Jean and Frank McKibben (1971) *Cookbook of Foods from Bible Days*. New Kensington, PA: Whitaker Books.

Mitchell, E. C. (1887) "American Explorers in Palestine." *The Old Testament Student* 6 (7): 213-19.

Morse, Kitty (1998) *A Biblical Feast: Ancient Mediterranean Flavors for Today's Table*. Chicago: La Caravane.

Nevil, Susan R. (1960) *The Biblical Zoo: The Story of a Very Special Zoo in the Land of the Bible*. Whitefish, MT: Literary Licensing.

O'Brien, Marian Maeve (1958) *The Bible Cookbook*. St. Louis: Bethany Press.

Paley, William (2006 [1802]) *Natural Theology*. Oxford: Oxford University Press.

Parks, Mary June and Burgess Parks (1981) *Cooking for the Lord: A Nutritional Guide Based on the Scriptures*. Lexington, KY: Parks Publishers.

Parmelee, Alice (1959) *All the Birds of the Bible: Their Stories, Identification and Meaning*. New York: Harper.

Robinson, Edward (1841) *Biblical Researches in Palestine, Mount Sinai and Arabia Petraea: A Journal of Travels in the Year 1838*. Boston: Crocker and Brewster.

Sandras, Eric (2006) *Plastic Jesus: Exposing the Hollowness of Comfortable Christianity*. Colorado Springs: NavPress.

Stratton, Porter, Gene (1909) *Birds of the Bible*. Cincinnati: Jennings and Graham.

Twain, Mark (1871) *The Innocents Abroad, or The New Pilgrim's Progress*. Hartford: American Publishing Company.

Vincent, John Heyl (1861) *Little Footprints in Bible Lands; Or, Simple Lessons in Sacred History and Geography, For the Use of Palestine Classes and Sabbath Schools*. New York: Carlton & Porter.

Vincent, John Heyl (1884) "Introduction." In *Biblical Geography and History*, J. L. Hurlburt, ed. Chicago: Rand, McNally, and Company.

Wood, John Georg (1888) *Story of the Bible Animals: A Description of the Habits and Uses of Every Living Creature Mentioned in the Scriptures, with Explanation of Passages in the Old and New Testament in Which Reference Is Made to Them*. Philadelphia: Charles Foster.

Zidon, Royi, et al. (2009) "Behavioral Changes, Stress, and Survival Following Reintroduction of Persian Fallow Deer from Two Breeding Facilities." *Conservation Biology* 23 (4): 1026–35.

Secondary References

Altick, Richard D. (1978) *The Shows of London*. Cambridge, MA: Belknap Press.
Arad, Pnina (2015) "Landscape and Iconicity: *Proskynetaria* of the Holy Land from the Ottoman Period." *The Art Bulletin* 100 (4): 62–80.
Ashley, Wayne (1999) "The Stations of the Cross: Christ, Politics, and Processions on New York City's Lower East Side." In *Gods of the City*, Robert A. Orsi, ed. 341–66. Bloomington: Indiana University Press.
Bachelard, Gaston (1964 [1958]) *The Poetics of Space*. Boston: Beacon.
Badone, Ellen and Sharon R. Roseman, eds. (2004) *Intersecting Journeys: The Anthropology of Pilgrimage and Tourism*. Urbana-Champagne: University of Illinois Press.
Bahktin, Mikhail (1981 [1934]) *The Dialogic Imagination: Four Essays*. Austin: University of Texas Press.
Bandak, Andreas (2014) "Of Refrains and Rhythms in Contemporary Damascus: Urban Space and Christian-Muslim Coexistence." *Current Anthropology* 55: s248–s261.
Barry, Andrew (1998) "On Interactivity: Consumers, Citizens, and Culture." In *The Politics of Display: Museums, Science, Culture*, Sharon Macdonald, ed. 85–102. London and New York: Routledge.
Bartal, Renana (2018) "Relics of Place: Stone Fragments of the Holy Sepulchre in Eleventh-Century France." *Journal of Medieval History* 44 (4): 406–21.
Bartal, Renana, Nina Bodner, and Bianca Kuhnel (eds) (2017) *Natural Materials of the Holy Land and the Visual Translation of Place, 500–1500*. London: Routledge.
Bartesaghi, Mariaelena and Chaim Noy (2015) "Interdiscursivity." *The International Encyclopedia of Language and Social Interaction*.
Baudrillard, Jean (1994) *Simulacra and Simulation*. Ann Arbor: University of Michigan Press.
Bauman, Richard (1986) *Story, Performance, and Event: Contextual Studies of Oral Narrative*. Cambridge: Cambridge University Press.
Bauman, Richard and Charles Briggs (1992) "Genre, Intertextuality, and Social Power." *Journal of Linguistic Anthropology* 2 (2): 131–72.
Beal, Timothy K. (2005) *Roadside Religion: In Search of the Sacred, the Strange, and the Substance of Faith*. Boston: Beacon.
Beal, Timothy K. (2010) *The Rise and Fall of the Bible: The Unexpected History of an Accidental Book*. New York: Harcourt Brace.

Bell, Catherine (1992) *Ritual Theory, Ritual Practice*. New York and Oxford: Oxford University Press.

Berns, Steph (2016) "Considering the Glass Case: Material Encounters between Museums, Visitors and Religious Objects." *Journal of Material Culture* 21 (2): 153–68.

Bial, Henry (2015) *Playing God: The Bible on the Broadway Stage*. Ann Arbor: University of Michigan Press.

Bialecki, Jon (2012) "Virtual Christianity in an Age of Nominalist Anthropology." *Anthropological Theory* 12 (3): 295–319.

Bialecki, Jon (2014) "Does God Exist in Methodological Atheism? On Tanya Luhrmann's *When God Talks Back* and Bruno Latour." *Anthropology of Consciousness* 25 (1): 32–52.

Bielo, James S. (2018) *Ark Encounter: The Making of a Creationist Theme Park*. New York: NYU Press.

Bielo, James S. (2020) "Experiential Design and Religious Publicity at D.C.'s Museum of the Bible." *The Senses and Society* 15 (1): 98–113.

Blanton, Anderson (2015) *Hittin' the Prayer Bones: Materiality of Spirit in the Pentecostal South*. Chapel Hill: UNC Press.

Blanton, Anderson (2019) "The 'Point of Contact': Radio and the Transduction of Healing Prayer." In *Language and Religion*, Robert Yelle, Courtney Handman, and Christopher Lehrich, eds. 404–17. Berlin: DeGruyter.

Bodner, Neta B. (2013) *Walking to "Jerusalem" from Vienna: A Seventeenth-Century Way of the Cross*. Jerusalem: Spectrum.

Bodner, Neta B. (2015) "Earth from Jerusalem in the Pisan Camposanto." In *Between Jerusalem and Europe: Essays in Honour of Bianca Kuhnel*, H Vorholt and R Bartal, eds. 74–93. London: Brill.

Bowman, Marion (2016) "The Contended Collector: Materiality, Relationality and the Power of Things." *Material Religion* 12 (3): 384–6.

Bowman, Marion (2020) "'Rehabilitating' Pilgrimage in Scotland: Heritage, Protestant Pilgrimage, and Caledonian Caminos." *Numen* 67 (5–6): 453–82.

Boylan, Anne M. (1988) *Sunday School: The Formation of an American Institution, 1790–1880*. New Haven: Yale University Press.

Boylston, Tom (2018) *The Stranger at the Feast: Prohibition and Mediation in an Ethiopian Orthodox Christian Community*. Berkeley: University of California Press.

Braverman, Irus (2013) "Animal Frontiers: A Tale of Three Zoos in Israel/Palestine." *Cultural Critique* 85: 122–62.

Bruner, Edward M. (1994) "Abraham Lincoln as Authentic Reproduction: A Critique of Postmodernism." *American Anthropologist* 96 (2): 397–415.

Bryman, Alan (1999) "The Disneyization of Society." *The Sociological Review* 47 (1): 25–47.

Buck, Roy C. (1977) "The Ubiquitous Tourist Brochure: Explorations in Its Intended and Unintended Use." *Annals of Tourism Research* 4 (4): 195–207.

Butler, Ella (2010) "God Is in the Data: Epistemologies of Knowledge at the Creation Museum." *Ethnos* 75 (3): 229–51.

Carter, Sarah Anne (2018) *Object Lessons: How Nineteenth-Century Americans Learned to Make Sense of the Material World*. New York and Oxford: Oxford University Press.

Chidester, David (2005) *Authentic Fakes: Religion and American Popular Culture*. Berkeley: University of California Press.

Cintron, Ralph (1997) *Angels' Town: Chero Ways, Gang Life, and Rhetorics of the Everyday*. Boston: Beacon.

Classen, Constance (2017) *The Museum of the Senses: Experiencing Art and Collections*. London: Bloomsbury.

Cohen, Erik (1985) "The Tourist Guide: The Origins, Structure and Dynamics of a Role." *Annals of Tourism Research* 12: 5–29.

Coleman, Simon (2000) *The Globalisation of Charismatic Christianity: Spreading the Gospel of Prosperity*. Cambridge: Cambridge University Press.

Coleman, Simon (2007) "A Tale of Two Centres? Representing Palestine to the British in the Nineteenth Century." *Mobilities* 2 (3): 331–45.

Coleman, Simon (2018) "On Praying in an Old Country: Ritual, Replication, Heritage, and Powers of Adjacency in English Cathedrals." *Religion* 49 (1): 120–41.

Coleman, Simon and John Eade (2004) "Introduction: Reframing Pilgrimage." In *Reframing Pilgrimage: Cultures in Motion*, Simon Coleman and John Eade, eds. London: Routledge.

Coleman, Simon and John Elsner (1995) *Pilgrimage: Past & Present in the World Religions*. Cambridge: Harvard University Press.

Coleman, Simon and John Elsner (2004) "Tradition as Play: Pilgrimage to 'England's Nazareth.'" *History and Anthropology* 15: 273–88.

Colligan, Mimi (2002) *Canvas Documentaries: Panoramic Entertainments in Nineteenth-Century Australia and New Zealand*. Melbourne: Melbourne University Publishing.

Colloredo-Mansfield, Rudi (2003) "Introduction: Matter Unbound." *Journal of Material Culture* 8 (3): 245–54.

Comment, Bernard (1999) *The Painted Panorama*. London: Reaktion Books.

Coole, Diana and Samantha Frost, eds. (2010) *New Materialisms: Ontology, Agency, and Politics*. Durham: Duke University Press.

Csordas, Thomas J. (1993) "Somatic Modes of Attention." *Cultural Anthropology* 8 (2): 135–56.

Dann, Graham (1996) *The Language of Tourism: A Sociolinguistic Perspective*. Boston: CAB International.

Davalos, Karen Mary (2004) "The Via Crucis in Chicago: a Reflection on/of Grace." *American Catholic Studies* 115 (2): 97–100.

Davis, John (1996a) *The Landscape of Belief: Encountering the Holy Land in Nineteenth-Century American Art and Culture*. Princeton: Princeton University Press.

Davis, Susan G. (1997) "The Theme Park: Global Industry and Cultural Form." *Media, Culture, and Society* 18 (3): 399–422.

DeConinck, Kate (2019) "Traversing Mass Tragedies: Material Religion Between the 9/11 and Newtown Memorials." *Journal of Global Catholicism* 3 (1): 126–52.

Donkin, Lucy (2017) "Earth from Elsewhere: Burial in *Terra Sancta* Beyond the Holy Land." In *Natural Materials of the Holy Land and the Visual Translation of Place, 500-1500*. Renana Bartal, Neta Bodner, and Bianca Kuhnel, eds. 109–26. London: Routledge.

Elisha, Omri (2017) "Proximations of Public Religion: Worship, Spiritual Warfare, and the Ritualization of Christian Dance." *American Anthropologist* 119 (1): 73–85.

Engelke, Matthew (2007) *A Problem of Presence: Beyond Scripture in an African Church*. Berkeley: University of California Press.

Engelke, Matthew (2010) "Religion and the Media Turn: A Review Essay." *American Ethnologist* 37 (2): 371–9.

Engelke, Matthew (2013) *God's Agents: Biblical Publicity in Contemporary England*. Berkeley: University of California Press.

Eyl, Jennifer (2019) "Anachronism as a Constituent Feature of Mythmaking at the BibleWalk Museum." In *Christian Tourist Attractions, Mythmaking, and Identity Formation*, Erin Roberts and Jennifer Eyl, eds. London: Bloomsbury.

Fader, Ayala, Henry Goldschmidt, Samuel Heilman, Barbara Kirshenblatt-Gimblett, Paul Rosenthal, and Jeffrey Shandler (2007) "Jewish Children's Museum: A Virtual Roundtable on Material Religion." *Material Religion* 3 (3): 405–28.

Farinacci, Elisa (2017) "The Israeli-Palestinian Separation Wall and the Assemblage Theory: The Case of the Weekly Rosary at the Icon of Our Lady of the Wall." *Journal of Ethnology and Folkloristics* 11 (1): 83–110.

Feldman, Jackie (2007) "Constructing a Shared Bible Land: Jewish Israeli Guiding Performances for Protestant Pilgrims." *American Ethnologist* 34 (2): 351–74.

Feldman, Jackie (2016) *A Jewish Guide in the Holy Land: How Christian Pilgrims Made Me Israeli*. Bloomington: Indiana University Press.

Feldman, Jackie and Jonathan Skinner (2018) "Tour Guides as Cultural Mediators: Performance and Positioning." *Ethnologia Europaea: Journal of European Ethnology* 48 (2): 5–13.

Feldman, Keith P. (2016) "Seeing Is Believing: U.S. Imperial Culture and the Jerusalem Exhibit of 1904." *Studies in American Jewish Literature* 35 (1): 98–118.

Fine, Elizabeth C. and Jean Haskell Speer (1985) "Tour Guide Performances and Sight Sacralization." *Annals of Tourism Research* 12: 73–95.

Flood, Finbarr Barry (2014) "Bodies and Becoming: Mimesis, Mediation, and the Ingestion of the Sacred in Christianity and Islam." In *Sensational Religion: Sensory Cultures in Material Practice*, Sally M. Promey, ed. 459–93. New Haven: Yale University Press.

Foliard, Daniel (2017) *Dislocating the Orient: British Maps and the Making of the Middle East, 1854-1921*. Chicago: University of Chicago Press.

Garriott, William and Kevin Lewis O'Neill (2008) "Who Is a Christian? Toward a Dialogic Approach in the Anthropology of Christianity." *Anthropological Theory* 8: 381–98.

Gertsman, Elina and Asa Simon Mittman (2017) "Rocks of Jerusalem: Bringing the Holy Land Home." In *Natural Materials of the Holy Land and the Visual Translation of Place, 500-1500*. Renana Bartal, Neta Bodner, and Bianca Kuhnel, eds. 157–71. London: Routledge.

Gibson, James J. (1977) "The Theory of Affordances." In *Perceiving, Acting, and Knowing*, R. Shaw and J. Bransford, eds. 67–82. Lawrence: Erlbaum.

Gillen, Julia (2013) "Writing Edwardian Postcards." *Journal of Sociolinguistics* 17 (4): 488–521.

Gillen, Julia (2017) "The Picture Postcard at the Beginning of the Twentieth Century: Instagram, Snapchat or Selfies of an Earlier Age?" In *Literacy, Media and Technology*. B Parry, C Burrnett, and G Merchant, eds. 11–24. London: Bloomsbury.

Gillen, Julia and Nigel Hall (2010) "Edwardian Postcards: Illuminating Ordinary Writing." In *The Anthropology of Writing: Understanding Textually-Mediated Worlds*, David Barton, ed. 169–89. London: Continuum.

Giumbelli, Emerson (2018) "Religious Tourism: Analytical Routes through Multiple Meanings." *Religion and Society: Advances in Research* 9: 24–38.

Goffman, Erving (1956) *The Presentation of Self in Everyday Life*. New York: DoubleDay.

Goffman, Erving (1974) *Frame Analysis: An Essay on the Organization of Experience*. Cambridge: Harvard University Press.

Goh, Robbie B. H. (2017) "The Jerusalem of Jesus: Space and Pentecostal-Evangelical Branding in Orlando's Holy Land Experience and Eureka Spring's Holy Land Tour." *Culture and Religion: An Interdisciplinary Journal* 18 (3): 296–323.

Gonzalez, Vincent (2014) *Born-Again Digital: Exploring Evangelical Video Game Worlds*. Doctoral Dissertation. Dept. of Religious Studies. Chapel Hill, NC: University of North Carolina-Chapel Hill.

Gordon, Beverly (1986) "The Souvenir: Messenger of the Extraordinary." *Journal of Popular Culture* 20 (3): 135–46.

Grazian, David (2012) "Where the Wild Things Aren't: Exhibiting Nature in American Zoos." *The Sociological Quarterly* 53 (4): 546–65.

Griffiths, Alison (2008) *Shivers Down Your Spine: Cinema, Museums, and the Immersive View*. New York: Columbia University Press.

Gross, Rachel B. (2019) "Table Talk: American Jewish Foodways and the Study of Religion." *Religion Compass* 13 (4): 1–10.

Gundaker, Grey (1993) "Tradition and Innovation in African-American Yards." *African Arts* 26 (2): 68–96.

Gundaker, Grey (2000) "The Bible *as* and *at* a Threshold: Reading, Performance, and Blessed Space." In *African Americans and the Bible: Sacred Texts and Social Textures*, Vincent L. Wimbush, ed., 754–72. New York: Continuum.

Gundaker, Grey (2014) "Ritualized Figuration in Special African American Yards." In *Materialities of Ritual in the Black Atlantic*, Akinwumi Ogundiran and Paula Saunders, eds. 236–57. Bloomington: Indiana University Press.

Gundaker, Grey (2016) "Edenic Gardens and African Landscapes." In *Refractions of the Scriptural: Critical Orientations as Transgression*, Vincent L. Wimbush, ed., 90–106. New York: Routledge.

Gundaker, Grey and Judith McWillie (2004) *No Space Hidden: The Spirit of African American Yard Work*. Knoxville: University of Tennessee Press.

Gutjahr, Paul (2001) "American Protestant Bible Illustration from Copper Plates to Computers." In *The Visual Culture of American Religions*, David Morgan and Sally M. Promey, eds. 267–86. Berkeley: University of California Press.

Handman, Courtney (2018) "The Language of Evangelism: Christian Cultures of Circulation Beyond the Missionary Prologue." *Annual Review of Anthropology* 47: 149–65.

Handman, Courtney (2019) "The Spatiotemporal Transformations of Lutheran Airplanes." *Signs and Society* 7 (1): 68–95.

Hanks, William F. (1987) "Discourse Genres in a Theory of Practice." *American Ethnologist* 14 (4): 668–92.

Harding, Susan F. (2000) *The Book of Jerry Falwell: Fundamentalist Language and Politics*. Princeton: Princeton University Press.

Harries, John (2017) "A Stone That Feels Right in the Hand: Tactile Memory, the Abduction of Agency and Presence of the Past." *Journal of Material Culture* 22 (1): 110–30.

Hasinoff, Erin (2011) *Faith in Objects: American Missionary Expositions in the Early Twentieth Century*. New York: Palgrave.

Hazard, Sonia (2013) "The Material Turn in the Study of Religion." *Religion and Society: Advances in Research* 4: 58–78.

Hein, Hilde (2000) *The Museum in Transition: A Philosophical Perspective*. Washington and London: Smithsonian Institution Press.

Hendricksen, Brett (2017) *The Healing Power of the Santuario de Chimayo: America's Miraculous Church*. New York: NYU Press.

Hicks, Ann (2009) "Garden of Hope." In *The Encyclopedia of Northern Kentucky*, Paul A. Tenkotte and James C. Claypool, eds. Lexington: The University Press of Kentucky.

Hicks-Keeton, Jill and Cavan Concannon (2018) "'Squint Against the Grandeur!': Waiting for Jesus at the Museum of the Bible." *The Bible & Critical Theory* 14 (2): 1–16.

Hiipala, Tuomo (2014) "Linguistic and Multimodal Insights into the Tourist Brochures." *Finnish Journal of Tourism Research* 10 (2): 2–9.

Hillis, Ken and Michael Petit with Nathan Scott Epley, eds. (2006) *Everyday eBay: Culture, Collecting, and Desire*. London: Routledge.

Howes, David (2015) "Introduction to Sensory Museology." *The Senses and Society*, 9 (3): 259–67.

Hyde, Ralph (1988) *Panoramania! The Art and Entertainment of the "All-Embracing" View*. London: Refoil Publications.

Irvine, Richard D.G. (2011) "The Architecture of Stability: Monasteries and the Importance of Place in a World of Non-Places." *Etnofoor* 23 (1): 29–49.

Irvine, Richard D.G. (2018) "Our Lady of Ipswich: Devotion, Dissonance, and the Agitation of Memory at a Forgotten Pilgrimage Site." *Journal of the Royal Anthropological Institute* 24: 366–84.

Isnart, Cyril and Nathalie Cerezales (2020) "Introduction." In *The Religious Heritage Complex: Legacy, Conservation, and Christianity*, Cyril Isnart and Nathalie Cerezales, eds. 1–14. London: Bloomsbury.

Jackson, Gregory S. (2009) *The Word and Its Witness: The Spiritualization of American Realism*. Chicago: University of Chicago Press.

Jaworski, Adam (2012) "Linguistic Landscapes on Postcards: Tourist Mediation and the Sociolinguistic Communities of Contact." *Sociolinguistic Studies* 4 (3): 569–94.

Kark, Ruth (1987) "Jerusalem in New England." *Ariel: A Review of Arts and Letters in Israel* 69: 52–61.

Kaufman, Suzanne K. (2004) *Consuming Visions: Mass Culture and the Lourdes Shrine*. Ithaca: Cornell University Press.

Kaell, Hillary (2012) "Of Gifts and Grandchildren: American Holy Land Souvenirs." *Journal of Material Culture* 17 (2): 133–51.

Kaell, Hillary (2014) *Walking Where Jesus Walked: American Christians and Holy Land Pilgrimage*. New York: NYU Press.

Kaell, Hillary (2017) "Seeing the Invisible: Ambient Catholicism on the Side of the Road." *Journal of the American Academy of Religion* 85 (1): 136–67.

Kaell, Hillary (2020) *Christian Globalism at Home: Child Sponsorship in the United States*. Princeton: Princeton University Press.

Keane, Webb (2014) "Rotting Bodies: The Clash of Stances toward Materiality and Its Ethical Affordances." *Current Anthropology* 55 (s10): s312–21.

Kerby, Lauren R. (2020) *Saving History: How White Evangelicals Tour the Nation's Capital and Redeem a Christian America*. Chapel-Hill: University of North Carolina Press.

Kersel, Morag M. and Yorke M. Rowan (2012) "Cultural Heritage, Archaeology, Tourism and the Miniature in the Holy Land." *Heritage & Society* 5 (2): 199–220.

Ketchell, Aaron (2007) *Holy Hills of the Ozarks: Religion and Tourism in Branson, Missouri*. Baltimore: Johns Hopkins University Press.

Kirshenblatt-Gimblett, Barbara (1998) *Destination Culture: Tourism, Museums, and Heritage*. Berkeley: University of California Press.

Klingman, Anna (2007) *Brandscapes: Architecture in the Experience Economy*. Cambridge: MIT Press.

Koerber, Susannah K. (2004) *Signs of the Times: Context and Connection in Southern Conservative Evangelical Protestant and Midwestern Roman Catholic Grassroots Art Environments*. Doctoral dissertation, Institute of the Liberal Arts. Atlanta: Emory University.

Kopytoff, Igor (1986) "Cultural Biography of Things: Commoditization as Process." In *The Social Life of Things: Commodities in Cultural Perspective*, Arjun Appadurai, ed. Cambridge: Cambridge University Press.

Krasniewicz, Louise (2015) "Miniature Exhibits at the World's Fairs." *Miniature Collector Magazine* (July).

Laestadius, Linnea (2017) "Instagram." In *The SAGE Handbook of Social Media Research Methods*, Luke Sloan and Anabael Quan-Haase, eds. London: SAGE.

Lasansky, D. Medina (2017) "The 'Catholic Grotesque' at the Sacro Monte of Varallo: the Protestant Aversion to a Graphic Space during the Late 19th and Early 20th Centuries." *The Senses and Society* 12 (3): 317–32.

Leatherbarrow, David (1987) "The Image and Its Setting: A Study of the Sacro Monte at Varallo." *RES: Anthropology and Aesthetics* 14: 107–22.

Lindsey, Rachel McBride (2017) *A Communion of Shadows: Religion and Photography in Nineteenth-Century America*. Chapel Hill: University of North Carolina Press.

Lindquist, Benjamin (2014) "Mutable Materiality: Illustrations in Kenneth Taylor's Children's Bibles." *Material Religion* 10 (3): 316–45.

Lindquist, Benjamin (2019) "Slow Time and Sticky Media: Frank Beard's Political Cartoons, Chalk Talks, and Hieroglyphic Bibles, 18760–1905." *Winterthur Portfolio* 53 (1): 41–84.

Linenthal, Edward (1995) *Preserving Memory: The Struggle to Create America's Holocaust Museum*. New York: Columbia University Press.

Liutikas, Darius (2015) "Religious Landscape and Ecological Ethics: Pilgrimage to the Lithuanian Calvaries." *International Journal of Religious Tourism and Pilgrimage* 3 (1): 12–24.

Long, Burke O. (2000) "Lakeside at Chautauqua's Holy Land." *Journal for the Study of the Old Testament* 92: 29–53.

Long, Burke O. (2003) *Imagining the Holy Land: Maps, Models, and Fantasy Travels*. Bloomington: Indiana University Press.

Lundberg, Anita (2008) "Material Poetics of a Malay House." *The Australian Journal of Anthropology* 19 (1): 1–16.

MacCannell, Dean (1976) *The Tourist: A New Theory of the Leisure Class*. Berkeley: University of California Press.

MacWilliams, Mark W. (2002) "Virtual Pilgrimages on the Internet." *Religion* 32 (4): 315–35.

Malley, Brian (2006) "The Bible in British Folklore." *Postscripts* 2 (2–3): 241–72.

Markantes, Charles G. (2005) "The Custer Cyclorama, Revisited." *Military Images* 27 (2): 21–31.

Marwick, Alice E. (2015) "Instafame: Luxury Selfies in the Attention Economy. *Public Culture* 27 (1): 137–60.

Mathews, Jana (2015) "Theme Park Bibles: Trinity Broadcasting Network's Holy Land Experience and the Evangelical Use of the Documentary Past." *Journal of Religion and Popular Culture* 27 (2) : 89–104.

McDannell, Colleen (1995) *Material Christianity: Religion and Popular Culture in America*. New Haven, CT: Yale University Press.

Meier, Allison C. (2018) "Cycloramas: The Virtual Reality of the 19th Century." *JSTOR Daily* (December, 2018).

Meikle, Jeffrey L. (2015) *Postcard America: Curt Teich and the Imaging of a Nation, 1931–1950*. Austin: University of Texas Press.

Mellinger, Wayne Martin (1992) "Postcards from the Edge of the Color Line: Images of African Americans in Popular Culture, 1893–1917." *Symbolic Interaction* 15 (4): 413–33.

Mesaritou, Evgenia, Simon Coleman, and John Eade (2016) "Introduction: Guiding the Pilgrim." *Tourist Studies* 16: 3–22.

Messenger, Troy (1999) *Holy Leisure: Recreation and Religion in God's Square Mile*. Philadelphia: Temple University Press.

Meyer, Birgit (2008) "Powerful Pictures: Popular Christian Aesthetics in Southern Ghana." *Journal of the American Academy of Religion* 76 (1): 82–110.

Meyer, Birgit (2014) "An Author Meets Her Critics: Around Birgit Meyer's 'Mediation and the Genesis of Presence: Toward a Material Approach to Religion.'" *Religion and Society: Advances in Research* 5: 205–54.

Meyer, Birgit (2015) *Sensational Movies: Video, Vision, and Christianity in Ghana*. Berkeley: University of California Press.

Meyer, Birgit (2019) "Recycling the Christian Past: The Heritagization of Christianity and national identity in the Netherlands." In *Culture, Citizenship and Human Rights*, Rosemarie Buikema, Antoine Buyse, Antonius C.G.M. Robben, eds. 64–88. London: Routledge.

Mikula, Maja (2017) "Miniature Town Models and Memory: An Example from the European Borderlands." *Journal of Material Culture* 22 (2): 151–72.

Minchew, Kaye Lanning (2014) "Callaway Family." *New Georgia Encyclopedia* (December 29).

Mitchell, Jon P. (2020) "How Landscapes Remember." *Material Religion* 16 (4): 432–51.

Mitchell, Margaret (2019). "'It's Complicated.' 'No, It's Not.': The Museum of the Bible, Problems and Solutions." In *The Museum of the Bible: A Critical Introduction*, eds. Jill Hicks-Keeton and Cavan Concannon, 3–36. Lanham, MD: Lexington Books.

Mohan, Urmila and Jean-Pierre Warnier (2017) "Marching the Devotional Subject: the Bodily-and-Material Cultures of Religion." *Journal of Material Culture* 22 (4): 369–84.

Morgan, David (1997) *Visual Piety: A History and Theory of Popular Religious Images*. Berkeley: University of California Press.

Morgan, David (1999) *Protestants and Pictures: Religion, Visual Culture, and the Age of American Mass Production*. Oxford: Oxford University Press.

Morgan, David (2007) *The Lure of Images: A History of Religion and Visual Media in America*. London and New York: Routledge.

Morgan, David (2009) "Aura and the Inversion of Marian Pilgrimage: Fatima and Her Statues." In *Moved by Mary: The Power of Pilgrimage in the Modern World*, Anna-karina Hermkens, Willy Jansen and Catrien Notermans, eds. 49–65. London: Ashgate.

Morgan, David (2012) *The Embodied Eye: Religious Visual Culture and the Social Life of Feeling*. Berkeley: University of California Press.

Morgan, David (2013) "Religion and Media: A Critical Review of Recent Developments." *Critical Research on Religion* 1 (3): 347–56.

Morgan, David (2014) "The Ecology of Images: Seeing and the Study of Religion." *Religion and Society: Advances in Research* 5: 83–105.

Morgan, David (2016) "On the Nature of Collecting." *Material Religion* 12 (3): 375–7.

Morgan, David (2017) "Material Analysis and the Study of Religion." In *Materiality and the Study of Religion: The Stuff of the Sacred*, Tim Hutchings and Joanne McKenzie, eds. 14–32. London: Routledge.

Moss, Candida and Joel Baden (2017) *Bible Nation: The United States of Hobby Lobby*. Princeton: Princeton University Press.

Musser, Charles (1993) "Passions and the Passion Play: Theatre, Film and Religion in America, 1880–1900." *Film History* 5 (4): 419–56.

Myrvold, Kristina, ed. (2010) *The Death of Sacred Texts: Ritual Disposal and Renovation of Texts in World Religions*. London: Routledge.

Murphy, Keith M. (2016). "Design and Anthropology." *Annual Review of Anthropology* 45: 433–49.

Newton, Richard (2020) "Hallowed Haunts: The National African American Museum as Sacred Space." *Religions* 11: 1–16.

Nielsen, Marie Vejrup (2021) "Building on the Gospel: The Moravian Settlement at Christiansfeld." In *The Bible and Global Tourism*, James S. Bielo and Lieke Wijnia, eds. London: Bloomsbury.

Ochs, Elinor (2012) "Experiencing Language." *Anthropological Theory* 12 (2): 142–60.

Oetterman, Stephan (1997) *The Panorama: History of a Mass Medium*. New York: Zone Books.

Oliphant, Elayne (2015) "Beyond Blasphemy or Devotion: Art, the Secular, and Catholicism in Paris." *Journal of the Royal Anthropological Institute* 21: 352–73.

Opas, Minna and Anna Haapaleinen (2017) "Introduction: Christianity and the Limits of Materiality." In *Christianity and the Limits of Materiality*. Minna Opas and Anna Haapalainen, eds. 1–36. London: Bloomsbury.

Orsi, Robert A. (2005). *Between Heaven and Earth: The Religious Worlds People Make and the Scholars Who Study Them*. Princeton: Princeton University Press.

Ousterhout, Robert G. (1981) "The Church of Santo Stefano: A 'Jerusalem' in Bologna." *Gesta* 20 (2): 311–21.

Padan, Yael (2019) "Seeing Is Believing: Miniature and Gigantic Architectural Models of Second Temple." *Journal of Tourism and Cultural Change* 17 (1): 69–84.

Paine, Crispin (2019) *Gods and Rollercoasters: Religion in Theme Parks Worldwide*. London: Bloomsbury.

Parezo, Nancy J. and Don D. Fowler (2009) *Anthropology Goes to the Fair: The 1904 Louisiana Purchase Exposition*. Omaha: University of Nebraska Press.

Patterson, Sara M. (2016) *Middle of Nowhere: Religion, Art, and Pop Culture at Salvation Mountain*. Albuquerque: University of New Mexico Press.

Patterson, Sara M. (2020) *Pioneers in the Attic: Place and Memory Along the Mormon Trail*. New York and Oxford: Oxford University Press.

Pena, Elaine A. (2011) *Performing Piety: Making Space Sacred with the Virgin of Guadalupe*. Berkeley: University of California Press.

Pena, Elaine A. (2017) "Time to Pray: Devotional Rhythms and Space Sacralization Processes at the Mexico-US Border." *Material Religion* 13 (4): 461–81.

Plate, S. Brent, ed. (2004) *Representing Religion in World Cinema: Filmmaking, Mythmaking, Culture Making*. New York: Palgrave.

Plate, S. Brent (2012) "What the Book Arts Can Teach Us about Sacred Texts: The Aesthetic Dimension of Scripture." *Postscripts* 8 (1–2): 5–25.

Plate, S. Brent, ed. (2015) *Key Terms in Material Religion*. London: Bloomsbury.

Plate, S. Brent (2016) "'The Stations of the Cross' in London: An Interview with Aaron Rosen." *Material Religion* 12 (2): 255–7.

Plate, S. Brent (2017) *Religion and Film: Cinema and the Re-creation of the World*, 2nd edition. New York: Columbia University Press.

Porter, Sarah (2019) "The Land of Israel and Bodily Pedagogy at the Museum of the Bible." In *The Museum of the Bible: Critical Perspectives*, Jill Hicks-Keeton and Cavan Concannon, eds. 121–42. Lanham, MD: Lexington Books.

Primiano, Leonard Norman (2016) "Collecting Vernacular Religious Material Culture." *Material Religion* 12 (3): 381–3.

Promey, Sally M., ed. (2014) *Sensational Religion: Sensory Cultures in Material Practice*. New Haven: Yale University Press.

Promey, Sally M. (2018) "Testimonial Aesthetics and Public Display." *The Immanent Frame* (February 8).

Promey, Sally M. (2019) "Elijah Pierce." In *Reflections: The American Collection of the Columbus Museum of Art*, eds. Nannette V. Maciejunes and M. Melissa Wolfe, 450–61. Athens, OH: Ohio University Press.

Rakow, Katja (2017) "The Bible in the Digital Age: Negotiating the Limits of 'Bibleness' of Different Media." In *Christianity and the Limits of Materiality*, Minna Opas and Anna Haapalainen, eds., 101–21. London: Bloomsbury.

Rakow, Katja (2020a) "The Light of the World: Mediating Divine Presence through Light and Sound in a Contemporary Megachurch." *Material Religion* 16 (1): 84–107.

Rakow, Katja (2020b) "The Material Dimension of the Bible from Print to Digital Text." In *The Oxford Handbook of the Bible and American Popular Culture*. Dan W. Clanton, Jr. and Terry R. Clark, eds. 414–32. New York and Oxford: Oxford University Press.

Ron, Amos S. and Jackie Feldman (2009) "From Spots to Themed Sites – The Evolution of the Protestant Holy Land." *Journal of Heritage Tourism* 4 (3): 201–16.

Ron, Amos S. and Dallen J. Timothy (2013) "The Land of Milk and Honey: Biblical Foods, Heritage, and Holy Land Tourism." *Journal of Heritage Tourism* 8 (2–3): 234–47.

Rogan, Bjarne (2005) "An Entangled Object: The Picture Postcard as Souvenir and Collectible, Exchange and Ritual Communication." *Cultural Analysis* 4: 1–27.

Rose, Kevin Stewart (2019) "'The World Food Crisis Is Not a Fad': The *More-with-Less* Cookbook and Protestant Environmental Spirituality." *Religion and American Culture: A Journal of Interpretation* 29 (2): 216–54.

Rose, Lena 2020 "'Nazareth Village' and the Creation of the 'Holy Land' in Israel-Palestine: The Question of Evangelical 'Orthodoxy.'" *Current Anthropology* 61 (3) (online first, May).

Ross, Scott (2019) "Being Real on Fake Instagram: Likes, Images, and Media Ideologies of Value." *Journal of Linguistic Anthropology* 29 (3): 359–74.

Rubel, Nora (2015) "A 'Jewish' Joy of Cooking? How a 20th Century Cookbook Containing Frog's Legs, Snails, and Ham Became a Beloved Jewish Icon." In *The Value of the Particuar: Lessons from Judaism and the Modern Jewish Experience*, Michael Zank and Ingrid Anderson, eds. 268–97. London: Brill.

Rubin, Rehav (2000) "When Jerusalem Was Built in St. Louis: A Large-Scale Model of Jerusalem in the Louisiana Purchase Exposition 1904." *Palestine Exploration Quarterly* 132 (1): 59–70.

Rubin, Rehav (2007) "Stephan Illes and His 3d Model-Map of Jerusalem (1873)." *The Cartographic Journal* 44 (1): 1–10.

Scarles, Caroline (2004) "Mediating Landscapes: The Processes and Practices of Image Construction in Tourist Brochures of Scotland." *Tourist Studies* 4 (1): 43–67.

Schaefer, Sarah C. (2017) "Illuminating the Divine: The Magic Lantern and Religious Pedagogy in the USA, ca. 1870–1920." *Material Religion* 13 (3): 275–300.

Schmidt, Leigh Eric (2000) *Hearing Things: Religion, Illusion, and the American Enlightenment*. Cambridge: Harvard University Press.

Sciorra, Joseph (1989) "Yard Shrines and Sidewalk Altars of New York's Italian-Americans." *Perspectives in Vernacular Architecture* 3: 185–98.

Shaffer, Marguerite (2001) *See America First: Tourism and National Identity, 1880–1940*. Washington, D.C.: Smithsonian Institution Press.

Shamir, Milette (2012) "Back to the Future: The Jerusalem Exhibit at the 1904 St. Louis World's Fair." *Journal of Levantine Studies* 2 (1): 93–113.

Shankar, Shalini and Jillian R. Cavanaugh (2012) "Language and Materiality in Global Capitalism." *Annual Review of Anthropology* 41: 355–69.

Shavel, Zur (2009) "Christian Pilgrimage and Ritual Measurement in Jerusalem." *Micrologus* 19: 131–50.

Sheehan, Jonathan (2005) *The Enlightenment Bible: Translation, Scholarship, Culture*. Princeton: Princeton University Press.

Siekierski, Konrad (2018) "Faith and Fatigue in the Extreme Way of the Cross in Poland." *Religion, State, & Society* 46 (2): 108–22.

Skinner, Jonathan (2016) "Walking the Falls: Dark Tourism and the Significance of Movement on the Political Tour of the West Belfast." *Tourist Studies* 16 (1): 23–39.

Smith, Ellen (2001) "Greetings from Faith: Early-Twentieth-Century American Jewish New Year Postcards." In *The Visual Cultures of American Religions*, eds. David Morgan and Sally M. Promey, 229–48. Berkeley: University of California Press.

Sponsler, Claire (2004) *Ritual Imports: Performing Medieval Drama in America*. Ithaca: Cornell University Press.

Stausberg, Michael (2011) *Religion and Tourism: Crossroads, Destinations, and Encounters*. London: Routledge.

Stevenson, Jill (2015) "Affect, Medievalism and Temporal Drag: Oberammergau's Passion Play Event." In *The Changing World Religion Map*, Stanley D. Brunn, ed. 2491–515. New York: Springer.

Stewart, Susan (1984) *On Longing: Narratives of the Miniature, the Gigantic, the Souvenir, Collection*. Durham: Duke University Press.

Stolow, Jeremy (2012) "Introduction: Religion, Technology, and the Things in Between." In *Deus in Machina*, Jeremy Stolow, ed. 1–22. New York: Fordham University Press.

Stromberg, Peter G. (2009) *Caught in Play: How Entertainment Works on You*. Stanford: Stanford University Press.

Thurston, Herbert S.J. (1914) *The Stations of the Cross: An Account of Their History and Devotional Purpose*. London: Burns & Oates.

Timothy, Dallen J. and Daniel H. Olsen, eds. (2006) *Tourism, Religion, and Spiritual Journeys*. London: Routledge.

Toumey, Christopher (1994) *God's Own Scientists: Creationists in a Secular World*. New Brunswick, NJ: Rutgers University Press.

Turner, Victor and Edith Turner (1978) *Image and Pilgrimage in Christian Culture*. New York: Columbia University Press.

Uecker, Jeffry (2012) "Portland's Gettysburg Cyclorama: A Story of Art, Entertainment, and Memory." *Oregon Historical Quarterly* 113 (1): 36–61.

Uricchio, William (2011) "A 'Proper Point of View': The Panorama and Some of Its Early Media Iterations." *Early Popular Visual Culture* 9 (3): 225–38.

Vanolo, Alberto and Nadine Cattan (2017) "Selling Cruises: Gender and Mobility in Promotional Brochures." *Tourist Studies* 17 (4): 406–25.

Vogel, Lester (1993) *To See a Promised Land: Americans and the Holy Land in the Nineteenth Century*. State College: Penn State University Press.

Watts, James W. (2019) *How and Why Books Matter: Essays on the Social Function of Iconic Texts*. London: Equinox.

West III, Thomas J. (2019) "The Spirit Is Willing, but the Flesh Is Weak: Embodied Transcendence and Sacred Spectatorship in *The Robe* (1953)." *Material Religion* 15 (3): 347–68.

Wharton, Annabel Jane (2006) *Selling Jerusalem: Relics, Replicas, Theme Parks*. Chicago: University of Chicago Press.

Whitcomb, Andrea (2010) "Remembering the Dead Be Affecting the Living: The Case of a Miniature Model of Treblinka." In *Museum Materialities: Objects, Engagements, Interpretations*, Sandra H. Dudley, ed., 39–52. London: Routledge.

Whitcomb, Andrea (2011) "Interactivity: Thinking Beyond." In *A Companion to Museum Studies*, Sharon MacDonald, ed., 353–61. London: Wiley-Blackwell.

Wijnia, Lieke (2020) "Relocated Pilgrimage: An Artistic Via Dolorosa in the Heart of Amsterdam." *International Journal of Religious Tourism and Pilgrimage* 8 (5): 70–82.

Wijnia, Lieke (2021) "Music, Scripture and the Sacred: Negotiating the Postsecular at a Dutch Arts Festival." In *The Bible and Global Tourism*, James S. Bielo and Lieke Wijnia, eds. London: Bloomsbury.

Williams, Sara A. (n.d.) "The Way of the Cross in the Ordinary: Ethnographic Attention to the Good as Invitational Ethics." Unpublished manuscript.

Wojcik, Daniel (1996) "'Polaroids from Heaven': Photography, Folk Religion, and the Miraculous Image Tradition at a Marian Apparition Site." *Journal of American Folklore* 109: 129–48.

Wojcik, Daniel (2008) "Outsider Art, Vernacular Traditions, Trauma, and Creativity." *Western Folklore* 67 (2/3): 179–98.

Woody, Howard (1998) "International Postcards: Their History, Production, and Distribution (circa 1895 to 1915)." In *Delivering Visions: Distant Cultures in Early Postcards*. Christraud M. Geary and Virginia-Lee Webb, eds. Washington, D.C.: Smithsonian Institution Press.

Index

affect 21, 27, 36, 43, 49–50, 63, 110, 132, 149, 160, 165, 168, 171–2, 179, 227, 230, 232–3, 236
affordances 3, 44, 60–1, 65, 119, 132, 142–4, 147, 149, 154, 159, 191, 236
agency 4, 18, 63, 69, 75, 109, 114–15, 119, 190, 192, 211
American Bible Society 167, 236
American Folk Art Museum 220, 224
Anglicans 82, 92, 235
archaeology 10, 31, 33–4, 70–1, 74, 92, 99, 104, 146, 202, 230, 232, 236, 240 n.1
architecture 22, 37, 70, 108, 144, 153, 165, 176, 180, 193, 230
Ark Encounter (Kentucky) 13, 48–56, 205
assemblages 115, 120, 137
attention economy 143–4, 147
authenticity 27, 31–4, 37, 59, 69, 84, 100, 103, 109, 127, 157, 162, 170, 179, 230
authority and authorization 2, 5–6, 9–10, 12, 18, 31, 35, 52, 54, 56, 72, 75, 87, 89, 99–101, 104–5, 120, 129, 137, 149–50, 167, 169, 172, 179, 195, 202, 206, 229–33
Ave Maria Grotto (Alabama) 14, 125, 127

Bakhtin, Mikhail 124
Baptists 25, 27, 34, 40, 44, 46, 69, 85, 99, 107, 200, 209
Barker, Robert 176
Bible Walk (Ohio) 68
Bible Walk (Pennsylvania) 67–8
Bibleland (Florida) 125–6, 128, 232
biblical
    animals 22–3, 90–7, 222
    birds 92–4
    botanicals 32, 80–9, 92, 104, 112, 137, 145, 177, 193
    cookbooks 101–4
    food 22–3, 71, 76, 98–105, 193
    gardens 13, 80, 84–8, 104, 145, 193, 233
    literalism 34, 49–56, 65, 91, 97, 215–16
    sand sculptures (Maryland) 58, 62–4
    zoo 90, 94–7
Biblical Arts Center (Texas) 131
Biblical Gardens (Wisconsin) 68, 128
Biblical History Center (Georgia) 87, 98–100, 127
Billy Graham Library (North Carolina) 167
Blue, Debbie 93
Bochart, Samuel 92
book of Job (Kentucky) 38–47

Camposanto of Pisa 110
Catherwood, Frederick 176
Catholicism and Catholics 10, 12, 17, 33, 44, 59–61, 63, 67, 71, 84, 94, 101, 108, 110, 112, 119, 153–7, 160, 177–8, 182, 206, 221, 224, 226, 231–2
chalk talks 36, 63
charismatic Christians 27, 33, 59, 64, 67–8, 102, 135, 227, 232, 241 n.27, 243 n.4
Christian nationalism 49, 100, 200
Christian Zionism 33, 64
Christus Gardens (Tennessee) 69, 125, 127
Church of Santa Croce (Italy) 110
Church of Santo Stefano (Italy) 9, 157
circulation 2, 12, 15, 27, 59, 70, 76–7, 104, 109, 115, 119–20, 131, 133, 141, 147, 149, 154, 167, 200, 204, 220, 226
Clear Creek Baptist Bible College (Kentucky) 34–6
Coers, Morris 107

Colbert, Stephen   220
Corey, Irene and Orlin   39
Creation Museum (Kentucky)   90–2, 205
creationism   49–56, 90–2, 94, 100
Curt Teich Company   135–6
cyclorama   4, 14, 126, 174–84, 194, 231

devotional labor   7, 61, 63, 108, 162, 183, 209, 221
Dickinson, Emily   111–12
Disney   50, 55, 165, 168
Drive-Thru Bible Garden (Georgia)   208–16, 231
Du Bois, Patterson   113

Eastern Orthodoxy   9, 17, 22, 71, 189, 232
eBay   14, 104, 114, 123, 239 n.9, 246 n.3, 247–8
entertainment   18, 39, 50, 52, 56, 143, 149, 168, 172, 179, 233
ephemera   15, 125, 132
erasure   21, 23, 33, 36, 195, 199, 210, 216, 220, 227
Ewing, Francis   83
experience economy   168, 171–2, 235
experiential design firms   7, 71, 146, 165–6, 169–72, 180, 189, 191–2, 230, 235–6
experiential frames   6–8, 23, 39, 44, 46–7, 52, 149, 161, 169, 188, 200, 230

Faith and Liberty Discovery Center   167, 236
Fatima shrine (Portugal)   61, 157
Field Museum (Chicago)   83
Fields of the Wood (North Carolina)   14, 125, 134–8, 231–2
fire (destruction by)   114, 177–8, 223

Garden of Hope (Kentucky)   13, 106–8, 198, 200–6, 231–2
Garden Tomb (Jerusalem)   108, 135, 137, 200, 232
genre   124–5
Goffman, Erving   7, 39, 142
Gray, Todd   105
Great Passion Play (Arkansas)   25–7
Greco, John   221

Greenwood Rising (Oklahoma)   234, 236
Grotto of the Redemption (Iowa)   61–2
guidebooks   14, 32, 36, 71–2, 124, 181

Harbaugh, Henry   92
Harris, Thaddeus Mason   82, 92
Hasselquist, Fredrik   82
heritage and heritagization   6, 9, 68–70, 175, 182–4, 231
Holy Land, USA (Connecticut)   218–28, 231
Holy Land, USA (Virginia)   110
Holy Land Experience (Florida)   27, 33, 69, 167, 240 n.1

iconicity   26, 50, 64, 70, 157, 162
imagineering   50–5, 75, 171, 180, 230
indexicality   32, 53, 63–6, 72, 104, 108, 113, 146, 158, 180
infrastructure   3, 12, 16, 18, 70, 129, 131, 137, 199
Instagram   15, 140–7, 160
interactivity   167–9
interdiscursivity   18, 232–3
intertextuality   52, 55, 70–6
intimacy   2, 18, 23, 31–2, 35–6, 77–8, 81, 85, 88, 92, 95, 101, 103–5, 109, 113, 127, 133–4, 191, 199, 201, 206, 227, 237
Israel Antiquities Authority   99, 111

King, Eleanor Anthony   84
King James Bible   41, 43, 134, 145
kitsch   220

landscape   3, 5–6, 9–11, 17, 22, 31, 33, 37, 43, 60, 64, 70, 74, 108–15, 119, 138, 144–5, 157, 176, 194, 213, 215, 222, 227, 230–1, 236
Legacy Museum (Alabama)   236
liberation theology   156–7
Linneaus, Carl   82
Lourdes shrine (France)   12, 61, 133–4, 157
Lutherans   82

McKibben, Jean and Frank   102
magic lanterns   23, 137

material religion
  and language analysis 7–8
  study of 2–5, 70, 76, 119
materiality 22, 24, 43, 49, 59–65, 69–70, 135, 153, 158, 180, 219, 222
media ideology 142–3, 147
mediation 8, 70, 124, 128, 199
Mennonites 25, 69, 71–2, 102
Methodists 27, 33, 40, 81, 84
miniatures 11, 22, 25, 30–7, 64, 233
miracles 67, 110, 120, 123, 133, 202–4
missionaries 25, 128, 138, 243 n.4
Missouri Botanical Gardens (St. Louis) 83
Mormons and Mormonism 17, 27
Morris, Robert 113–14
Mount Royal Cross 222
Musee Historique Canadienne (Quebec) 69
Museum of the Bible (Washington, D.C.) 13, 66, 70–7, 105, 110, 127, 140–7, 164, 169–73, 187–8, 230, 235
museums 7, 31, 33, 125, 166–7, 172, 193, 195, 234

National Center for Civil and Human Rights (Georgia) 234–5
National Geographic Tomb of Christ Experience (Washington, D.C.) 186, 188–9, 233
National Historical and Bible History Wax Museum (Washington, D.C.) 128
National Museum of African American History and Culture (Washington, D.C.) 234, 236
National Underground Railroad Freedom Center (Ohio) 166, 234, 236
Nazareth Village (Israel) 71–3
Noah's ark 21, 24, 36, 60, 62, 91, 206, 209, 215, 230

object lesson 25, 31, 36–7, 69, 107–8, 112–13
O'Brien, Marian Maeve 101
orientalism 23–4, 28, 33, 36, 179
outsider art 210, 220

Palestine Park (New York) 10–11, 14, 25, 27, 81, 110, 233

Parks, Mary June and Burgess 102
Parmelee, Alice 93
participatory pedagogy 23
Pierce, Elijah 60
pilgrimage 6–7, 9–10, 23, 42, 64, 81, 94, 100, 107, 109–10, 113, 123–4, 127–8, 131, 133, 136, 145, 154, 157, 162, 171, 177–8, 182, 187, 189, 192, 194, 199, 201, 223, 235
play 35–6, 63, 75, 100, 160–1, 168, 180, 233
postcards 130–8, 142
Protestants and Holy Land 4, 23, 71–2, 74, 194

racialization 60, 132, 166, 210–11, 213, 216, 234–7
Robinson, Edward 10, 31–2
Rosenbaum, Art 212
Ruth, John 208–16

Sacred Mount of Varallo (Italy) 9–10, 157, 232
Saint-Anne-de-Beaupre shrine (Quebec) 122–3, 126, 157, 178
St. John Paul II National Shrine (Washington, D.C.) 167
Salvation Mountain (California) 228
Sandtner, Jacob 31
santa casa 10
scala santa 10, 123, 222
Schluckbildchen 101, 104
science 10, 18, 31–2, 35, 37, 49–50, 72, 81–2, 85, 100, 102, 104, 115, 189, 192, 195, 213, 233
secularity 6, 17, 44–6, 123, 127, 183–4, 210, 228, 231
Sedlec Monastery (Czech Republic) 110
selfies 141–7, 160
sensory indexicality 32, 74–5, 77–8, 86, 89, 100–2, 104–5, 114–15, 145, 236
Seventh-Day Adventists 27
Shrine of Christ's Passion (Indiana) 127, 152, 157–60
Shrine of Our Lady of La Leche (Florida) 125
Shrine of Our Lady of the Snows (Illinois) 127, 155

smell   26–7, 78, 85–6, 89, 100–1, 103, 230
sound   7, 43, 49, 70, 73–4, 77, 86, 93–4, 119, 131, 145, 158–9, 167, 171–3, 180–1, 188, 190–1, 230, 236
souvenirs   23, 34, 49–50, 100, 112, 120, 128–9, 131–2, 135, 206
Stations of the Cross   9, 23, 61, 153–62, 230
stereoscope   14–15, 23, 137, 154, 184
Stratton-Porter, Gene   93
Sunday school   11, 36, 63, 81, 83, 85, 112–13
supersessionism   27–8, 170

Tabernacle in the Wilderness   20–1, 24–7, 36, 64, 69, 138, 230
Temple of Solomon (Brazil)   64–6, 77, 110
temporality   69, 111, 137, 177–8
Themed Entertainment Association   165–6, 248
Tisch Family Zoological Gardens (Israel)   95–7

Tomlinson, A. J.   135
tour guides   34, 36, 71, 84–5, 100, 199–206, 211–15, 246 n.16
tourism   6–7, 11–12, 25, 33, 36, 41, 63–4, 69, 72, 91, 97, 100, 104–5, 112, 120, 123–5, 127–8, 131–4, 141, 162, 166, 183, 199, 201, 223, 231, 234–5, 240 n.1
Turner, Edith and Victor   119
Twain, Mark   109

UNESCO   9

Vincent, John Heyl   11, 81, 113
virtual reality   145, 184–94, 233, 236

Warsaw Biblical Gardens (Indiana)   84, 86–7
Wax Museum   68, 128
World's Fairs   21, 25, 33, 41, 132, 177, 222, 240 n.2

yard work   210–12

www.ingramcontent.com/pod-product-compliance
Lightning Source LLC
Chambersburg PA
CBHW052217300426
44115CB00011B/1731